FAMILY ANALYSIS

A *Questionnaire*
and a *Ditto Master Code Sheet*
accompany this laboratory manual.

FAMILY ANALYSIS

Readings and Replication of Selected Studies

MURRAY A. STRAUS

University of New Hampshire

105899

Rand McNally & Company · Chicago

RAND McNALLY SOCIOLOGY SERIES

Edgar F. Borgatta, *Advisory Editor*

1-4-71-MW-3.55

Preface

The history of laboratory manuals and workbooks in sociology has not been a happy one. A number have appeared over the years, but none has been much used. I hope that this book, which is a "laboratory manual" rather than a workbook and which presents a different approach to laboratory work in sociology, will fare better, and that it may, perhaps, symbolize a turning-point in the teaching of sociology.

The deficiency of workbooks is that they have not provided the student with a series of experiments or empirical research projects. Rather, most have been exercise books to provide the student with opportunities for repetition and verbal application of the textbook and lecture materials. It is obvious that familiarity with the concepts and their symbolic manipulation, which the workbooks in family sociology have stressed, are essential. But, since such concepts must be based on, and tested by, empirical observation, this manual will attempt to be more than descriptive; it will provide, in addition, an opportunity for the student to manipulate empirical observations in relation to theory. Such an experience provides an understanding of the process of scientific inquiry which is an essential part of a liberal education in this age of social science research.

Thus, in contrast to the workbooks, the present laboratory manual focuses on a series of significant research articles which are reprinted at the beginning of the problems in this book. Only the second problem, which has been designed to familiarize the student with the procedures, is descriptive; all of the subsequent problems are analytical, in that they enable the student himself to demonstrate the validity of certain propositions about the relationships between variables. At the same time these problems, which are replications of the reprinted articles, are simple enough to be within the command of the typical student in family sociology, and only one of the problems uses statistics beyond percentages and means.

Each of the replications can be completed within a two-hour laboratory period. If, however, a laboratory period is not possible, the necessary tabulations can be done in the usual class period, and the student can then complete his analysis and write the laboratory report as an outside assignment which will also require about one hour. It is also possible to carry out the laboratory problems entirely as outside assignments; further explanation of this procedure is given in Appendix A, pages 193–197. Still another alternative, which is also explained further in Appendix A, is to present the data tabulation as a classroom demonstration, putting the resulting tabulations on the chalk board so that they are available to the students, who can then write up the laboratory report as an outside assignment. This last procedure is preferable when the class is large, and the lecture group is not subdivided into small discussion sections which meet separately.

Part I discusses the role of empirical research in family sociology and the social sciences generally and describes the procedures to be followed in all the problems in this manual. Part II introduces the student to elementary notions of quantification and the measurement of data on the family. Part III contains a series of problems dealing with the interrelationships between the family and other social systems, particularly the occupational and religious systems. These problems will enable the student to prove for himself that, for example, a wife's participation in the occupational world is related to her role within the family. The problems in Part IV allow the student to demonstrate empirically the ways in which one aspect of the internal structure of the family influences other aspects. The final section, Part V, is concerned with the processes by which families are formed and the consequences for subsequent family patterns of variations in these processes.

An integral part of this manual is the Questionnaire on the family which each student is asked to complete. The Questionnaire provides all of the data necessary to carry out the laboratory problems and also makes the problems of personal interest to the students, since the data refer, at least in part, to themselves. This empirical material is also theoretically oriented at a modest level of theory. Thus, it meets the scientific requirements for a laboratory experience. I have found that this combination of elements—materials of personal interest, problems of genuine scientific importance, and an objective and empirical approach to their analysis—constitutes an effective method of instruction in sociology.

MURRAY A. STRAUS
Durham, New Hampshire

CONTENTS

APPENDICES

Part I　THE WHY AND HOW
OF LABORATORY WORK
IN FAMILY SOCIOLOGY

What Laboratory Experience Accomplishes

Any field of study which lays claim to the title of science must be capable of providing a laboratory experience for its students. By "laboratory experience" I obviously do not mean white-coated workers and elaborate equipment, nor even a specific place called a laboratory. I mean simply the opportunity for you to experience directly the modes of establishing knowledge in the field you are studying.

No university—and, indeed, no first-rate high school—attempts to teach the physical and biological sciences without the aid of such a systematic laboratory experience, because, in the last analysis, a science depends on the evidence provided by sensory observation. If the evidence for the propositions in a field is not observable or demonstrable by a trained researcher, or by students working under proper guidance, it is likely that the field in question can be more properly classified as something other than a science.

Until recent years, family sociology has been as much a field of social philosophy as a social science. Even now its claim to be a science is just barely admissible, for much of what is contained in the typical textbook on the sociology of the family clearly does not meet the criteria of a science—it is not based on objectively verifiable *and* verified evidence. Yet tremendous progress has been made in that direction during the past decade, so much so that it is now possible to provide students of the family with an opportunity to demonstrate for themselves the empirical validity of some of the propositions of the field. Such a demonstration of the verifiability or objectivity of the content of family sociology is the central objective of the laboratory problems presented in this manual.

Specifically, the laboratory problems in this book are replications of published research studies. You will approach each problem by reading the original research which is reprinted at the beginning of the problem. Then, using data which you yourself have obtained and coded, you will repeat the essential steps of the investigation. Besides fulfilling the central objective of demonstrating the verifiability of sociological research, I hope that this laboratory experience will also provide a number of other advantages; among the most important are the following:

1. Replicating the creative process of research can be an intellectually enjoyable experience. The thrill of discovering that "it works" is something which many of you have experienced in the chemistry or physics laboratory. This book offers the same opportunity in sociology. Of course, there are also potential frustrations: if your procedures are careless, or if there are sampling variations, your laboratory results may differ from the findings of the original research. And just as generations of freshmen chemistry students have fudged a little to make their "laws" work out as expected, you may be tempted to do likewise with these problems if you place too much emphasis on confirming the hypothesis.

2. The concrete experience with empirical research provided by these problems should make courses in statistics and research methods more meaningful and facilitate learning in these areas, even though no statistics more complicated than percentages and means are used, except in one problem. If you have had the experience provided by these laboratory problems you should have an elementary but vivid understanding of hypothesis-testing, quantification, analysis of data, and the interpretation of research findings. As a result, you will be in a better position to understand the meaning and utility of the techniques taught in courses in statistics and research methods than are students who have not had such laboratory experience.

3. Replication of some of the earlier research efforts in family sociology will provide a better understanding of the substantive content of those topics dealt with in the laboratory problems. For example, you will probably find yourself much more aware of the relationship between social class and parent-child interaction after you have worked Problem 3 which deals with this issue.

4. Your attempts to replicate certain research findings in these twelve problems will increase your ability to read and understand the reports on new research in the sociological journals—a skill which it has become crucial to master because of the rapid and accelerating rate of growth of new knowledge in sociology. Without this skill, knowledge laboriously acquired is likely to become obsolete within a relatively few years. And experience has shown that few students—even "A" students—have this skill. The brief reports written for each of the laboratory problems, and the similar procedures for abstracting published articles, together lay bare the essential structure of a research report and provide a most effective method for acquiring the ability to read and understand research reports. These skills will also help you to understand those parts of the texts in family sociology which are based on and report empirical research.

5. Because many more variables are coded in the first laboratory problem than are used in the subsequent problems, a variety of data and, therefore, possible problems for term papers, are available. Your instructor will probably require some small-scale empirical papers of all graduate students, and he may also assign such papers for undergraduates. Directions for such projects are given in Appendix C.

In addition, although the five laboratory problems listed below had to be eliminated from this manual because of space limitations, the questions which would supply the data required for replication of the original studies have been retained in the Questionnaire for the use of interested instructors or students:

A. Social Class and Socialization for Achievement Roles (Kohn, 1959)
B. Religion and Preference for Male Children (Dinitz, Dynes, and Clarke, 1954)
C. Sex and Generation Differences in Spousal Role Expectations (Hartley, 1959–1960)
D. Maternal Employment and the Child's Personality (Hoffman, 1961)
E. Age at Marriage and Number of Children (Population Reference Bureau, 1961)

6. Finally, it is hoped that the laboratory method of instruction will have certain indirect but important long-term effects on the field of family sociology. For one thing, it may help recruit those of you who are scientifically minded into a career in sociological research. Perhaps it will also encourage both teachers and students of family sociology to demand objectively verifiable and verified propositions as the basis for the content of their textbooks and in their own thinking. In short, I hope that this manual will not only increase your knowledge and understanding as a student, but that it will also contribute to the long-term development of the field of family sociology.

Some Misconceptions About Laboratory Work in Sociology

There is a tendency in sociology to regard research experience as suitable only for advanced students, in part because research experience is often conceived of as *original* research. But in other fields of science, students commonly obtain their first research experience by repeating the experiments on which long-established discoveries are based; thus, for example, a student in laboratory psychology may be required to plot a maze-learning curve.

Similarly, the laboratory work developed in this manual is not intended to be original research leading to the discovery of something new; it attempts simply to give you first-hand experience with the scientific method as it can be applied to the study of the family. In short, this laboratory experience is not for advanced research, or for *any* research in the sense of original discovery; it is simply a way of learning to understand the scientific mode of analysis—an essential part of liberal education in this age of social science research.

Another element which has delayed the introduction of laboratory work in sociology is our tendency to associate the laboratory with the equipment, manipulations, and physical setting of the biological or physical science laboratory. Obviously, sociologists have little need of test tubes and pressure gauges, but we do need some means of obtaining the observations which are the basis for scientific knowledge, and we do need some kind of measuring instruments. Such instruments are provided in this manual, together with a set of problems to which the measurements can be applied, and a system for enabling you to order the observations conveniently, and in a way which will answer the research problem or hypothesis.

The technique used to obtain the necessary observations of family behavior is to ask each of you to fill out a Questionnaire on the basis of your observations of the behavior of your own family. This Questionnaire has been specifically designed to obtain the data necessary for an objective and quantitative test of the hypotheses posed in each of the laboratory problems. The techniques of measurement are simply the assignment of numbers to the observations reported in the Questionnaire and the construction of a few Likert, or summated rating, scales.

This is all you need to test empirically a wide variety of propositions. And, in fact, correlational or cross-sectional designs using self-reported data constitute the methodology of the vast majority of published research findings on the family. Obviously, these methods have severe limitations. Ideally we would like to construct laboratory problems based on experimentation in the literal sense, and to make use of laboratory observation in the literal sense. Both of these techniques are now coming into use in sociological research on the family (Borgatta and Crowther, 1965; O'Rourke, 1964; Straus, 1968), but practical considerations have forced their omission from this manual. Thus, even though all of the problems are empirical, I have deliberately refrained from using the term "experiment" to describe them.

Outline of Laboratory Procedures

1. INITIAL LABORATORY PERIOD

The first laboratory session is devoted to obtaining the data needed for all subsequent problems. Sociology, like all sciences, depends on the analysis of observed phenomena. Every student has the opportunity to make the observations necessary for the laboratory problems in this manual in the course of his interaction with his own family. Thus, in the first laboratory session each of you will be asked to report your observations of your family in a standardized form—as the answers to the Questionnaire at the end of this manual.

(You will complete the Questionnaire anonymously, of course.)

2. SECOND LABORATORY PERIOD

This period is devoted to quantifying the observations reported in the Questionnaire and recording the results on a code sheet. The purpose of the code sheet is to present the data in a form which is more convenient to sort and tabulate than the original Questionnaires. It is recommended that you code the data during a two-hour class period or two one-hour periods, so that the instructor can assist you, but, if necessary, you may also do the coding as an outside assignment.

3. SUBSEQUENT LABORATORY PROBLEMS

All subsequent laboratory sessions follow a standard procedure. *First, before* you come to the laboratory period, you are asked to read a research report which has been reprinted from a sociological journal. The purpose of each laboratory problem is to repeat, or *replicate,* in simplified form, a main finding of that article. If you attempt to replicate the study without reading the original report in advance, it will be difficult, and of much less value as a learning experience. *Second,* you will write down a brief hypothesis based on the findings of the article you have just read and any other information you have. *Third,* you will tabulate the relevant data from the code sheets, to determine whether they reveal patterns similar to those identified in the original research and, thus, support the hypothesis which you have based on that research. *Fourth,* you will write a brief Laboratory Report in which you describe the sample, the variables used, and the findings, and provide a brief discussion or interpretation of them.

4. SEQUENCE OF PROBLEMS

Theoretically, the laboratory problems may be done in any sequence which fits the course outline, once the data have been coded (Problem 1). In practice, however, it is desirable for you to build up grad-

ually your familiarity and skill with these materials and this mode of analysis. For this reason, Problem 2 is restricted to a description of the characteristics of the sample and requires no cross tabulation; it is also used to eliminate from the sample the data for over-age students or students from broken homes. Following this, I would recommend that you go on to Problem 3 before you do any of the others, since it is restricted to a simple cross-tabulation. In addition, you will find it very helpful to prepare an abstract of the reading for Problem 3 before actually doing the problem. Forms and instructions for abstracting are given in Appendix B. With the experience of the first three problems behind you, you will then be ready to deal with the various complications which occur in subsequent problems, such as the use of social class as a control variable in Problem 4, and the use of two dependent variables in Problem 6.

REFERENCES

Borgatta, Edgar F., and Crowther, Betty. *A Workbook for the Study of Social Interaction Processes.* Chicago: Rand McNally, 1965.

Dinitz, Simon, Dynes, Russell R., and Clarke, Alfred C. "Preference for Male or Female Children: Traditional or Affectional?" *Marriage and Family Living,* 16 (1954), pp. 128–130.

Hartley, Ruth. "Some Implications of Current Changes in Sex Role Patterns," *Merrill-Palmer Quarterly of Behavior and Development,* 6 (1959–1960), pp. 153–164.

Hoffman, Lois W. "Effects of Maternal Employment on the Child," *Child Development,* 32 (1961), pp. 187–197.

Kohn, Melvin L. "Social Class and Parental Values," *American Journal of Sociology,* 64 (1959), pp. 337–351.

O'Rourke, John F. "Field and Laboratory: The Decision-Making Behavior of Family Groups in Two Experimental Conditions," *Sociometry,* 26 (1963), pp. 422–435.

Population Reference Bureau. "Spotlight on Marriage," *Population Bulletin,* 17 (1961), pp. 61–79.

Straus, Murray A. "Communication, Creativity, and Problem-Solving Ability of Middle- and Working-Class Families in Three Societies," *American Journal of Sociology,* 73 (1968), pp. 417–420.

Part II

QUANTIFICATION
AND DESCRIPTION
OF THE FAMILY

PRINCIPLES OF MEASUREMENT

Leonard S. Kogan

The business of the research worker is to contribute toward the answering of questions, the testing of hypotheses, and the making of decisions. These objectives are, of course, shared with many others who would not ordinarily consider themselves, nor be considered by others to be, research workers. An agency administrator, for example, may answer more questions, test more hypotheses, and make more decisions in a single day than a research worker may do in a year.

What is the nature of the difference between persons who are designated as research workers and others who commonly share the same general aims? Without attempting to answer this question in detail, it may be suggested that much of the difference lies in the *methods* by which the research worker goes about his business. Although his methods may at times be regarded as finicky or fussy, the research worker prefers to describe them as systematic and scientific. As this book well testifies, the conscientious research worker is a strong advocate of the old adage "Look before you leap!" Although the pressure of circumstances all too often may make him depart from his ideals, he tends to worry about such things as the definition of concepts, the specification of populations, the framing of sampling plans, and the explication of underlying assumptions. As we shall see, of all the things he worries about, one of the most important is the area of concern commonly referred to by the term *measurement*.

Philosophically speaking, the research worker may be regarded as a naïve interactionist. He shuttles between the so-called real world and the world of ideas or concepts. To a large degree the *theory of measurement* has to do with delineating rules and procedures whose application is designed to increase the probability that "goings-on" in the world of concepts will correspond to "goings-on" in the world of reality. In more sophisticated language, the philosopher of science speaks of this correspondence in terms of the degree of isomorphism between the empirical or object system on the one hand and the abstract or model system on the other.

Reprinted from SOCIAL WORK RESEARCH by Norman A. Polansky, editor, pp. 87–105, by permission of the author and The University of Chicago Press. Copyright © 1960 by The University of Chicago Press.

The Purpose and Function
of Measurement

WHAT IS MEANT BY MEASUREMENT

As might be expected, definitions of measurement vary. Perhaps the most commonly cited authority in this connection is the mathematical physicist, N. R. Campbell, who defines measurement as "the process of assigning numbers to represent qualities" (7, p. 267). Another classical definition is that of the mathematician-philosopher Bertrand Russell, to whom "Measurement of magnitudes is, in its most general sense, any method by which a unique and reciprocal correspondence is established between all or some of the magnitudes of a kind and all or some of the numbers, integral, rational, or real as the case may be" (29, p. 176). In more recent years, and with special influence on concepts of measurement in the social and behavioral sciences, there is the definition of measurement as "the assignment of numerals to objects or events according to rules" by the psychologist S. S. Stevens (36, p. 22). In 1958, Stevens stated, very appealingly, "In its broadest sense, measurement is the business of pinning numbers on things." He then added, "More specifically, it is the assignment of numbers to objects or events in accordance with a rule of some sort" (37, p. 384). In the same year, Torgerson, the psychologist, agreed essentially with Campbell and Russell in stating that measurement refers to the *properties* of objects rather than to the objects themselves: "Measurement of a property . . . involves the assignment of numbers to systems to represent that property" (41, p. 14).

These definitions all agree in considering that measurement involves the assigning of symbols to things or, more precisely, to the properties of things according to specified rules and operations. This idea is very close to what we ordinarily mean by language and, indeed, in the broadest of senses, the use of collective nouns, adjectives, and adverbs is a first step in the development of measurement procedures. More narrowly, however, the type of language usually associated with the concept of measurement is that of *numerals* and, even more narrowly, that of *numbers*. Just as there is room for discussion about whether or not there can logically be such a thing as non-numerical measurement, there is also debate about what may properly be included in the thing to be measured. Classical measurement theory, by and large, is concerned with the world of physics, i.e., "fundamental" dimensions such as length, weight, and time duration or "derived" dimensions such as density and velocity. While the world of physics plays a most important role in social work and its concerns (for example, the age and weight of a child or the area of his bedroom), the social worker

is also concerned with many other "worlds"—the psychological world, the sociological world, the economic world. The social worker must, perforce, deal with data from any and all of these worlds, and hence we must assume that what is to be measured in social work research includes such things as physical objects, persons, groups, institutions, and events.

All this does not mean, however, that measurement procedures are identical as we move from one domain to another. Within physics, as Campbell admits, measuring temperature is not the same as measuring length. The length of an object can be measured directly by placing a foot rule alongside it, but temperature is measured indirectly by noting the height (or length) of a column of mercury in a tube. The foot is a small piece (standard unit) of length but one degree is not a small piece of temperature in the same direct sense.

As noted above, the social work researcher will be dealing frequently with physical magnitudes, but perhaps more often he will be interested in psychological and sociological variables in such realms as motivation, racial conflict, family friction, and the like. One of the "real world" systems which he commonly encounters is concerned with money. Objectively speaking, money has many of the characteristics of length, i.e., as one foot plus one foot equals two feet, so one dollar plus one dollar equals two dollars. Nevertheless, in psychological and sociological (not to mention economic) terms, we know that the value of a dollar does not remain constant. For example, one may question whether a dollar added to an income of $25,000 means the same to the recipient as a dollar added to an income of $250. We must hasten to add, moreover, that, psychologically speaking, even height and length cannot be assumed to have a constant significance, viz., a woman who is six feet tall will not be as pleased with her height as a man of the same height will be.

THE ROLE OF MEASUREMENT IN
SCIENTIFIC RESEARCH

The assignment of reference symbols to the properties of "objects" results in several major kinds of data. The first kind involves situations in which the results consist of the number of observations which fall into each of a set of mutually exclusive categories. The measurement operation in this case is one of classification and the data consist of "counts" or frequency per class. Such data are commonly referred to as attributive, classificatory, qualitative, or *enumerative*. A second major kind of data occurs when it is possible to assume that the property being studied varies from less to more, either discretely or along a continuum, and the numbers assigned to various "amounts" of the property depict their ordering or magnitude. The measurement operation in this case consists of ranking the objects with respect to the specified property or assigning numbers which indicate the relative or absolute "amounts" of the property each object possesses. Data resulting from these operations are called quantitative or *metric,* although a further distinction is commonly made between *ordered* and *metric* data.

Progress in a particular area of research can often be judged roughly by the relative prevalence of classificatory, ordering, or metrical concepts in the field. We say roughly because at times the introduction of apparent quantification may not be justified in terms of the "sensitivity" of available techniques. However, when there is adequate experimental justification, the benefits to be derived are marked. Among the advantages, for example, are the following:

Increased Precision of Description. Although classification is probably the first significant step in the development of a science, it is often useful to distinguish among things which are grouped together in a given classification. A certain group of parents, for example, might be categorized as "rejecting," but it would be of greater value to describe each parent in terms of the degree to which such behavior is exhibited. In this instance attention is directed to observations within a category. In other instances attention may be given to differences between categories. To call one set of cases *short-term* and another *long-term,* technically speaking, simply tells us that they differ at some arbitrary point. The number of interviews per case would tell us not only that one group of cases received more contact than another but also how much more.

Increased Communicability of Research Operations and Results. In general, as we move from classificatory to metrical concepts, it becomes necessary to be more rigorous in the specification of measurement procedures. This results both in greater possibilities for exact repetition of studies and also in greater clarity of presentation and interpretation of findings. It is commonly said that numbers are the only universal language. Be that as it may, we can infer more about the standard of living of a particular family when we know family income, expenditures, rent, etc., than when we know only that the family is or is not receiving public assistance.

Increased Possibilities for Discovering and Establishing Relationships among Phenomena. The long-run objective of scientific research is to develop principles which will account for what has already been observed in the empirical world and predict what has not yet been observed. Again, as one moves from classificatory to metrical data, there is greater opportunity for discovering regularities in our data. With classificatory data it is possible to detect non-random associations between classifications. Ranked data permit statements regarding direction of association. Metrical data allow for the quantitative expression of functional relationships. Not only are there advantages in the matter of the discovery and expression of possible relationships, but numbers, when properly applied to empirical phenomena, make possible the use of the full armamentarium of mathematics in constructing and testing theories aimed at explaining, predicting, and controlling the "real world."

Elements of Measurement Theory

The purpose of this section is to present an overview of the conceptual framework which, whether recognized or not, lies behind the application of measurement procedures. It is a curious world, perhaps three interpenetrating worlds, of theoretical models, number systems, and empirical data. One can only hope that the serious student will gain a desire to penetrate more deeply in these worlds through some of the references listed at the end of the chapter.

THEORETICAL MODELS AND THE WORLD OF REALITY

The research worker shuttles between the real world and the world of concepts. The real world provides his empirical evidence, the world of concepts a scheme or map for "making sense" out of the portion of the real world which he is seeking to account for, explain, or predict. In modern terminology the conceptual scheme or map is known as a *theoretical model.* Depending on the stage of development of the particular science or area of research, the model consists of more or less clearly defined constructs and more or less logical relationships or connections among the constructs. If the theoretical model is to be useful, there is the necessity of specifying rules connecting at least some part of the conceptual system with the world of reality. If all works well, these rules permit passage between the world of reality and the hypothetical world of the theoretical model. Then the connections within the theoretical model permit further passage among the constructs, finally emerging as *predictions* about some other part of the empirical system. If the predictions are found to be substantially correct, the theoretical model is strengthened; otherwise, there is a need to check where it went wrong and make corrections.

RULES OF CORRESPONDENCE

The rules connecting the theoretical model and the world of reality are called *rules of correspondence* (41). It is largely with regard to these rules that measurement plays its significant role. At their weakest, the rules of correspondence between constructs in the model and empirical observations are judgmental assumptions on the part of the investigator; at their best, the rules take the form of rigorous operational definitions which specify the connections between the constructs and the observations. A strong contribution to such rigor is possible when the properties of the empirical system can be "measured" to permit the expression of the construct in numerical terms.

POSTULATES BASIC TO THE REAL NUMBER SYSTEM AND COMPLETE MEASUREMENT

The ideal situation in measurement exists when numbers can be assigned to the properties of "objects" and the numbers can then be manipulated according to the rules of mathematics. The traditional viewpoint in measurement, as expressed by Campbell, is that justification for treating numerical data as numbers, i.e., addition and the derivative procedures of subtraction, multiplication, and division, occurs when operations with objects in the physical world can be carried out which duplicate the additive properties of the number system. Thus, for example, it is possible to "prove" that a line four feet in length plus a line two feet in length equals a line six feet in length by placing the two lines end to end and applying a foot rule to the new line. Such possibilities for direct attack on measuring the properties of objects are very limited (length, weight, time, and perhaps electrical resistance), and in the physical world most properties are measured in an indirect fashion.

Within the scope of this chapter no attempt will be made to present a detailed account of the properties of numbers and the concomitant requirements for so-called complete measurement. In general, these postulates may be grouped into three major classes having to do, respectively, with what is meant by equivalence, order, and additivity.

Some Postulates regarding Equivalence

a) Either $A = B$ or $A \neq B$ (Equivalence, Non-equivalence)
b) If $A = B$, then $B = A$ (Symmetry)
c) If $A = B$ and $B = C$, then $A = C$ (Transitivity)

Some Postulates regarding Ordinality

a) If $A \neq B$, then either $A > B$ or $A < B$ (Connectedness)

b) If $A > B$, then $B \not> A$ (Asymmetry)
c) If $A > B$ and $B > C$, then $A > C$ (Transitivity)

Some Postulates regarding Additivity

a) $A + B = B + A$ (Commutative Law)
b) If $A = P$ and $B = Q$, then $A + B = P + Q$ (Axiom of Equals)
c) $A + (B + C) = (A + B) + C$ (Associative Law)

(In the statements given, the symbol $\neq$ means "not equal to," $>$ means "greater than," $<$ means "smaller than," and $\not>$ means "not greater than."

The reader who is not emotionally conditioned against simple equations should immediately conclude that the propositions stated above are self-evident (the labels for the propositions are for reference purposes and should not be allowed to influence this conclusion). And the propositions are indeed self-evident to anyone familiar with elementary arithmetic. In general, this should suggest that difficulties in problems of measurement do not occur within the self-contained realm of numbers but in formulating rules of correspondence between the numerical model and the "thing" measured which permit the numerical model to be tested empirically.

Scales of Measurement

Torgerson (41) summarizes the major characteristics of the real number series, some of which were stated as postulates in the preceding section, as follows:

Numbers are ordered.

Differences between numbers are ordered. That is, the difference between any pair of numbers is greater than, equal to, or less than the difference between any other pair of numbers.

The series has a unique origin indicated by the number 0. These Torgerson calls, respectively, the characteristics of *order*, *distance*, and *origin*. They are based on the fact that numbers form a sequence going from lesser to greater, that differences (distances) between numbers may be directly compared, e.g., $6 - 4 = 3 - 1$, and, finally, that numbers begin at zero, so that any number represents the distance from zero to the number. To these three characteristics we would add the elementary characteristic of uniqueness, non-equality, or *non-equivalence*, namely, that different numbers are not equal to each other. Torgerson, following Campbell and Russell, rejects classification of objects or events as a form of measurement. In this he is in disagreement with the well-known views of Stevens (35, 36, 37), who conceives of classification as the most primitive form of measurement. Torgerson's main point is that in measurement the numbers assigned should refer to relative degrees of a property shown by different objects and not to the objects themselves. We shall agree with the more liberal point of view and assume that classification does warrant conception as a measurement procedure.

Elaborating the classification of scales given by Torgerson to include Stevens' nominal scale, although we shall call it *nominal classification*, six major types

TABLE 1. *Six Major Types of Scales of Measurement**

	Non-Equivalence	*Order*	*Distance*
No natural origin	Nominal classification	Ordinal scale with arbitrary origin	Interval scale
Natural origin	None/some scale	Ordinal scale with natural origin	Ratio scale

* Order includes the property of non-equivalence; distance includes the properties of non-equivalence and order. Stevens' system of classification consists of the nominal scale, the ordinal scale (without regard to origin), the interval scale, and the ratio scale. Torgerson omits the column labeled "Non-Equivalence." Adapted from Torgerson (41).

of scales are presented in Table 1. The type of scale is based on the characteristics of the number system possessed by the scale.[1]

Nominal Classification. In the so-called nominal scale, numerals are assigned to objects or classes of objects. A nominal scale, for example, may be used to identify different objects within a group, e.g., numbers of baseball players, or classes of objects which contain comparable items, e.g., different numerals to label groups of individuals according to religion or national origin. Another example would be the use of numerals to designate various categories of a psychiatric or psychosocial diagnostic classification.

A slightly more complicated example of assigning numerals to objects would be the use of a six-digit number to identify different cases which are carried by a social agency. If within each case, the father were further assigned the numerals 01, the mother 02, the oldest child 03, and so on, each individual's number might be regarded as having a major classification in which the first six numerals are assigned to different families, while a numeral in the 7th and 8th place would identify different members of each family and constitute a minor classification. The utility of such a use of numerals can be seen when it is noted, for example, that all individuals receiving a 0 and a 2 in the 7th and 8th position of the number would be mothers.

While identification of things which are alike and discrimination between things which are unlike are the basic operations underlying all measurement, there are several reasons why the usual nominal scale should

probably be regarded simply as a classification system and not as a scale in the sense that the remaining five categories in Table 1 refer to scales. In the first place the numerals used for distinguishing different classes exhibit none of the properties or relationships of real numbers except the tautology that no two different numbers are alike. This means that any other set of different symbols, e.g., letters of the alphabet or different colors, could be utilized to label the classes rather than numbers. The advantage of numerals is their familiarity, convenience, and large supply.

In the second place, and somewhat paradoxically, a nominal classification containing more than two classes is too complicated to be regarded as a unidimensional scale. This is because there is no restriction on the kind or number of properties which may be used in establishing the classification system. Thus, a commonly used psychiatric classification (1) is based on a consideration of many properties such as symptoms, occurrence of trauma, course of development, and so on. Although this is an extreme example, it serves to illustrate that it should not be concluded automatically that classification is necessarily simpler than measurement.

The key to the matter is actually the term *unidimensional scale*. Before one proceeds to deal with the complexities of scales attempting to deal simultaneously with more than one property, it is logical to discuss scales which deal with only a single property. Except for nominal classification, the scales designated in Table 1 refer to the use of numbers to represent differing degrees or amounts of a particular property.

The None/Some Scale. The simplest scale dealing with a single property appears to be what may be called an absence/presence or none/some scale. It is simply a dichotomous or two-category affair, one category for objects which are characterized by absence of a given property and the second category for objects which possess that property.[2] In its most literal form, the first category should represent "zero amount" of the property and the second category "100% amount" of the property. However, since few objects of research interest show such "all or none" characteristics with respect to a particular property, in practice objects are assigned to the first category if they possess a non-discriminable or negligible amount of the given property and to the second category if they show a discriminable or minimal amount of the property. Thus, a number of sounds may be classified as "not audible" or "audible," a group of individuals may be classified as "not casework clients" or "casework clients," or a group of cases in a social agency may be divided into those which have closed on an unplanned basis versus those which have closed on a planned basis.

In most if not all instances, a nominal classification consisting of more than two categories may be resolved into a group of none/some scales by considering each category successively as the "some" category and combining all other categories into a single "none" category. To give an oversimplified example, an investigator may have classified a group of cases into three categories, depending on whether the major problem was in the economic area, the family relationships area, or the physical health area. The three-category classification consists of three none/some scales, one, for example, based on cases which do not show an economic problem and cases which do show an economic problem. This example also illustrates a useful device for handling classification systems in which a given case may fall into more than one category. Thus, some cases might have been regarded as possessing not only an economic problem but a physical health problem, and perhaps also a family relationships problem. In such instances where the total count in a classification system may exceed the number of cases, the entries in each none/some scale consist of the number of cases falling into a particular category, e.g., possessing an economic problem, while the number of cases in the second category consists of the difference in count between the total number of cases and those which fall into the specified category.

According to the logic of the none/some scale, many commonly used dichotomies, such as male-female, aggressive-passive, or accepting-rejecting, which are designated by what may ostensibly seem to be two different properties, may be reducible to unidimensional none/some form by designating one of the categories as the none category and the other one as the some category. Thus, a male-female classification becomes a none/some scale if the categories are taken to represent non-males and males.

In instances where utilization of a none/some scale is applicable it is common to assign the number 0 to the none category and the number 1 to the some category. Whereas the use of the number 0 is inherent within the system, the second number may be arbitrarily chosen as any number but zero. In many uses both numbers may be chosen arbitrarily, with the same results as far as relationship of the dichotomous variable to other variables is concerned. However, in addition to the computational convenience, which is provided by use of 0 and 1 for the value of each category, the resulting frequency distribution is immediately interpretable in terms of proportions or percentages.

Ordinal Scale with Arbitrary Origin. In measurement with an ordinal scale the numbers used for representing various amounts or degrees of a given property correspond to order of magnitude. Thus, a group of children might be arranged in order of height from left to right along a wall with the smallest child assigned the number 1, the next-to-smallest child number 2, and so on. The numbers would indicate the rank order of the children with respect to height. Since the only purpose of the numbers is to indicate that each child is taller than the child to his right and shorter than the child to his left, any other set of numbers might have been chosen which show this fact, e.g., 2, 8, 9, 16, and so on.

Examples of situations where a set of objects is ordered with respect to degree or magnitude of a particular property are very common. Horses are ranked in order of finishing a race. Chickens in a barnyard may be ranked in order of who pecks whom. Students, unfortunately, are often ranked in terms of how well they please the teacher.

The foregoing examples represent situations in which separate objects are completely ranked. In other instances, classes of objects rather than single objects are ranked or ordered in terms of a particular characteristic or property. An oft-cited example is Mohs' ten-step scale of the comparative hardness of minerals (what will scratch what), in which talc has rank 1, gypsum has rank 2, all the way to diamond, with rank 10. The sociological literature on social stratification abounds in scales purporting to rank different individuals in terms of social class, such as Warner's six-step scale comprising lower-lower, upper-lower, lower-middle, upper-middle, lower-upper, and upper-upper classes (43).

Ordinal Scale with Natural Origin. Torgerson (41) points out that in some instances one of the classes of an ordinal scale may logically be assigned the number 0 to represent zero amount of the property under consideration. A commonly used type of item in research schedules is one which describes the relative frequency of a particular kind of behavior in terms of "never occurs," "occurs rarely," "occurs occasionally," and so on. With such a ranking scale it would be logical to assign the number 0 to the category "never occurs."

In other cases the category which could logically be assigned the number 0 might occur somewhere toward the middle of the scale rather than at the lower end. For example, the steps on an attitude scale may run from "dislikes very much" at one end to "likes very much" at the other end, with a neutral point in the middle representing the attitude "neither likes nor dislikes." The neutral attitude may be considered the natural origin of the scale and be assigned the number 0. Scales of this kind are commonly referred to as *bipolar* in nature.

Interval Scale. In measurement with an interval scale (sometimes called a *cardinal* scale), not only does the order of the numbers in the scale correspond to the order of magnitude of the property, but the difference between any pair of numbers assigned to two magnitudes bears a functional relationship to the difference between the two magnitudes. Such scales are said to have a common unit of measurement so that it is permissible to say that one object has less or more of a given property than a second object and how many units less or more.

Many examples of interval scales exist in the physical world. Temperature as measured either by the centigrade or Fahrenheit scale is one example. In the centigrade scale the unit of measurement is the degree, representing 1/100 of the distance between the freezing point of water set at 0° and the boiling point of water set at 100°. The arbitrariness of the magnitude of the unit of measurement in an interval scale is seen from the fact that in the Fahrenheit scale each degree represents 1/180 of the distance between the freezing point of water (set at 32°) and the boiling point of water (set at 212°).

Calendar time is also measured by an interval scale, with arbitrary origin at the birth of Christ. The common unit of measurement is the year, which allows us to say that the same amount of time elapsed between A.D. 1700 and A.D. 1800 as between A.D. 1850 and A.D. 1950. (Surplus or deficit in family income as compared with public assistance budget standards could similarly be regarded as distances on an interval scale.)

Ratio Scale. If an interval scale has a natural origin at number 0, representing zero amount of the property being measured, the type of scale is called a ratio scale. In this case, the numbers assigned to various degrees or amounts of the property bear a direct relationship to the absolute amount of the property. With such a scale we can say not only that one object has so many units more of a property than a second object but also that the first object is so many times as "big" as the second object. Thus, a tree one hundred feet in height is twice as tall as a tree fifty feet in height, or a boy who weighs one hundred pounds is twice as heavy as a boy who weighs fifty pounds. This is in contrast, for example, to the ordinary temperature scale where it is not meaningful to say that a temperature of 50° F. is twice as hot as a temperature of 25° F.

Interestingly enough, the counting of objects generally gives rise to ratio scale measurement. Thus, a social worker with a caseload of twenty cases has twice as large a caseload as one with ten cases. The property of the group of objects in this connection is *numerosity* (15). Numerosity is an especially interesting

property because it illustrates so clearly the process of abstracting from "nature" which is characteristic of research data. In counting, the number 1 is assigned to each object and each is added. In most research uses of counts, e.g., items per class in a nominal classification or frequencies per class interval in a frequency distribution, the objects counted are alike in some property under consideration but generally they differ in other properties about which the investigator is not concerned. Just as the individual who has fifty dollars is not usually concerned with differences in the serial numbers or state of cleanliness of his bills, so the decision above that a worker with twenty cases has twice as large a caseload as one with ten cases would take no cognizance, for example, that the second worker might be seeing his clients twice as often as the first one.

THE CONCEPT OF MULTIDIMENSIONAL SCALING

The preceding discussion of scales of measurement was directed almost entirely to what is called the unidimensional scale. We were concerned only with the possibilities of assigning meaningful numbers to different degrees or amounts of a single property which was assumed to vary from less to more on a single continuum. Frequently multidimensional variables are assumed arbitrarily to be unidimensional or are forced into apparent unidimensionality. For example, *social class*, when based on combining the individual's occupation, amount of education, income, etc., may be regarded as reducing several variables to what is treated as a unidimensional property. Similarly, most indexes of *social need* have been based on the arbitrary combination of two or more factors (44).

In general, the problem of multidimensional scaling has to do with the assignment of a set of numbers to represent varying orders or amounts of two or more properties possessed by a group of objects and the relationships among the properties. To give a simple geometric illustration suggested by Green (14) in terms of a portion of the theoretical framework postulated by Ripple (28), a client's motivation may be considered to be a function of both his discomfort and hope. The variable (property) under consideration is *motivation*. In terms of motivation, let us assume that three clients, A, B, and C, have been judged (assuming further that this complex variable could be measured on an interval scale) to show the following differences: $A - B = 4$, $B - C = 3$, and $A - C = 5$. These differences could obviously not occur (except in error) if motivation were a unidimensional variable, i.e., if A, B, and C were points on a single straight line. However, if A, B, and C are actually located at the vertices of a right triangle (in two-dimensional space), the differences become consistent (the rule of Pythagoras says so!). Thus, A and B differ 4 units in discomfort but not at all in hope, B and C differ 3 units in hope but not at all in discomfort, and A and C differ in both discomfort and hope.

Problems relating to multidimensional scaling can take many forms. In some cases the objective may be to analyze a complex variable into a number of unidimensional variables, e.g., by methods of factor analysis.[3] In other cases the problem is more directly related to unidimensional scaling, that is, the establishment of the order among values or of distances between values is the aim of the investigator. Further discussion of this topic is beyond the scope of this chapter. The interested reader is directed to the introductory account by Guilford (16), the student to Torgerson (41).

Measurement Scales and Statistics

The classical requirements for complete measurement necessitate empirical demonstration that various degrees of a specified property behave in the same manner as the number system. This could be interpreted to mean that the characteristic of additivity of quantities of the property should be confirmable experimentally. As noted previously, this requirement is probably directly demonstrable by physical operations for only a few so-called extensive dimensions in the physical world, such as length and weight.

What then is left with regard to possibilities for measurement in the non-physical world? The stock in trade of the social work researcher, as well as of his colleagues in such related fields as psychology and sociology, abounds in properties of persons and groups, such as attitude toward receiving help or family cohesiveness. That such properties are not amenable to complete measurement in the classical sense of physically demonstrable additivity seems hardly debatable. Stated in such terms, most non-physical properties or objects, persons or events can probably at best meet formal requirements for ordinality—if that![4]

There is a growing body of opinion that psychological and sociological variables having to do with aptitudes, attitudes, personality characteristics, properties of groups, and the like can be measured at best on ordinal scales. This opinion commonly takes the form of insistence that only certain types of statistical procedures are permissible, depending on the strength of measurement, i.e., type of scale, of the variables involved. For example, two recent statistical books (31, 34) have promulgated this point of view, acknowledging the conception of Stevens (36). Table 2 lists examples of permissible statistics given by Stevens in the framework of his hierarchy of scales (37). In each instance, statistics permissible for a given type of scale are permissible for "stronger" scales, e.g., the median

TABLE 2. *Type of Scale and Permissible Statistics*[*]

Scale	Permissible Statistics
Nominal	Number of cases Mode "Information" measures Contingency correlation
Ordinal	Median Percentiles Order correlation (type *O:* interpreted as test of order)
Interval	Mean Standard deviation Order correlation (type *I:* interpreted as *r*) Product moment (*r*)
Ratio	Geometric mean Harmonic mean Per cent variation

[*] Based on Stevens (37).

is permissible not only for the ordinal scale but also for the interval and ratio scales.

Specifically, much discussion has centered on the so-called misuse of interval scale statistics for data in which equality of units has not been clearly established. This might mean, for example, that a group of children may be ranked by means of an I.Q. test but differences in their actual scores should not be taken seriously.[5] At its extreme, this point of view would hold that computing means, standard deviations, and product moment correlation coefficients cannot be justified for most psychological and sociological variables, and this would also hold for much data in social work research.[6] In terms of tests of "significance" and other methods of statistical inference, the same point of view would advocate the abandonment of classic *parametric* statistical methods largely based on normal distribution assumptions in favor of so-called *nonparametric* or distribution-free methods, which to a considerable extent make use of classifications or ranks rather than scores (31, 34).

One of the strongest statements of the contrasting viewpoint is that of Burke, who concluded after an analysis of the relationship between scales of measurement and statistics that "the properties of a set of numbers as a measurement scale should have no effect upon the choice of statistical techniques for representing and interpreting the numbers" (5, p. 75). This article produced a rejoinder by Senders, who concluded: "Since psychologists are presumably more interested in the behavior they describe with numbers than in the numbers themselves, they will learn more if their statistical techniques correspond with the properties of the set of numbers as a measurement scale than if these properties"—as Burke asserts—"have no effect upon the choice of statistical techniques for representing and interpreting the numbers" (31, p. 424).

Whether statistical methods must be consistent with the scale properties of the data being analyzed cannot be gone into here. Much as I would like to, I can offer no simple solution to the dilemma. It seems clear that statistical methods, whether parametric or nonparametric, like mathematics in general, are self-contained systems independent of reality considerations. And yet the value of statistical procedures when applied in research depends on the degree to which the results of the statistical manipulations lead to useful and meaningful decisions or contributions to knowledge. The "safe" approach, since in general fewer assumptions are made, may appear to be to use nonparametric rather than parametric techniques whenever a relevant method is available. At the same time the investigator must be aware that in adopting the safe approach, he may be discarding data and weakening his chances of detecting significant differences or relationships. At present, moreover, most nonparametric methods do not lend themselves to an estimation of the magnitude of experimental effects or strength of relationships.

It may be expected that in the future a clearer rationale will be developed for choice of particular statistical techniques for particular kinds of data. Even at present it appears that on a practical level, especially for larger samples, differences in conclusions reached by employment of nonparametric or parametric methods may be negligible. Questions of what to measure and how to measure, as well as problems of sampling, control, and relevance to theory, are more pressing.

Assessing the Adequacy of Measurement Procedures

Perhaps the richest source of specific techniques of interest to the social work researcher is to be found in the methodological literature on psychometrics and sociometrics, especially in the areas of psychophysical methods, attitude-scale construction, and test development. Some major references to this large body of literature are to be found at the end of the chapter.

Much of what has been said up to this point has presumed that the properties being studied have been measured with perfect success except for the relative degree of refinement, i.e., scale of measurement, to which the particular set of data was amenable within the techniques available to the investigator. In other words, it has been assumed that the operation of classification, ordering, or quantification has been carried out without error and that the investigator has achieved the results he set out to obtain. These two considerations—the degree to which measurements are free from error, and the degree to which one gets what he is looking for—have been referred to as the *reliability* and the *validity* of measurement. Over the years each of these terms has accrued many synonyms (20). It should be noted that the most common synonyms in use today are *precision* and *relevance*. In addition to these basic considerations, the adequacy of a particular measurement procedure must also be evaluated in terms of certain more mundane criteria which may be grouped under such headings as *practicality* and *feasibility*.

Practicality and feasibility have to do with such things as cost in time, money, and effort in using the instrument or procedure, the need for special training, and the ease of scoring and interpretation of results, and may include attention to matters of ethics in collecting information or seeing that a research procedure does not interfere with practice objectives or administrative policies with respect to the group of clients or institutions being studied. It can readily be seen that a whole volume could be devoted to discussion of practicality and feasibility in the development and application of measurement procedures. We shall not elaborate further on these matters in the present chapter except to emphasize that the research worker's technical competence founders all too often on the twin reefs of practicality and feasibility.

THE GENERAL CONCEPT OF RELIABILITY

Although secondary to problems of the validity or relevance of measures, we shall speak of reliability or precision first, since reliability is a necessary if not sufficient condition for the establishment of adequate validity. Here we are primarily concerned not with what is being measured but rather with *how well* whatever is being measured is measured. We may ask of our data, for example, how close we would come to the same results if we repeated the measurements a number of times. Would each of a group of boys have remained classified as delinquent or non-delinquent? Would a sample of families have been ranked in the same order with respect to social class status? Would a group of clients have been judged to show the same amount of movement? In each instance, it may be noted, the particular procedures used may not have done a good job of "getting at" delinquency, social class, or movement, but in considering reliability of measurement we are postponing this crucial question and are concerned only with the reproducibility or repeatability of our results.

In most theoretical discussions of reliability it is assumed that the measurements involved are in the form of scores which can be handled by the usual processes of arithmetic. As a matter of fact, the measurements perhaps most common to such discussions (18, 39) have been based on so-called objective tests in which an individual is presented with a number of items from which his score is derived by counting the number of correct responses. In the light of the preceding description of requirements for measurement one may question the degree to which distributions of such scores approach interval-scale form, based as they are on assumptions such as the normal distribution of traits and equivalence of items in a test. However, for purposes of the present discussion of reliability and validity, we will assume that, generally, the results of the measurement procedure have been expressed in the form of scores and will note that, generally, the principles involved can be applied to classification or ranking, as the case may be.

THEORETICAL DEFINITION OF RELIABILITY AND STANDARD ERROR OF MEASUREMENT

All measurement is characterized by error or, more accurately, by variability. Hypothetically, one might take an infinite number of measurements of a particular property of a particular thing and assume reasonably that some measure of central tendency for the set of measurements represents the "true value" for the thing measured, and some measure of variability could be used to summarize the variations around the true value. With a dichotomous classification, for example, the true value might be assumed to be the modal category for the particular thing, and variability might be expressed in terms of the proportion of instances in which the thing was classified in the modal category. For a property expressed in scores, the true value for the particular thing could be represented by the mean of the repeated measures and the variability or errors of measurement by the standard deviation of the repeated measures.

Another hypothetical approach to the concept of reliability begins with a similar postulate, that any observed score can be thought of as consisting of two parts (15, 16, 39) expressed by the equation:

$$X_o = X_t + X_e,$$

(where X_o = the observed or obtained score; X_t = the true score; and X_e = the "error" component). If it is then assumed that the errors in a set of measures are distributed independently and randomly, it is easy to show that the variance (square of the standard deviation) of the observed scores is equal to the variance of the "true" scores plus the variance of the errors, or in equation form:

$$\sigma_o^2 = \sigma_t^2 + \sigma_e^2.$$

With slight manipulation this equation will read:

$$\frac{\sigma_t^2}{\sigma_o^2} = 1 - \frac{\sigma^2}{\sigma_o^2}.$$

The reliability of a set of measures (symbolized by r_{11}) is then defined as either side of the above equation, i.e.,

$$r_{11} = \frac{\sigma_t^2}{\sigma_o^2} = 1 - \frac{\sigma_e^2}{\sigma_o^2}$$

(definition of coefficient of reliability), or, in words, the coefficient of reliability of a set of measures is defined either as the ratio of the true variance to the observed variance or as one minus the ratio of the error variance to the observed variance. Further manipulation would indicate that

$$\sigma_e^2 = \sigma_o^2 (1 - r_{11})$$

and

$$\sigma_e = \sigma_o \sqrt{1 - r_{11}}$$

(definition of standard error of measurement).

The two definitions above, i.e., the coefficient of reliability and the standard error of measurement, represent the two most common ways in which the reliability or precision of a set of measures is expressed when the measures are in the form of scores. The coefficient of reliability expresses reliability in terms of a ratio of variances, implicitly interpretable as an index of association between pairs of repeated measurements, while the standard error of measurement expresses reliability as the standard deviation of the distribution of "errors" of measurement.[7]

METHODS OF ESTIMATING RELIABILITY

It should be emphasized that the above definitions of the coefficient of reliability and the closely related standard error of measurement are completely hypothetical. In the development and application of measurement procedures, we can at best estimate hypothetical reliability. The number of approaches to estimation of reliability are almost legion, depending on such factors as the nature of the measurement instrument, the possibilities for repeated measurement, the effect on the object of repeated measurement, the conditions under which measurement occurs, and so on.

In the realm of objective psychological tests the estimation of a coefficient of reliability is most commonly based on one or the other of five major methods: (1) immediate retest with the same test; (2) delayed retest with the same test; (3) immediate retest with an equivalent or parallel form of the original test; (4) delayed retest with an equivalent or parallel form of the original test; and (5) internal analysis of a test given on one occasion.

Comparison of these methods would quickly reveal that one should not expect to obtain the same coefficient from each of them. For example, one might reasonably expect that a correlation based on retesting a group of subjects with the *same* test would tend to be higher than a correlation based on retesting with an equivalent but *different* form of the test. The magnitude of a particular estimate of reliability depends, as will be recalled from the theoretical definition, on the relative proportions of the observed variance assigned to "true" variance and "error" variance. In the example above, retesting a group of subjects with the same test means that the content of the test has been held constant and this condition will tend in general to "inflate" the estimate of true variance while lowering the estimate of error variance.

Thorndike and Hagen (40) have described the relationships between the five principal methods for estimating test reliability and three major sources of variation or fluctuation in obtained scores. Table 3 is a slightly modified version of one of their tables, showing a summary comparison of the different procedures. This table shows clearly that each procedure takes account of certain sources of variation in estimating reliability, while neglecting other sources of variation.[8] It may be noted that in this analysis of relations between procedures for estimating reliability and sources of variation the method of using immediate retest with a parallel form is similar to estimation based on a single test.

The sources of variation indicated in Table 3 may be subdivided and extended almost without end. Thorndike's original table also includes changes in the individual's speed of work which are pertinent for a timed test. Other possible sources of variation, for example, might be differences due to different testers or to different scorers of the test. In other contexts sources of variation might be referred to as interviewer, observer, judge, or case reader "error," leading, for example, to the concept of *inter-judge reliability,* generally measured by some coefficient of agreement between independent judges.[9]

Enough has certainly been said to convince the reader that reliability is a very general concept covering a wide range of possibilities for estimation and interpretation. And yet it must be emphasized that only the surface of the subject of reliability has been scratched. Other factors such as the variability and general level of the group on the particular property or characteristic, as well as the number of items used in obtaining the score for an individual, are also reflected in the estimate of reliability (15, 16, 19). A reliability coefficient standing by itself tells us very little about the dependability of measurement with a particular instrument or research procedure. In order

TABLE 3. *Sources of Variation Represented in Different Procedures for Estimating Reliability**

Procedures for Estimating Reliability	Sources of Variation in Scores		
	Variation Arising within Measurement Procedure Itself	Changes in the Individual from Day to Day	Changes in the Specific Sample of Items
Immediate retest (same test)	✕		
Retest after interval (same test)	✕	✕	
Parallel test form (without time interval)	✕		✕
Parallel test form (with time interval)	✕	✕	✕
Subdivision or item analysis of single test	✕		✕

* Based on Thorndike and Hagen (40).

properly to evaluate a quantitative statement about the reliability of a measurement procedure (regardless of whether the procedure yields a classification, an ordering, or a metric), we should know in complete detail the method used for estimating the reliability, the characteristics of the persons, objects, or events comprising the sample studied, the conditions under which measures were obtained, and any other information pertinent to application and interpretation of the procedure. As noted at the beginning of this section, reliability of measurement is secondary in importance to the validity or relevance of measures to be discussed below. High reliability or precision does not guarantee relevance of the measures to the purpose at hand; but negligible or low reliability of a measure may frequently destroy relevance.[10]

The Concept of Validity

In a broad sense the validity or relevance of a measurement procedure is based on the degree to which the aims or purposes of making the measurements are accomplished. Since the aims of making a set of measurements may vary in number, kind, and scope, it follows that in general we must speak of the *validities* rather than the *validity* of a measurement procedure.

Many attempts have been made to classify the major types of validity underlying measurement procedures. Upon analysis, such attempts at classifying types of validity appear to be efforts at classifying major purposes of measurement. The types of validity refer in turn to the kinds of evidence one should collect in order to demonstrate that the specified purpose or purposes have been met.

Evidence for validity usually comes from one or both of two major sources. On one hand, there is what may be called the *logical* or *rational* approach to problems of validity. Secondly, there is the *empirical* or *statistical* approach in which evidence is sought by de-

TABLE 4. *Major Types of Validity**

Types of Validity	Evidence Required
Concurrent validity	Measures correspond to measures of concurrent criterion performance or status.
Predictive validity	Predictions made from measurement procedure are confirmed by evidence gathered at some subsequent time.
Content validity	Content of measurement procedure samples or relates to class of situation or subject matter about which conclusions are to be drawn.
Construct validity	Certain explanatory constructs or concepts, i.e., theory, account for measures obtained.

* Based on (2).

termining the relationship of one's measures to other measures or variables.

Logical or rational approaches to determination of validity involve critical examination and analysis of the form, structure, and content of the measurement procedure in terms of what the investigator has aimed or claimed to measure. We may ask, for example, how clear and unambiguous are any definitions or instructions used? Was the sequence of steps taken by the investigator in developing his instrument a logical, well-planned sequence?

The empirical or statistical approach to validity is based on determining the relationship of the measures in hand to something outside the measures themselves. The "something outside" is called a *criterion*.[11] Psychological testers have long devoted themselves to the construction of instruments designed to have a diagnostic or prognostic function. It is well known, for example, that aptitude and ability tests have been developed which "predict" with reasonable success how well an individual will do in college, in medical school, or as a jet pilot. Most often empirical validity is reported in terms of a correlation known as a *validity coefficient*, but the expression of relationship between a measurement instrument and a criterion may take many forms depending on the nature of the data.

Beyond classifying evidences of validity as either logical or empirical, there have been other more elaborate classifications of types of validity. Anastasi (3), for example, discusses the validity of tests under the headings of face validity, content validity, factorial validity, and empirical validity. Guilford (15) speaks of validity by assumption, intrinsic validity, relevant validity, and face validity. Kogan (20), in an attempt to be humorous, collected a list which included twenty-five kinds of validity from a hurried survey of the literature.

A very useful contribution toward clarification of the conceptual framework of validity was made several years ago by a joint committee of the American Psychological Association, the American Educational Research Association, and the National Council on Measurements Used in Education (2). The purpose of this group was to develop a manual specifying the kinds of information which should accompany publication of tests or other "devices for diagnosis and evaluation."

The conclusions of the committee about major types of validity are presented in slightly modified summary form in Table 4. It will be noted that empirical validity has been subdivided into *concurrent* or *predictive* validity, depending on whether the criterion data are coexistent with or subsequent in time to the measures being validated. The distinction between concurrent and predictive validity is important primarily for practical reasons, e.g., the necessity of follow-up to establish predictive validity. To complete subclassification of empirical validity on the basis of the temporal relation between the measures and the criterion, one should add *postdictive validity* to the list to designate situations in which the aim is to "predict" prior events or conditions, e.g., testing an adult to determine his relationship to his mother during his childhood.

It may seem at first glance that what was previously referred to as rational or logical validity has been subdivided into *content* validity and *construct* validity. But this is not the case. Although content and construct validity depend to considerable degree on rational analysis and judgment, they are strengthened by empirical data-gathering operations. In social work research, for example, Hunt and Kogan (19) have described both the logical considerations and empirical procedures underlying development of the *Movement Scale,* and Ripple (28) has summarized how an instrument was designed to measure motivation, capacity, and opportunity in relation to clients' use of case-work service. It should be noted that in the opinion of some investigators the most efficient method of determining the construct validity of an instrument is by the procedures of factor analysis (15).[12]

The various concepts embraced under the rubric of *validity of measurement* are of basic importance because they force us to think both *behind* as well as *beyond* the particular measures obtained from a particular procedure. They focus our attention not only on clarifying *what* is being measured but the connections between what is measured and other phenomena in the world. The ultimate criteria of the adequacy of measurement and, indeed, the adequacy of research in general, stem from the utility of what is done. Measurement in social work research should produce accurate information which is meaningful and useful for both theory, practice, and progress in social work.

Summary

Measurement, as described in this chapter, refers to the process of using numbers to represent properties of objects according to specified rules. In the context of social work research the "objects" whose properties are the subject of measurement may be persons, groups, institutions, and the like. Depending on which characteristics of the number system (non-equivalence, order, distance, origin) the measures can be shown to possess, scales of measurement may be classified into six major categories: nominal classification, none/some scale, ordinal scale with arbitrary origin, ordinal scale with natural origin, interval scale, and ratio scale. All but the first of these categories refer to unidimensional scales.

Measurement considerations play a significant role in relation to the formulation and testing of theoretical models as well as in the choice of appropriate methods of statistical analysis. In general, as one moves from classificatory to metrical procedures, advantages are gained in terms of increased precision, communicability, and possibilities for discovering and establishing relationships among variables.

In addition to the scale of measurement attainable, the adequacy of a measurement technique should be assessed for practicability, feasibility, reliability, and validity. Reliability refers to a cluster of concepts relating to the precision, reproducibility, or stability of a set of measures. Validity or relevance depends on how well the purposes of the measurement procedure are met and is based on a combination of rational and empirical operations. Finally, the success of a measurement technique must be judged according to its demonstrated utilities.

NOTES

[1] Coombs (8) has developed a number of more elaborate classifications of scales of measurement, including such "in-between" types as the partially ordered scale and the ordered metric scale. Coombs further distinguishes kinds of scales both in terms of objects themselves as well as distances between objects. For a criticism of this approach see Torgerson (41).

[2] It should be pointed out that some authors regard properties classifiable only as "absent" or "present" as *non-scalable* properties.

[3] Factor analysis is a method of accounting for the intercorrelations among a group of variables by determination of a smaller number of underlying factors. See Guilford (16) for an introductory account of factor theory and techniques. For an application of factor analysis in social work research see Shyne and Kogan (33).

[4] Many attempts have been made in psychological research to establish *psychologically equal* units using the concept of equal distance or equal probability rather than additivity. For accounts of the large variety of methods employed see Edwards (13), Guilford (15), and Torgerson (41).

[5] It should be noted that Stevens (37) suggests that intelligence-test "standard scores" may be amenable to "interval scale" statistics. He also assumes that certain psychophysical scales relating to loudness and brightness may be handled as ratio scale data.

[6] See Bush (6) for presentation of this point of view of social work research.

[7] For a criticism of the "truth-error" conception of reliability see the significant paper by Tryon (42).

[8] Distinctions are commonly made between the kinds of reliability coefficients resulting from different procedures for estimating reliability, e.g., a coefficient of *stability* is based on retest after a time interval and a coefficient of *equivalence* is based on "simultaneous" testing with a comparable instrument (2).

[9] Several of the papers presented in the Conference on Use of Judgments in Social Work Research (32) were in large part devoted to discussions of inter-judge reliability, with special reference to research utilizing case records.

[10] See Guilford (15, 16) for a description of the theoretical relationship between reliability and validity of measures.

[11] It should be pointed out that criteria, too, are beset with problems of the appropriate scale of measurement as well as adequacy with respect to reliability, validity, and practicality. The best predictor in the world cannot predict a completely unreliable criterion.

[12] See note 3 above.

REFERENCES

1. AMERICAN PSYCHIATRIC ASSOCIATION. *Mental Disorders: Diagnostic and Statistical Manual.* Washington: American Psychiatric Association, 1952.
2. AMERICAN PSYCHOLOGICAL ASSOCIATION. "Technical Recommendations for Psychological Tests and Diagnostic Techniques," *Psychological Bulletin Supplement,* 51 (1954), 1–38.
3. ANASTASI, A. *Psychological Testing.* New York: Macmillan Co., 1954.
4. ARROW, K. J. "Mathematical Models in the Social Sciences," *The Policy Sciences,* ed. D. Lerner and H. D. Lasswell. Stanford: Stanford University Press, 1951.
5. BURKE, C. J. "Additive Scales and Statistics," *Psychological Review,* 60 (1953), 73–75.
6. BUSH, R. R. "The New Look in Measurement Theory," *Use of Judgments as Data in Social Work Research,* ed. A. W. Shyne. New York: National Association of Social Workers, 1959.
7. CAMPBELL, N. R. *Foundations of Science.* New York: Dover Publications, 1957 (formerly *Physics: The Elements.* Cambridge: Cambridge University Press, 1920).
8. COOMBS, C. H. "Theory and Methods of Social Measurement," *Research Methods in the Behavioral Sciences,* ed. L. Festinger and D. Katz. New York: Dryden Press, 1953.
9. ———, RAIFFA, H., and THRALL, R. M. "Some Views on Mathematical Models and Measurement Theory," *Psychological Review,* 61 (1954), 132–44.

10. Cronbach, L. J., and Gleser, G. C. *Psychological Tests and Personnel Decisions*. Urbana: University of Illinois Press, 1957.

11. _____, and Meehl, P. E. "Construct Validity in Psychological Tests," *Psychological Bulletin*, 52 (1955), 281–302.

12. Cureton, E. E. "Validity," *Educational Measurement*, ed. E. F. Lindquist. Washington: American Council on Education, 1950.

13. Edwards, A. L. *Techniques of Attitude Scale Construction*. New York: Appleton-Century-Crofts, Inc., 1957.

14. Green, B. F. "Attitude Measurement," *Handbook of Social Psychology*, ed. G. Lindzey. Cambridge, Mass.: Addison-Wesley Publishing Co., 1954.

15. Guilford, J. P. *Psychometric Methods*. 2d ed. New York: McGraw-Hill, 1954.

16. _____. *Fundamental Statistics in Psychology and Education*. 3d ed. New York: McGraw-Hill, 1956.

17. _____, and Comrey, A. L. "Measurement in Psychology," *Theoretical Foundations of Psychology*, ed. H. Helson. New York: Van Nostrand Co., 1951.

18. Gulliksen, H. *Theory of Mental Tests*. New York: John Wiley & Sons, 1950.

19. Hunt, J. M., and Kogan, L. S. *Measuring Results in Social Casework*. New York: Family Service Association of America, 1952.

20. Kogan, L. S. "Validity, Reliability, and Related Considerations," *Use of Judgments as Data in Social Work Research*, ed. A. W. Shyne. New York: National Association of Social Workers, 1959.

21. Lazarsfeld, P. F. (ed.). *Mathematical Thinking in the Social Sciences*. Glencoe: Free Press, 1954.

22. _____. "Problems in Methodology," *Sociology Today*, ed. R. K. Merton, L. Broom, and L. S. Cottrell. New York: Basic Books, 1959.

23. Lindquist, E. F. (ed.). *Educational Measurement*. Washington: American Council of Education, 1950.

24. Lindzey, G., and Borgatta, E. F. "Sociometric Measurement," *Handbook of Social Psychology*, ed. G. Lindzey. Cambridge, Mass.: Addison-Wesley Publishing Co., 1954.

25. Loevinger, J. "Objective Tests as Instruments of Psychological Theory," *Psychological Reports*, 3 (1957), 635–94.

26. Lorge, I. "The Fundamental Nature of Measurement," *Educational Measurement*, ed. E. F. Lindquist. Washington: American Council on Education, 1950.

27. Riley, M., Riley, J., Toby, J., *et al. Sociological Studies in Scale Analysis*. New Brunswick: Rutgers University Press, 1954.

28. Ripple, L. "Motivation, Capacity and Opportunity as Related to the Use of Casework Service: Theoretical Base and Plan of Study," *Social Service Review*, 29 (1955), 172–93.

29. Russell, B. *Principles of Mathematics*. 2d ed. New York: Norton & Co., 1938.

30. Senders, V. L. "A Comment on Burke's Additive Scales and Statistics," *Psychological Review*, 60 (1953), 423–24.

31. _____. *Measurement and Statistics*. New York: Oxford University Press, 1958.

32. Shyne, A. W. (ed.). *Use of Judgments as Data in Social Work Research*. New York: National Association of Social Workers, 1959.

33. _____, and Kogan, L. S. "A Study of Components of Movement," *Social Casework*, 39 (1958), 333–42.

34. Siegel, S. *Nonparametric Statistics for the Behavioral Sciences*. New York: McGraw-Hill, 1956.

35. Stevens, S. S. "On the Theory of Scales of Measurement," *Science*, 103 (1946), 677–80.

36. _____. "Mathematics, Measurement, and Psychophysics," in *Handbook of Experimental Psychology*, ed. S. S. Stevens. New York: John Wiley & Sons, 1951.

37. _____. "Measurement and Man," *Science*, 127 (1958), 383–89.

38. Stouffer, S. A., *et al. Measurement and Prediction*. Princeton: Princeton University Press, 1950.

39. Thorndike, R. L. "Reliability," in *Educational Measurement*, ed. E. F. Lindquist. Washington: American Council on Education, 1950.

40. _____, and Hagen, E. *Measurement and Evaluation in Psychology and Education*. New York: John Wiley & Sons, 1955.

41. Torgerson, W. S. *Theory and Methods of Scaling*. New York: John Wiley & Sons, 1958.

42. Tryon, R. C. "Reliability and Behavior Domain Validity: Reformulation and Historical Critique," *Psychological Bulletin*, 54 (1957), 229–49.

43. Warner, W., Meeker, M., and Eels, K. *Social Class in America*. Chicago: Science Research Associates, 1949.

44. Zimbalist, S. E. "Index-Making in Social Work," *Social Service Review*, 31 (1957), 245–57.

CODING THE QUESTIONNAIRE

Our objective in this laboratory problem is to convert the information recorded in the Questionnaire into quantitative form. Quantification is desirable for most types of scientific research since it permits us to use statistics in our analysis of the data. Statistical analysis is, of course, only one form of analysis, but, because of its explicit and objective rules and its precision, it has many advantages, some of which are discussed in the reading for this laboratory problem.

When the terms *quantification* or *measurement*

are used, there is a tendency to think of them in physical terms rather than in behavioral terms. As a result, many people do not see how it is possible to quantify family behavior. But, as Kogan's article suggests, any type of family behavior can be measured or quantified. While there are many complicated techniques for measurement, all that is really necessary is a system for "the assignment of numerals to objects or events in accordance with a rule of some sort." This is the sense in which you will be measuring family behavior in this laboratory assignment.

The set of rules which you will use for this purpose is known as a *code*, and the process of converting the observations to numerical form by means of this set of rules is known as *coding*. In modern research, coding is almost always designed to record the data on punched cards, so that the researcher can use computers and IBM card-sorting machines to process the data. Obviously, in a course like this all of you cannot have access to IBM machines to process your data. So, instead of coding the data onto IBM punched cards, we will code it on an ordinary sheet of paper which has been ruled off into 130 boxes, or cells (see the Coding Worksheet, page 25). One item of information is coded in each box. What is accomplished by this process?

1. Almost all the observations of the rather long Questionnaire are entered on a single sheet of paper. This is much easier to work with than the original bulky Questionnaire. It will enable you to sort and tabulate the set of code sheets in a way similar to the way in which IBM cards are sorted and tabulated.
2. All the data are expressed in an unambiguous numerical form which will permit you to use simple statistics, such as the mean or average.
3. In a number of cases a series of observations of the same phenomenon are combined into a single score, which may also be called a scale or index. This type of quantification usually results in a more reliable and valid measure than one based on a single observation.

Coding Instructions

1. Your instructor will shuffle and distribute the Questionnaires so that each student is coding a Questionnaire filled out by some other student. Coding someone else's Questionnaire gives you a more realistic coding experience. It also lets you sign your name *as a coder,* so that your coding work can be checked, although the Questionnaires themselves are anonymous to protect the respondent's privacy.

2. Tear out from this laboratory manual the Coding Worksheet, page 25, which has been ruled into 130 numbered boxes.

3. Turn to the Code on page 27. The numbers in the *first* column of the Code refer to the numbers of the questions in the Questionnaire. The numbers in the *second* column of the Code are the numbers of the 130 boxes on the Coding Worksheet. IMPORTANT: The question numbers are usually, *but not always,* the same as the box numbers.

4. Begin to code the information given in the Questionnaire by writing in Box 1 of the Coding Worksheet the number of the answer circled in response to Question 1; this is the score for Question 1. For example, if the answer chosen is 1 (Male), you should write a 1 in Box 1; if it is 2 (Female), you should write 2. Question 1 is a *precoded* item; that is, the number of the answer circled for this question in the Questionnaire is the number to be coded on the Coding Worksheet. Such items are marked (P) in the Code.

5. To code Question 2 (Age), simply write the age given as the answer to Question 2 in Box 2. This item is an example of *direct coding;* here the numerical answer given in the Questionnaire is simply transferred directly to the appropriate box on the Coding Worksheet. Items to be coded directly are marked (D) in the Code.

6. Proceed to code Question 3 in Box 3, Question 4 in Box 4, and so on, up through Question 9 which is coded in Box 9. All of these items are precoded. Question 10, however, and a number of the questions which follow are not precoded. For example, the number to be coded in Box 10 is the total number of different categories circled in response to Question 10, excluding category a. Instructions for coding those questions which are not precoded and cannot be coded directly will be found in the Code. These and other items which might cause difficulty in coding are marked with an asterisk (*) in the Code.

7. You should exercise great care in coding, since all subsequent results depend on the accuracy of the coding. A high level of coding error is likely to spoil your results in later problems.

8. After all the coding has been completed, copy your coding from the Coding Worksheet onto the Ditto Master Code Sheet which your instructor will supply. Be sure to remove the protective tissue sheet in the Ditto Master before you begin. WRITE ALL NUMBERS IN LARGE, CLEAR, LEGIBLE FIGURES. A ball point pen works very well. A pencil may also be used. But whatever you use, PRESS HARD! Do not make any unnecessary checks or marks on the Ditto Master.

TO MAKE A CORRECTION ON THE DITTO MASTER: Use a razor blade to scrape off from the back of the Ditto Master the incorrect number. Then write in the correct code number TO ONE SIDE OF THE ORIGINAL NUMBER. Do not write over the incorrect number because the carbon underneath it has already been used.

9. When the numbers in all the boxes have been copied onto the Ditto Master Code Sheet, write in your section or course number, the date, the Questionnaire number, and your name in the blanks at the top of the Ditto Master. Then REPLACE the protective tissue and turn in your Ditto Master Code Sheet to your instructor.

CODING WORKSHEET

SECTION/
COURSE NO. _____ DATE _____ QUESTIONNAIRE NO. _____ CODER'S NAME _____

1	2	3	4	5	6	7	8	9	10
11	12	13	14	15	16	17	18	19	20
21	22	23	24	25	26	27	28	29	30
31	32	33	34	35	36	37	38	39	40
41	42	43	44	45	46	47	48	49	50
51	52	53	54	55	56	57	58	59	60
61	62	63	64	65	66	67	68	69	70
71	72	73	74	75	76	77	78	79	80
81	82	83	84	85	86	87	88	89	90
91	92	93	94	95	96	97	98	99	100
101	102	103	104	105	106	107	108	109	110
111	112	113	114	115	116	117	118	119	120
121	122	123	124	125	126	127	128	129	130

REMOVE TISSUE BEFORE WRITING

CODE FOR QUESTIONNAIRE

KEY
for
Coding
Instructions

P: This item has been *precoded*; thus, you should simply enter in the box on the Coding Worksheet the answer number which has been circled on the Questionnaire.

D: This item can be *coded directly*; thus, you should enter in the box on the Coding Worksheet the numerical answer which has been written in on the Questionnaire.

*: The asterisk (*) indicates that the coding for this item is marked by some unusual feature. Read the Coding Instructions carefully and be sure you understand them before you code this item.

+: When a question has not been answered on the Questionnaire, you should insert a + in the appropriate box on the Coding Worksheet.

Question No.	Box No.	Item and Coding Instructions
1	1	Sex: P
2	2	Age: D
3	3	Race: P
4	4	Class standing: P
5	5	Grade-point average: D

I. YOUR FAMILY

Question No.	Box No.	Item and Coding Instructions
6	6	Parent referent: P
7	7	Family composition: P
8	8	Regular home: P
9	9	Marital status of parents: P
10	10*	Total in household: If only (a) is circled, code as 0. If (a) is *not* circled, count the number of answers circled, and enter that total in the box. If no answer is circled, code as +.
11	11	Number of brothers: D
12	12	Number of sisters: D
13	13	Total number of children in family: D
14	14	Birth order: P
15	15	Father's age at marriage: D
16	16	Mother's age at marriage: D
17	17*	Difference in parents' ages: D (Check to make sure that the answer in Question 16 has been subtracted from the answer in Question 15, and that the + or — sign is correct.)
18	18	Length of parents' marriage: D
19	19	Father's education: P
20	20	Mother's education: P
21	21	Parents' place of birth: P
22	22	Geographic mobility: P
23	23	Residence during childhood: P

Question No.	Box No.	Item and Coding Instructions

II. YOUR PARENTS' WORK

Question No.	Box No.	Item and Coding Instructions
24	24	Father's occupational classification: Read the occupation written in in Question 24 and check to see if you agree with the category circled by the respondent. If you do not agree or are not sure it is correct, ask your instructor if the occupational code should be changed.
25	25	Father's job satisfaction: P
26	26*	Mother's full-time employment: If (0) is circled, code as 0. If (0) is *not* circled, count the number of answers checked, and enter the total in the box.
27	27*	Mother's part-time employment: If (0) is circled, code as 0. If (0) is *not* circled, count the number of answers checked, and enter the total in the box.
28	28	Mother's occupational classification: Read the occupation written in in Question 28 and check to see if you agree with the category circled by the respondent. If you do not agree or are not sure it is correct, ask your instructor if the code should be changed.
29	29	Mother's job satisfaction: P
30	30	Mother's desire to work: P
31	31	Father's willingness to have mother work: P
32	32	Mother's satisfaction in homemaking: P
33	33	Father's father's occupational classification: Follow instructions given in Question 28.
34	34	Mother's father's occupational classification: Follow instructions given in Question 28.
35	35	Father's religious preference: P
36	36	Mother's religious preference: P
37	37	Your religious preference: P
38	38	Father's political preference: P
39	39	Mother's political preference: P
40	40	Your political preference: P

III. DATING AND MARRIAGE

Question No.	Box No.	Item and Coding Instructions
41	41	Present dating status: P
42	42	Marital status: P
43	43	Age at first date: D
44	44	Frequency of dates: P
45	45	Willingness to marry someone of a different religion: P

IV. YOU AND YOUR PARENTS

Question No.	Box No.	Item and Coding Instructions
46–47	46*	Trait desired most by father: Enter in the box the *letter* of the trait ranked (1) in column A (*Father*)
46–47	47*	Trait desired second by father: Enter in the box the *letter* of the trait ranked (2) in column A (*Father*)
48–49	48*	Trait desired most by mother: Enter in the box the *letter* of the trait ranked (1) in column B (*Mother*)
48–49	49*	Trait desired second by mother: Enter in the box the *letter* of the trait ranked (2) in column B (*Mother*)

Question No.	Box No.	Item and Coding Instructions
50	50	Hours per week spent on household tasks: D
51	51	Hours employed per week: D
52	52	Changes desired in mother: P
53	53	Changes desired in father: P
52 & 53	54*	Rejection of parents: Add the scores in boxes 52 and 53 and enter the total in box 54.
55	55	Marital happiness of parents: P
56	56	Popularity in high school: P
57	57	Childhood happiness: P

V. PARENT PRACTICES

Each of the scores for items 58–75 is based on the answers to two questions. If only one question in a pair has been answered, double that answer and enter it in the appropriate box on the Scoring Worksheet. If neither question in a pair has been answered, score as +.

Question No.	Box No.	Item and Coding Instructions
V: a & b	58*	Nurturance: Father: Add the circled answer numbers to items (a) and (b) in column A (Father), and enter the total in box 58.
V: a & b	59*	Nurturance: Mother: Add the circled answer numbers to items (a) and (b) in column B (Mother), and enter the total in box 59.
V: c & d	60*	Instrumental companionship: Father: Add the circled answer numbers to items (c) and (d) in column A (Father), and enter the total in box 60.
V: c & d	61*	Instrumental companionship: Mother: Add the circled answer numbers to items (c) and (d) in column B (Mother), and enter the total in box 61.
V: e & f	62*	Principled discipline: Father: Add the circled answer numbers to items (e) and (f) in column A (Father), and enter the total in box 62.
V: e & f	63*	Principled discipline: Mother: Add the circled answer numbers to items (e) and (f) in column B (Mother), and enter the total in box 63.
V: g & h	64*	Prescription of responsibility: Father: Add the circled answer numbers to items (g) and (h) in column A (Father), and enter the total in box 64.
V: g & h	65*	Prescription of responsibility: Mother: Add the circled answer numbers to items (g) and (h) in column B (Mother), and enter the total in box 65.
V: i & j	66*	Power: Father: Add the circled answer numbers to items (i) and (j) in column A (Father), and enter the total in box 66.
V: i & j	67*	Power: Mother: Add the circled answer numbers to items (i) and (j) in column B (Mother), and enter the total in box 67.
V: k & l	68*	Physical punishment: Father: Add the circled answer numbers to items (k) and (l) in column A (Father), and enter the total in box 68.
V: k & l	69*	Physical punishment: Mother: Add the circled answer numbers to items (k) and (l) in column B (Mother), and enter the total in box 69.
V: m & n	70*	Pressure for achievement: Father: Add the circled answer numbers to items (m) and (n) in column A (Father), and enter the total in box 70.
V: m & n	71*	Pressure for achievement: Mother: Add the circled answer numbers for items (m) and (n) in column B (Mother), and enter the total in box 71.

Question No.	Box No.	Item and Coding Instructions
V: o & p	72*	Deprivation of privileges: Father: Add the circled answer numbers for items (o) and (p) in column A (*Father*), and enter the total in box 72.
V: o & p	73*	Deprivation of privileges: Mother: Add the circled answer numbers for items (o) and (p) in column B (*Mother*), and enter the total in box 73.
V: q & r	74*	Expressive rejection: Father: Add the circled answer numbers for items (q) and (r) in column A (*Father*), and enter the total in box 74.
V: q & r	75*	Expressive rejection: Mother: Add the circled answer numbers for items (q) and (r) in column B (*Mother*), and enter the total in box 75.

VI. MARITAL ROLES

Question No.	Box No.	Item and Coding Instructions
VI: 1	76*	Wife's role: Mother's view of most important role: Enter the letter identifying the item ranked (1) in column A (*Mother's View*).
VI: 1	77*	Wife's role: Mother's view of second most important role: Enter the letter identifying the item ranked (2) in column A (*Mother's View*).
VI: 1	78*	Wife's role: Your view of most important role: Enter the letter identifying the item ranked (1) in column B (*Your View*).
VI: 1	79*	Wife's role: Your view of second most important role: Enter the letter identifying the item ranked (2) in column B (*Your View*).
VI: 2	80*	Husband's role: Father's view of most important role: Enter the letter identifying the item ranked (1) in Column A (*Father's View*).
VI: 2	81*	Husband's role: Father's view of second most important role: Enter the letter identifying the item ranked (2) in column A (*Father's View*).
VI: 2	82*	Husband's role: Your view of most important role: Enter the letter identifying the item ranked (1) in column B (*Your View*).
VI: 2	83*	Husband's role: Your view of second most important role: Enter the letter identifying the item ranked (2) in column B (*Your View*).
84: a & b	84*	Favorableness to marriage: Add the answer numbers circled in response to questions 84a and 84b, and enter the total in box 84.
85	85*	Favorableness to wife's employment: Count the number of "Yes" answers and enter that number in box 85.
86	86	Sex of child preferred: P
87	87	Responsibility for aged parents: P

VII. YOUR PERSONALITY AND YOUR PARENTS' PERSONALITIES

Each of the scores for items 88–96 and 100–114 is based on the answers to *two* questions. If only one question in a pair has been answered, double that answer and enter it in the appropriate box on the Scoring Worksheet. If neither question in a pair has been answered, score that item as +.

Question No.	Box No.	Item and Coding Instructions
VII: a & b	88*	Inclusion expressed: Yourself: Add the circled answer numbers for items (a) and (b) in column A (*Yourself*), and enter the total in box 88.
VII: a & b	89*	Inclusion expressed: Father: Add the circled answer numbers for items (a) and (b) in column B (*Father*), and enter the total in box 89.
VII: a & b	90*	Inclusion expressed: Mother: Add the circled answer numbers for items (a) and (b) in column C (*Mother*), and enter the total in box 90.

Question No.	Box No.	Item and Coding Instructions
VII: c & d	91*	Inclusion wanted: Yourself: Add the circled answer numbers for items (c) and (d) in column A (Yourself), and enter the total in box 91.
VII: c & d	92*	Inclusion wanted: Father: Add the circled answer numbers for items (c) and (d) in column B (Father), and enter the total in box 92.
VII: c & d	93*	Inclusion wanted: Mother: Add the circled answer numbers for items (c) and (d) in column C (Mother), and enter the total in box 93.
VII: e & f	94*	Control expressed: Yourself: Add the circled answer numbers for items (e) and (f) in column A (Yourself), and enter the total in box 94.
VII: e & f	95*	Control expressed: Father: Add the circled answer numbers for items (e) and (f) in column B (Father), and enter the total in box 95.
VII: e & f	96*	Control expressed: Mother: Add the circled answer numbers for items (e) and (f) in column C (Mother), and enter the total in box 96.

Control Expressed by Father and Mother:
Calculations for Complementary-Needs Laboratory Problem

	97*	Squares: Father: Square the score in box 95 and enter in box 97.
	98*	Squares: Mother: Square the score in box 96 and enter in box 98.
	99*	Cross-Products: Multiply the score in box 95 by the score in box 96 and enter the product in box 99.

Question No.	Box No.	Item and Coding Instructions
VII: g & h	100*	Control wanted: Yourself: Add the circled answer numbers for items (g) and (h) in column A (Yourself), and enter the total in box 100.
VII: g & h	101*	Control wanted: Father: Add the circled answer numbers for items (g) and (h) in column B (Father), and enter the total in box 101.
VII: g & h	102*	Control wanted: Mother: Add the circled answer numbers for items (g) and (h) in column C (Mother), and enter the total in box 102.
VII: i & j	103*	Affection expressed: Yourself: Add the circled answer numbers for items (i) and (j) in column A (Yourself), and enter the total in box 103.
VII: i & j	104*	Affection expressed: Father: Add the circled answer numbers for items (i) and (j) in column B (Father), and enter the total in box 104.
VII: i & j	105*	Affection expressed: Mother: Add the circled answer numbers for items (i) and (j) in column C (Mother), and enter the total in box 105.
VII: k & l	106*	Affection wanted: Yourself: Add the circled answer numbers for items (k) and (l) in column A (Yourself), and enter the total in box 106.
VII: k & l	107*	Affection wanted: Father: Add the circled answer numbers for items (k) and (l) in column B (Father), and enter the total in box 107.
VII: k & l	108*	Affection wanted: Mother: Add the circled answer numbers for items (k) and (l) in column C (Mother), and enter the total in box 108.
VII: m & n	109*	Achievement: Yourself: Add the circled answer numbers for items (m) and (n) in column A (Yourself), and enter the total in box 109.
VII: m & n	110*	Achievement: Father: Add the circled answer numbers for items (m) and (n) in column B (Father), and enter the total in box 110.
VII: m & n	111*	Achievement: Mother: Add the circled answer numbers for items (m) and (n) in column C (Mother), and enter the total in box 111.

VII: o & p	112*	Anxiety: Yourself: Add the circled answer numbers for items (o) and (p) in column A (*Yourself*), and enter the total in box 112.
VII: o & p	113*	Anxiety: Father: Add the circled answer numbers for items (o) and (p) in column B (*Father*), and enter the total in box 113.
VII: o & p	114*	Anxiety: Mother: Add the circled answer numbers for items (o) and (p) in column C (*Mother*), and enter the total in box 114.

VIII. THE LAST WORD

VIII: a	115*	Ultimate power index: Add the circled answer numbers for all the items in column A (*The Final Say*), and divide the total by 6 (or by the number of items answered), rounding to one decimal place. Enter this figure in box 115.
VIII: a	116*	Shared power index: Count (do NOT add) the number of times the answer (3) has been circled in column A (*The Final Say*), and enter the total in box 116. Code as +, however, if less than 5 items have been answered.
VIII: b	117*	Parents' agreement: Add the circled answer numbers in column B (*Parents' Agreement*), and divide the total by 6 (or by the number of items answered), rounding to one decimal place. Enter this figure in box 117.
VIII: c	118*	Your influence: Add the circled answer numbers in column C (*Your Influence*), and divide the total by 6 (or by the number of items answered), rounding to one decimal point. Enter this figure in box 118.

VALUES AND LIMITATIONS OF FAMILY RESEARCH USING STUDENT SUBJECTS

Judson T. Landis

Perhaps the chief limitation of research studies using students in college classes as subjects is the fact that college students are a select group rather than a representative sample of the population. The conscientious researcher needs to be careful to state clearly the limits of his sample when presenting findings. There is sometimes a tendency to apply such findings indiscriminately to a broader population than the sample warrants.

A possible limitation of research using college student subjects is that when the researcher secures the cooperation of students in his own classes, in which rapport exists between professor and students, it cannot be known with certainty whether the students' interest and enthusiasm for cooperating in the research may have some effect toward skewing the responses and findings. In fact, it must probably be assumed that in any research which requires the giving of information about personal experiences, attitudes, or other

factors in individual experience, the rapport established between researcher and informant may possibly influence the nature of the responses. It would seem that that possibility may be a limitation of much sociological research and not peculiar to research using college students. Limitations of questionnaire and interview techniques would apply with student subjects in the same measure as with other groups of subjects. Moreover, research with student subjects does have some special advantages which seem to outweigh limitations.

Until of late, sociological research has tended to give disproportionate attention to two social classes: (1) the upper middle, better educated classes represented by an undue proportion of college and university people whose cooperation is relatively easy to secure, and (2) the unfortunates in society who could be pressured into cooperating because of circumstances such as poverty, unemployment, delinquency, or other factors that made them available to researchers. In the earlier history of the teaching of social problems much of the information about society came from studies

Reprinted by permission of the author and the National Council on Family Relations from *Marriage and Family Living*, 19 (1957), pp. 100–105.

of people who had been in difficulty with the law or who were dependent upon society. The samples were skewed away from the "average" citizen. The point here is that there was nothing wrong with the findings of research with the specialized groups. Findings were often valid for the groups studied. What was, and is, needed is further research with other groups to complete the picture.

In the field of family sociology, researchers at first had to move slowly because of social prejudices and taboos. Family sociologists have had to find their research subjects among very special groups, one of which readily at hand was the college student group. (Since the research findings were being used with college students and with the upper middle classes who do most of the reading of research on marriage and the family, sociologists were actually using the best possible sample for their consuming public. The researcher working with industrial workers would naturally wish to do his research with industrial workers rather than some other groups or even with a cross-sectional sample of the population.) We recognize that the main family researches have dealt with the more highly educated people and with the upper middle classes; we have almost no research which could be considered representative of the entire population. I would not criticize the studies which have been made of special groups in society in any field of the social sciences. We cannot know too much about any one segment of society. As research findings extend to other groups, eventually a more complete picture of society as a whole will emerge.

A special value in research with student subjects is that it offers opportunities to compare findings of research among middle class young people with findings about those in other segments of society. To illustrate: Little research has been done on the subject of children's contacts with adult sexual deviation. What information was available had been gained from children whose cases had been handled in the courts. Those cases usually represented families from lower socio-economic levels, unstable families, and families with delinquency records. Since sexual deviation is a topic which is not generally discussed or admitted openly, it would be difficult to study a representative sample of children in the matter of their experiences with adult sexual deviation. However, I was able to get 2,000 of my students to participate in a study in which they reported their experiences with adult deviation.[1] The findings from this study indicate that findings of the earlier studies taken from court cases are not necessarily valid for children from other social classes.[2] The study indicates the need for repeating research with many different groups before any over-all conclusions can be reached.

Earl Koos, Mirra Komarovsky, Robert Angell, Ruth Cavan, and others have investigated family crises.[3] In general their studies have focused upon the lower socio-economic groups. There has been little study of family crises among the upper classes. Studies which focus upon crises among college-educated families would help to fill in the gaps in our understanding of family crises. College students might well be used as subjects for a project dealing with ways in which families meet crises.

Some of the early conclusions about sexual behavior among young people came from studies of delinquent boys and girls. Whyte gives us a picture of sexual behavior in an urban Italian community.[4] Winston Ehrmann and Lester Kirkendall are filling a gap with their studies of sexual behavior of college students.[5]

Research with student subjects serves a special purpose in that it becomes an entering wedge for doing research in areas which have been closed to research in the past and with groups not previously reached. We are able to do research with non college populations today because of the pioneering of those who worked with college students or who used college students to distribute their questionnaires in the 1920's and 1930's. Ernest Burgess and Leonard Cottrell, Katherine Davis, Paul Wallin, and others all contributed to make it possible for those of us today to study non college populations. Many of us will continue to do new researches which will be the entering wedge for research with wider populations. I mentioned the sexual deviation research which I have just completed. I believe enough has been learned through this research project with students so that the study could be repeated now with a non college group.

Another project in this category: For years I had received questions from the students in my family sociology classes asking why more information was not available on emotional changes which may accompany the menstrual cycle in women. Some 400 women in my classes were asked to participate in research on this subject by keeping daily records of any changes they were aware of in physical, mental, and emotional well-being for a period of from one to three months.[6] The experience of doing this research led me to believe that it would be almost impossible to get any other group of subjects to cooperate in keeping such daily records for any appreciable length of time. Cooperation through to the end of such a project required a select group of women, and one in which the researcher could furnish strong motivation for continuing their daily records. The problem in doing this research is not so much that it is in a taboo field, but that it is difficult to get a group of women to take the time to keep daily records of their physical and emotional states. With college subjects the professor can furnish the motivation from day to day so that the subject will make the necessary daily records. In such an area of research, our information will for some time probably have to come from highly selected groups. And who can say that fluctuations accompanying the cycle in college women are any different from the emotional fluctuations accompanying the menstrual cycle in non college women? It is simply that the information can be gotten from college women while it probably could not be gotten from other groups except with groups such as psychiatric or medical patients. One other study on this subject is by Therese Benedek and Boris Rubenstein which is a detailed endocrinological-psychoanalytical study of 15 women who were under psychoanalytic treatment.[7]

We must recognize that for the time being there are certain researches that can be done with limited groups because of the problems involved in getting subject cooperation, or because of the taboo nature of the research, and for such researches the student population may be an excellent source. As long as we recognize the limitations of our samples, then significant results can come from using college students, and eventually the researches can be repeated more extensively with non college groups.

Research done among students at a university serves specifically to make possible research in a larger population. If university researchers have investigated sexual deviation behavior and found that one-third of the students have had such experiences with adults, then community leaders can see some point in allowing a study in this area throughout the community. With Shirley and Thomas Poffenberger, a few years ago I studied husband-wife adjustment to first pregnancy among college student couples in Michigan.[8] Detailed information was gained on all aspects of adjustment to pregnancy, including the sexual adjustment. Thomas Poffenberger is now repeating this study with all the women who come to the hospital in Davis, California, to have their babies.

The value of student research in getting research methods accepted in communities is something which should not be overlooked. If students have participated in research at college, then they will be more willing to participate and to see the value of research as community members.

Another value to be derived from using students as subjects for research is in the development of research instruments. Since students are willing subjects, the researcher can use them as an experimental group for the testing of questionnaires, schedules, interview techniques, case histories, and other techniques. The researcher gets not only valuable assistance in building his instruments for research but also valuable insight into what can and what cannot be gained through his proposed research. If he finds an instrument inadequate with a college group, then he knows it is probably not usable with another less-informed group. At one time I considered doing a study which would have required student subjects to give the economic level of each of their parents before marriage and the present income of the father, in addition to certain other information on the past and present economic standing of the family. Testing the instruments with students, I found that most students had no idea as to the economic level from which their parents had come, and further, only a few students have any specific idea of their parents' present income. Needless to say, the project was abandoned. Many studies have been attempted with non college groups which would have been abandoned early or greatly improved if the researcher had used his students as guinea pigs in the research before going into the field with his study.

A common criticism of research with college student subjects is that there is no overall plan or design that is applied from university to university. Professors in widely separated colleges are doing piece-meal projects, each of which seems to have no relationship to what anyone else is doing. Some people argue that it would be better to work as organized groups with a common goal and method. Granted that the ideal research situation would be coordinated, cooperative, large scale projects which would produce overall pictures, but such projects would require the expenditure of massive funds, as well as almost unlimited time and human energy. Up to now, if the research-minded college professor had restrained himself from going ahead to do research using his students as subjects while he waited for the ideal research situation, we would still have little research information. We can hope that that ideal situation will come to exist, but in the meantime individual projects with college students have produced much basic and fundamental knowledge in family sociology. Attempts at large scale, group-planned, and group-executed studies of family life have not yet been able to make very extensive contributions. Rather it has been the individual professor, plodding along, getting ideas and setting up hypotheses, and subjecting them to empirical research with the groups at hand—in many cases university students —who has contributed the most to our knowledge.

It seems to me that for some time it will be necessary for most family sociologists to follow this jigsaw pattern of research. There are so many variations in family life that it will be necessary to do detailed studies of many special groups—the Negro family in the south and in the north, in the country and in the city; the Mexican family; the rural family; the Jewish family; and so forth. Family sociologists must continue to do what studies they can with students and their families. As these studies are done, expanded, and repeated with different groups, our jigsaw or crazy-quilt way of doing research gradually will produce the overall picture. An easier, quicker, or better way has not yet been made effective.

The check on the reliability of the jigsaw pattern of research with student subjects comes through professors in different universities doing repeat studies with their students. Willard Waller investigated the rating and dating complex on one campus.[9] William M. Smith, Jr., and Robert O. Blood, Jr., repeated the study with students at their respective universities.[10] Robert F. Winch has been investigating a theory of complementary needs in mate selection with 25 couples who were college graduates.[11] To check on the reliability of his findings repeat studies have been done by Charles Bowerman and B. R. Day studying 60 student couples either engaged or going steady and by Thomas Ktsanes studying 25 college married couples.[12] One repeat study found support for the Winch theory of complementary needs, the other did not. The Burgess-Cottrell-Wallin marital prediction schedule was formulated largely on the basis of information furnished by people with some college education. The schedule has now been tried out with people of various nationalities, various racial and socio-economic backgrounds.

Although it appears that there is no research design, one might say that a design is emerging in which studies of students of one college are repeated with those of other colleges; eventually non college people are studied. Although this may not be the most efficient way to get the job done, it may in the final analysis result in a very satisfactory product. Certainly many students and professors will have taken part in fitting together the jigsaw of family research.

There may be certain universals in human relationships which are true at all socio-economic levels. Some factors may be basic in parent-child and in husband-wife relationships and it may make little difference whether one studies college students, their parents' marriage, or the marriages of the non college population. Some situations produce frustrations and tension in a parent-child relationship or in a marriage. One might compare these universals in human relationships to universal laws in the field of germ disease. In general if people are exposed to certain disease germs they are likely to contract the disease whether they have college or non college backgrounds. It is true that a population which is better housed and has better nutrition might have greater resistance to certain germs than a poorer population, but the characteristics of the disease and its effect on its victims when it does strike can be known nevertheless. Similarly, any of our family research which is getting at universals is worthwhile regardless of the population studied. All of the researches which have attempted to get at the meeting of personality needs in marriage are contributing to our understanding of a universal.

The research of Nelson Foote and his students at the Family Study Center in the field of identity and interpersonal competence may be getting at a universal which should apply to all class levels.[13] My own research on time to adjust in marriage was perhaps getting at a universal in marriage adjustment.[14]

Further, there may be universal reactions to traumatic experiences in relationships and the pattern of reaction may be similar in the different socio-economic levels of society. To illustrate: Clifford Kirkpatrick and Theodore Caplow studied the reactions of college students to broken love affairs.[15] If their study were repeated among a non college population of college age young people, a similar pattern of reaction might be expected to be found. Non college people, like college people, probably react to the trauma of a broken love affair by such behavior as preserving keepsakes, dreaming about the partner, frequenting or avoiding places of common association, and the others found by Kirkpatrick and Caplow among college students. It seems that Kirkpatrick and Caplow were getting at basics in psychological reactions to frustrating experiences in human relationships. The fact that their subjects were college students should have no effect at all upon the findings, except that possibly the researchers could do the research with fewer handicaps by using college subjects than would have been the case with other subjects.

The studies of Willard Waller and William Goode on adjustment to divorce, done largely with non college subjects, revealed reactions to marriage failure.[16] The same patterns of reactions would be likely to be found if one studied the divorced in college classes. All of the many studies on family crises such as unemployment, war separation, death, unwanted pregnancy, illegitimacy, mental illness, crime, and alcoholism, are contributing to an understanding of human reactions which cut across social class.

Those studies which have focused upon the positive values in parent-child and in husband-wife relationships have doubtless revealed elements in human relationships which cut across all levels in society. The educational film "Roots of Happiness" has been considered one of the best by many because it brings out these values for all social classes and yet the film pictures family life among poor Puerto Rican families. The mutual respect of husband and wife for each other seems to be basic whether it be among rural Puerto Rican families, farm or city families in the United States, or a college student population. The lack of conflict in the home contributes to the security of children in poor or rich families, educated or uneducated. The mutual satisfaction of affectional and sexual needs is basic in the marriages of college students as well as among their non college friends; and it takes both groups time to arrive at a mutually satisfactory sexual adjustment.

It may appear that I have departed from my topic, "Values and Limitations of Family Research Using Student Subjects," since I have been referring to some researches among non student groups. My point in doing this is to make clear that research among college students is significant if the researcher constantly asks himself this question: "Is this getting at a universal in human relationships?" If the answer is yes, then there is no reason to feel apologetic for using students as subjects any more than if the researcher were using nurses, farmers, or industrial workers as his subjects.

If a project is not getting at a universal, then does it meet one of the other criteria mentioned earlier? Does it give research information which is valuable for comparison with findings from a different social class? Would the research serve as an entering wedge for doing research with a wider population? Does it serve as a pilot study for doing research with groups, or possibly with a representative sample of the whole population? Most research using student subjects can be of great value if directed to meet one of the above objectives.

In the final analysis, research with college students, like all other research, comes back to the specific carefulness, conscientiousness, and ability of the individual researcher. In thinking through this subject I believe that what it adds up to is this: Research using college subjects has no special limitations that are not encountered in any field of research using an unrepresentative sample. It does have some special values which are not always found in research using other subjects and in other fields.

NOTES

[1] Judson T. Landis, "The Nondelinquent Child and The Sexual Deviate," *Proceedings of the Pacific Sociological Society,* Research Studies of the State College of Washington, 23 (June, 1955), pp. 92–101. Entire study to be published soon in *The Psychiatric Quarterly.*

[2] *California Sexual Deviation Research,* California State Department of Mental Hygiene, March, 1952, January, 1953.

[3] Earl Koos, *Families in Trouble,* New York: King's Crown Press, 1946; Mirra Komarovsky, *The Unemployed Man and His Family,* New York: The Dryden Press, Inc., 1940; Robert C. Angell, *The Family Encounters the Depression,* New York: Charles Scribner's, 1936; Ruth S. Cavan and Katherine H. Ranck, *The Family and the Depression,* Chicago: University of Chicago Press, 1936.

[4] William F. Whyte, "A Slum Sex Code," *American Journal of Sociology,* 49 (July, 1943), pp. 24–31.

[5] Winston W. Ehrmann, "Student Cooperation in a Study of Dating Behavior," *Marriage and Family Living,* 14 (November, 1952), pp. 322–326.

[6] This study is to be published in *Social Problems.*

[7] Therese Benedek, *Studies in Psychosomatic Medicine—Psychosexual Functions in Women,* New York: The Ronald Press Company, 1952.

[8] Judson T. Landis, Thomas Poffenberger, and Shirley Poffenberger, "The Effects of First Pregnancy Upon the Sexual Adjustment of 212 Couples," *American Sociological Review,* 15 (December, 1950), pp. 767–772. Also, Shirley Poffenberger, Thomas Poffenberger, and Judson Landis, "Intent Toward Conception and the Pregnancy Experience," *American Sociological Review,* 17 (October, 1952), pp. 616–620.

[9] Willard Waller, "The Rating and Dating Complex," *American Sociological Review,* 2 (October, 1937), pp. 727–734.

[10] William M. Smith, Jr., "Rating and Dating: a Re-Study," *Marriage and Family Living,* 14 (November, 1952), pp. 312–316; Robert O. Blood, Jr., "A Retest of Waller's Rating Complex," *Marriage and Family Living,* 17 (February, 1955), pp. 41–47.

[11] Robert F. Winch, "The Theory of Complementary Needs in Mate-Selection," *American Sociological Review,* 20 (October, 1955), pp. 552–555.

[12] Thomas Ktsanes, "Mate Selection on the Basis of Personality Type," *American Sociological Review,* 20 (October, 1955), pp. 547–551; C. E. Bowerman and B. R. Day, "A Test of the Theory of Complementary Needs," *American Sociological Review,* 21 (October, 1956), pp. 602–605.

[13] Nelson N. Foote and Leonard S. Cottrell, Jr., *Identity and Interpersonal Competence,* Chicago: University of Chicago Press, 1955.

[14] Judson T. Landis, "Length of Time Required to Achieve Adjustment in Marriage," *American Sociological Review,* 11 (December, 1946), pp. 666–677.

[15] Clifford Kirkpatrick and Theodore Caplow, "Courtship in a Group of Minnesota Students," *The American Journal of Sociology,* 51 (1945), pp. 114–125.

[16] Willard Waller, *The Old Love and the New,* New York: Horace Liveright, 1930; William J. Goode, *After Divorce,* Glencoe: The Free Press, 1956.

FAMILY COMPOSITION AND SOCIAL CLASS

Problem

The heart of any science is the explanation—determination of cause and effect. In relation to the family, we want to know what causes families to be the way they are, and what the consequences of various patterns of family organization are for the individual family members and for society as a whole. For example, why do some families have many children and others few? and what are the consequences of being part of a family with many children, or with few?

Most of the laboratory problems in this manual

are concerned with *analytical* issues such as these, but this first problem is largely descriptive. We are starting out with a descriptive problem such as this one, not only because its simplicity makes it easier to learn the procedures to be used in laboratory work. More important, it is essential to know what a few of the major characteristics of the sample are, because some of them may affect the outcome of subsequent laboratory problems, and because this information will enable us to judge the extent to which our sample is representative (or unrepresentative) of the population as a whole.

The set of code sheets you have before you contain data for a sample drawn from a population which is composed of the families of students attending the university or college which you attend. This is *not* a very representative sample, partly because it is made up of the families of students in one or two courses only, and also because it is further restricted to families from just that fraction of the population who send their children to college. Therefore, this sample has a number of special characteristics, and generalizations reached on the basis of subsequent laboratory problems may be limited to this population, or, at most, to other populations which closely resemble it.

Such variables as family composition and socioeconomic status influence many aspects of the family. You will have the opportunity to demonstrate this in subsequent laboratory work. But in this problem, you will simply describe the distribution of your sample on these key variables (by tabulating the responses to Questions 2, 7, and 24), and compare your results first with your own guesses about the family composition and socioeconomic status or social class of your classmates, and then with the national statistics. The first of these comparisons will give you practice in stating and testing a simple hypothesis, and the second will provide information on the extent to which a college-student sample is typical of the population as a whole.

In carrying out this laboratory problem, you will be learning some elementary techniques of empirical social research: first, how to pose a hypothesis; and second, how to organize the data necessary to test the hypothesis by manipulating the code sheets, putting data into tabular form, and converting raw data to percentages.

Hypothesis

A hypothesis is a statement of what you expect the research to show. It can be based on logic, theory, prior research, or just plain hunch. The purpose of a hypothesis is both to provide a reminder or a guide to help you stick to the main point of the research, and also to help you maintain objectivity by having you state your presuppositions in advance.

In this problem you are to base the hypothesis on your own estimate of what the population of the college you attend is like. That is, state briefly your estimates of the following: (1) the social-class distribution of your classmates (i.e., about what percentage are from middle-class, farm, and working-class families); and (2) about what percentage are from "unbroken" families (both parents alive and living together).

See Appendix B (page 198) for general information on writing an hypothesis. On page 45 you will find the form for the Laboratory Report for Problem 2; on it write out your hypothesis *before* going on to the next steps of this problem.

Empirical Indicators for Problem 2

2. Age at last birthday:_____years

7. At the time you finished high school, your parents were:
   1 Both living together
   2 Divorced
   3 Separated
   4 Father was dead
   5 Mother was dead
   6 Temporarily living apart, for reasons other than marital problems (only if this situation had existed for one year or longer; otherwise circle 1 above)

24. What was your father's occupation at the time you graduated from high school, or what was it before his retirement (please specify)?

   _____

   In addition please circle the answer category which best fits his occupation.
   1 Professional (architect, chemist, doctor, etc.) or managerial position (department head, postmaster, police chief, etc.)
   2 Proprietor, except farm (i.e., owner of a business)
   3 Clerical or sales position
   4 Farmer (owner-operator or renter)
   5 Skilled workman or foreman (machinist, carpenter, etc.)
   6 Semiskilled or unskilled workman (truck driver, factory worker, etc.)
   7 Homemaker, or not employed outside the home
   + Don't know

Data Analysis

To save time and increase accuracy, you should work in pairs on the sorting and tabulating of the code sheets for this problem (and all others).

A. AGE

Sort out, clip together, and put aside all code sheets for persons aged 30 or over (age is coded directly in Box 2). This step is necessary because a person who is now 30 or over cannot be expected to remember what went on when he was 17 or 18, and the information which he supplies may be unreliable.

B. FAMILY COMPOSITION

1. *Sort* the code sheets into separate piles on the basis of the scores in Box 7 which gives the marital status of the parents at the time the student was a senior in high school. By referring to the question which was coded in Box 7, you will see that there are six possible categories and that scores of 1 in Box 7 indicate those students whose parents were both living together, scores of 2 indicate divorced parents, and so on. Note that there may be no code sheets falling into certain categories.

2. *Count* the number of code sheets in each pile and enter this information on Table 1 of the Tabulation Form under "*Frequency—f.*" Then total the column to find the total size of the sample. Divide up this and other parts of the problem so that you and your partner each do part of the job. Remember to copy your partner's work onto your own Tabulation Form.

3. *Calculate* the percentage of families falling in each category, and enter the percentages on Table 1 under "%." Use the percentage tables given in Appendix D, pages 211–216, and express your results as whole percentages only (i.e., 83.1 remains 83 per cent, 83.7 becomes 84 per cent, and so on). Do not be concerned if, because of rounding, the percentages total to only 99 per cent or to 101 per cent.

The first five or six people who finish this step should enter the percentage from unbroken families on the chart your instructor has drawn on the chalkboard.

4. *Paper clip* and put aside all cases falling in any category of Box 7 except 1. These are the broken, or single-parent families. In all subsequent problems, except Problem 8, we will not use these broken families, since the inclusion of the single-parent families introduces complications and may, in occasional instances, bias the results we obtain. For example, divorced mothers are more likely to be employed. Therefore, a study of the effects of the mother's employment might be confounded by, or tied in with, the effects of a divorce in the family if we did not separate out the divorced groups.

C. SOCIAL CLASS

Social class is one of the characteristics in which sociologists are most interested, and there are a number of ways of classifying families with regard to this important dimension. We will base our classification of this sample on one factor only—the occupation of the

respondent's father. This is one of the simplest methods of determining social class, and it is not without some inadequacies; nevertheless, the occupational classification of the father is probably the best *single* indicator of social class available to us.

1. *Tabulate* on Table 2 the father's occupational classification (coded in Box 24). Remember that you should use only code sheets for respondents who are under 30 and are from unbroken families.

It is not always necessary to sort the code sheets into separate piles to tabulate a piece of information. An alternative is to write tally marks (卌 11) on the Tabulation Form under "Tally" as you go through the set of code sheets. Then total the tally marks for each category based on the father's occupational classification and write these numbers under "*Frequency—f.*"

2. *Calculate* what percentage of the total sample falls in each occupational category and enter your results on Table 2 under "%."

3. *Combine* the six occupational categories into the three broad social-class groups shown at the right of Table 2. To do this, add the percentages within each of the three broad groupings, and enter these combined percentages on Table 2.

The first five or six people who complete this step should enter their findings on the chart your instructor has drawn on the chalkboard (i.e., enter the percentages who are white-collar, farm, and blue-collar).

Laboratory Report

Complete the remainder of the Laboratory Report for Problem 2. Refer to Appendix B (Outline for Preparing Laboratory Reports and Abstracts, pages 198–200), to find out what should go into each part of the report. In addition to the general instructions in Appendix B, the following points apply to this problem:

1. Problem 2 is purely descriptive; that is, there is no *independent* or *dependent* variable.

2. If your sample contains code sheets from other classes, your instructor will supply information about that part of the sample.

3. Confine your Summary of Findings to the following:

(a) The proportion of the sample from unbroken homes

(b) The proportions of the sample who are middle class, working class, and farm

4. In the Discussion for Problem 2, give primary attention to the following:

(a) Compare your findings with what you predicted in the hypothesis, and state whether you think the hypothesis is supported or refuted by the findings. Do *not* change the hypothesis to fit the findings. The purpose of a hypothesis is to help guide the research and the evidence can prove it to be wrong.

(b) Compare your findings with the statistical data available for more representative samples, as reported in Tables A and B. To what degree

is your sample representative of the nation? Of course, the institution you are attending would be very unusual if it were representative of the national distribution on socioeconomic status. It is important to keep this in mind in all subsequent work with this sample. Most state universities, for example, are representative of the middle levels of our society only; they do

TABLE A. *Percentage Distribution of All Children under 18 by Family Status, April, 1955*

Family Status of Child and Marital Status of Parent	Percentage of All Children (1955)
No relative present in household	0.8%
Living with relative other than parent	1.8
Living with one or both parents	97.4
Living with both parents	86.9
Living with father only	1.1
Living with mother only	9.4

Source: Metropolitan Life Insurance Company, *Statistical Bulletin,* 37(1956), Table 2, p. 3.

TABLE B. *Percentage Distribution of Occupations Reported for Males 14 Years Old and Over for the United States, 1960*

Occupation	Percentage	Class Status
Professional, technical, and kindred workers	10.1	White-collar = 35.3%
Managers, officials, and proprietors (except farm)	12.7	
Clerical and kindred workers	6.7	
Sales workers	5.8	
Farmers and farm managers	5.7	Farm = 9.4%
Farm laborers and foremen	3.7	
Craftsmen, foremen, and kindred workers	17.7	Blue-collar = 55.3%
Operatives and kindred workers	18.4	
Private household workers	.1	
Service workers, except private household	6.1	
Laborers, except farm and mine	7.6	
Unemployed	5.4	
TOTAL	100.0%	100.0%

Source: U.S. Bureau of the Census, *Statistical Abstract of the United States* (Washington: Government Printing Office, 1963), Table 286, p. 219, and Table 303, p. 231.

not usually represent, to any significant extent, the really top level, nor do they generally represent the lowest level.

(c) State how you think the characteristics of this sample will affect the degree to which you will be able to generalize from your conclusions in the laboratory problems which follow.

5. Tear out both the Tabulation Form and the Laboratory Report and hand them in to your instructor.

REFERENCES

Glick, Paul C., Heer, David M., and Beresford, John C. "Family Formation and Family Composition: Trends and Prospects," in Marvin B. Sussman, ed. *Sourcebook in Marriage and the Family*. Boston: Houghton Mifflin, 1963. Pp. 30–40.

Population Reference Bureau. "Spotlight on Marriage," *Population Bulletin*, 17 (1961). Also in Marvin B. Sussman, ed. *Sourcebook in Marriage and the Family*. Boston: Houghton Mifflin, 1963. Pp. 3–15.

SECTION/COURSE NO._____ DATE_____ NAME_____

TABLE 1. *Marital Status of Parents*

Family Composition (Box 7)	Frequency f	%
1 Both living together		
2 Divorced		
3 Separated		
4 Father was dead		
5 Mother was dead		
6 Temporarily living apart		
TOTAL		100%
No answer		✕

TABLE 2. *Father's Occupational Classification*

Father's Occupational Classification (Box 24)	Tally	Frequency f	%	
1 Professional or managerial position				White-collar or middle class = ____ %
2 Proprietor, except farm				
3 Clerical or sales position				
4 Farmer				Farm = ____ %
5 Skilled workman or foreman				Blue-collar or working class = ____ %
6 Semiskilled or unskilled workman				
7 Homemaker or not employed outside the home				
TOTAL			100%	
No answer			✕	

SECTION/COURSE NO._____ DATE_____ NAME_____

Family Composition and Social Class

HYPOTHESIS: _____

_____

_____

_____

_____

_____

_____

_____

_____

SAMPLE: _____

_____

_____

_____

_____

_____

_____

_____

SUMMARY OF FINDINGS: _____

_____

_____

_____

_____

_____

_____

_____

DISCUSSION: _____

Part III

INTERRELATIONS
OF THE FAMILY AND
OTHER SOCIAL SYSTEMS

ADOLESCENT-PARENT ADJUSTMENT—SOCIO-ECONOMIC
LEVEL AS A VARIABLE

F. Ivan Nye

The present study developed from the general hypothesis that socio-economic level is one of the variables in the differential adjustment of adolescents to parents. More specifically: (1) adolescents are better adjusted to parents in high socio-economic level than in low socio-economic level families, and (2) socio-economic level differences in adolescent-parent adjustment are not explained by other factors mutually associated with socio-economic level and adolescent-parent adjustment.

Pertinent Previous Studies

Contributions to the sociology of parent-adolescent interaction may be divided conveniently into two groups: (1) general sociological theory which can be

applied to the special area of parent-adolescent interaction, and (2) empirical research in that special area of sociology.

Principal contributions to general theory have been made by Reuter,[1] Parsons,[2] Merton,[3] Davis,[4] Dinkel,[5] and Green.[6] While they stress somewhat different points, a wide common base can be found for agreement that adolescent behavior of today is a result of the nature of present-day American society and particularly of two aspects of it: (1) its urban industrial character which has made the adolescent's labor of little or no value and his maintenance and education a heavy drain on the financial resources of the family, and (2) the extremely rapid rate of social change which gives the adolescent many experiences that the parent did not have and with which parents, institutions as presently constituted, and the mores are unable to cope in an organized manner.

The principal contributions to empirical research have been made by Cavan,[7] and Stott,[8] who have contributed to the comparison of residence groups,[9] and Havighurst[10] to the comparison of age groups. No

Reprinted by permission of the author and the American Sociological Association from the *American Sociological Review,* 16 (1951), pp. 341–349.

* The writer wishes to acknowledge the assistance of Judson T. Landis, who combined the function of major professor during the research with critic during the preparation of the manuscript; also to acknowledge valuable suggestions from C. P. Loomis, Duane Gibson, and Charles Proctor during the course of the project.

previous study of socio-economic level as a variable in adolescent-parent adjustment has come to the writer's attention.[11]

Construction of a Measurement Instrument

The present study began in 1946 in Salem, Oregon. The city high school was experiencing a "wave" of vandalism, insubordination, and absenteeism. The teachers felt that most of the adolescents' school adjustment problems could be traced to unsatisfactory adjustment in the home.

A check list of parental behavior items was prepared, but what proved to be more significant was a number of open-ended questions such as: On what subject would you like more freedom from parents? More information? More advice? More direction? Finally, and most productive, What advice do you think most important to give parents of children your age?

Of the mass of information secured from the above questions there was little indication which behavior and attitudes were really important to adolescent-parent adjustment and which were perhaps annoying or common but not important. To test its significance, each attitude and behavior item was formed into an objective multiple-choice question. The resulting anonymous questionnaire was administered to 572 high school students in six Washington high schools.[12] Each of the items was tested for association with the adolescent's evaluation of his relationship to his parents as measured by the question: "Do you consider your relationship to your parents: Ideal . . . , Very Satisfactory . . . , Satisfactory . . . , Unsatisfactory . . . , Very Unsatisfactory . . . ?"

Some of the behavior and attitudes mentioned by adolescents showed no significant correlation with the adolescent's own feeling about his adjustment and were dropped. These included what the adolescent felt about the regulation of child's spending money, control of adolescent eating, and amount of work required of the child.

After the elimination of non-significant behavior and attitude items, an objective form for the measurement of adolescent-parent adjustment was constructed, consisting of 31 adolescent-mother, 31 adolescent-father, and six adolescent-parent items. For convenience these items were grouped into five general areas: (1) feeling of being loved and accepted by parents, (2) parents' trust and confidence in the child, (3) child's feelings about the personalities of the parents, (4) socialization of the child, (5) adjustment to groups outside family.[13] Each of the items was stated in a form similar to the following example: "When my father makes me do something, he tells me why it's necessary: Always . . . , Almost Always . . . , Sometimes . . . , Seldom . . . , Never . . ."

An arbitrary system of weighting was adopted after a close correlation was found between it and the sigma system.[14] Since in the above example it was found that the largest per cent of the best adjusted adolescents checked "always" it was given the highest weight, 5, "almost always" the next highest, 4, etc. An additional check of this weighting was made by employing a variation of the Criterion of Internal Consistency in which quartiles formed by totaling scores from all the scale items were substituted for adjustment as measured by responses to a single question.[15]

Sample and Methodology

The sample consists of 1472 adolescents from grades eight and eleven of fifteen of the public schools of Michigan.[16] It includes 423 farm, 183 open country non-farm, 238 village,[17] 173 small town (2,500 to 10,000 population), 208 fringe, and 216 city adolescents, and 5 who did not indicate residence. The instrument was administered in the classroom to students taking required subjects. All were administered by the writer personally. The forms were strictly anonymous, a point which was stressed to reduce inhibitions to answering family questions.

The joint sponsorship of the Division of Education of Michigan State College and the State Department of Public Instruction with the Department of Sociology helped secure full cooperation on the part of teachers and school administrators, who in turn helped motivate the students. A combination of high motivation and the use of class time made possible a hundred per cent return. For various reasons eighteen returns were not used,[18] which left approximately ninety-nine per cent usable.

Socio-economic level was determined by weighting equally the occupation of the head of the family, estimated income, church attendance of each of the parents, education of each of the parents, number of memberships in organizations, and working status of the mother. The high correlation between objective measures of socio-economic level and the judgment of judges has been demonstrated by Kaufman,[19] Warner,[20] and indirectly by Hollingshead.[21]

Validity and Reliability

A number of tests of validity were employed both to individual scale items and to the scale as a whole. These included: (1) The correlation betweeen each item and the feeling that the adolescent has of his relationship to his parents was checked (association significant above the 1% level was required). (2) Each item was checked by the Criterion of Internal Consistency (C.R. of 3.0 was required). (3) Factor analysis was made of twenty-eight scale items from all areas of the scale.[22] (4) Parents scored themselves on the same scale and a correlation of .40 with children's score was obtained. (5) Scores were correlated with the ten areas of the California Mental Health Analysis—intermediate form—and significant correlations were obtained for nine of the ten areas (r ranging from .60 to .20). (6) The subjective evaluations by experts on three campuses and of some 2,000 adolescents in Washington and Michigan were utilized. (7) A positive correlation of .67 between the scale scores and the subjective self-evaluation of the group scoring lowest on the scale was obtained.[23]

The split-half check of reliability employing the Kudor-Richardson formula yielded an uncorrected correlation of .92.[24]

Test of the Hypotheses

Hypothesis one is stated: Adolescents are better adjusted to parents in high than in low socio-economic level families. Three tests were made: (1) by comparing mean scores of the high and low socio-economic groups, (2) a Chi-square check of the distributions of high and low socio-economic level adolescents on each individual scale item, and (3) by the distribution of high and low socio-economic level adolescents in high, middle, and low adjustment quartiles.

The possible range of scores on the scale is 1.00 to 5.00. The highest socio-economic group showed a mean score of 3.96 compared to 3.66 for the lowest socio-economic group, a difference which is 7.02 times its standard error (a C.R. of 2.0 is generally considered adequate).

Of the 68 items in the scale, 48 or 70.6% show significant differences. All the items differing significantly show higher distributions for the high socio-economic group. Some items show slightly higher

TABLE 1. *Significance of Differences Between Responses of High and Low Socio-Economic Level Adolescents to All Adolescent-Parent Items*

Scale Sections	Difference Significant Above 5%	Difference Not Significant
Love and security items	9	2
Status items	9	3
Socialization	7	9
Parent personality items	11	4
Outside family items	12	2
	48	20
Items favoring high socio-economic level families		48
Items favoring low socio-economic level families		0

distributions for the low socio-economic group, but these differences are below the 5% level. The better adjustment of the high socio-economic group is distributed throughout all of the areas of the scale (see Table 1). Adolescents from the higher socio-economic level families score higher on feeling of being loved and secure, feelings that parents trust and have confidence in them, socialization including disciplinary relationships, attitudes toward the parent's personality, and relationships in interaction affecting the adolescent's contact with groups outside the family.

Likewise the hypothesis is supported by the distribution of high and low socio-economic level adolescents into high, middle, and low adjustment quartiles (shown in Table 2).

The hypothesis is supported above the 1% level of probability by a comparison of the mean adjustment scores of the two groups and by a comparison of the distribution of high and low socio-economic level adolescents into high, middle, and low adjustment quartiles, and above the 5% level of probability by forty-eight single items of the scale.

The above analysis, while it is convincing as stated, is of limited usefulness in establishing a causal relationship. Since a number of other variables are

TABLE 2. *Distribution of High, Medium, and Low Socio-Economic Level Adolescents into High, Middle, and Low Adolescent-Parent Adjustment Quartiles*

Adjustment Quartile	High Socio-Economic Level		Medium Socio-Economic Level		Low Socio-Economic Level		Total
High quartile	109	(38%)	220	(23%)	19	(12%)	348
Middle quartiles	133	(47%)	505	(52%)	70	(46%)	708
Low quartile	43	(15%)	250	(25%)	64	(42%)	357
	285	100%	975	100%	153	100%	1413

$X^2 = 65.4$; $P < .01$.

TABLE 3. *The Distribution of City and Farm Adolescents among High, Middle, and Low Adolescent-Parent Adjustment Quartiles*

Adjustment Quartile	Farm		City		Total
High quartile	84	(20%)	66	(31%)	150
Middle quartiles	205	(49%)	105	(49%)	310
Low quartile	130	(31%)	43	(20%)	173
	419	100%	214	100%	633

$X^2 = 13.2$; $P < .01$.

significantly associated with both adolescent-parent adjustment and socio-economic level, it becomes necessary to inquire whether the observed socio-economic differences may not be explained by variables associated with socio-economic level. More formally, this hypothesis is stated: Socio-economic level differences in adolescent-parent adjustment are not explainable by factors mutually associated with socio-economic level and adjustment. To test this hypothesis the factors of residence, broken families, family size, and working status of the mother are analyzed in the following discussion.

Residence as a Factor

Residence is significantly associated with adolescent-parent adjustment. This is shown by: (1) a comparison of mean scores of city, 3.896, and farm, 3.732 (C.R. of the difference to its standard error is 3.62), (2) a significant difference in the distribution of city and farm adolescents into high, middle, and low adjustment quartiles (shown in Table 3).

Residence is also significantly associated with socio-economic level.[25] This is indicated by the finding that there is a rank order correlation of .45 between items significantly different between farm-city and high-low socio-economic level. The association is significant, also, as shown by a Chi-square check of the distribution of farm and city families into high and low socio-economic levels.[26]

Since it has been established above that residence is significantly associated with both socio-economic level and adolescent-parent adjustment, it becomes necessary to determine whether all or some major portion of the socio-economic differences are explainable by residence. This check is made by holding residence constant. This is accomplished by testing the distribution of high and low socio-economic level adolescents among high, middle, and low adjustment quartiles within the farm and city samples separately (shown in Table 4).

Since socio-economic differences remain above those required at the 1% level of probability, we may state with confidence that differences in adolescent-parent adjustment observed between high and low socio-economic level are not explained by residence differences.

Broken Homes

Proportion of broken homes[26a] is significantly associated with both level of adolescent-parent adjustment and with socio-economic level. The association between broken homes and adolescent-parent adjustment is above the 1% level (shown in Table 5). The association between incidence of broken homes and

TABLE 4. *Comparison of High, Medium, and Low Socio-Economic Level Adolescent-Parent Adjustment, with Residence Constant*

Adjustment Quartile	Farm						City				Total
	High Socio-Economic Level		Medium Socio-Economic Level		Low Socio-Economic Level		High Socio-Economic Level		Medium Low Socio-Economic Level		
High quartile	18	(37%)	61	(23%)	6	(8%)	28	(40%)	37	(25%)	150
Middle 2 and 3	25	(51%)	147	(55%)	33	(44%)	34	(49%)	76	(53%)	315
Low quartile	6	(12%)	87	(33%)	36	(48%)	8	(11%)	31	(22%)	168
	49	100%	295	100%	75	100%	70	100%	144	100%	633

X^2 for total table is 31.54 with six degrees of freedom; $P < .01$.

TABLE 5. *The Distribution of Adolescents from Broken and Unbroken Homes among High, Middle, and Low Adolescent-Parent Adjustment Quartiles*

Adjustment Quartile	Broken Families		Unbroken Families		Total
High quartile	53	(19%)	303	(27%)	356
Middle 2 and 3	133	(48%)	577	(50%)	710
Low quartile	90	(33%)	267	(23%)	357
	276	100%	1147	100%	1423

$X^2 = 12.7$; $P < .01$.

socio-economic level is also above the 1% level of probability.[27]

Since broken homes are significantly associated with both socio-economic level and adolescent-parent adjustment, it is possible that this factor can explain the observed socio-economic differences. To determine whether all or some major portion of the socio-economic differences are explained by a different per cent of broken homes in the high and low socio-economic level groups, broken homes are held constant. This is accomplished by testing the distribution of high and low socio-economic level adolescents among high, middle, and low adjustment quartiles within the broken and unbroken family samples separately (shown in Table 6).[28]

Since socio-economic differences remain above those required at the 1% level of probability, we may state with confidence that differences in adolescent-parent adjustment observed between high, medium, and low socio-economic levels are not explained by differing proportions of broken homes in the three socio-economic levels. Table 6 indicates further that

socio-economic status is a much more significant variable in unbroken than in broken homes. If broken homes were considered alone, the importance of socio-economic level would remain problematical.

Size of Family

Size of family is significantly associated with both socio-economic level[29] and adolescent-parent adjustment. The association between size of family and adjustment is above the 1% level of probability (see Table 7).

Since size of family is associated with both adolescent-parent adjustment and socio-economic level, size of family is held constant to determine whether size of family can explain observed differences between socio-economic levels (shown in Table 8).

Since socio-economic differences remain above those required at the 1% level of probability, it may be stated with confidence that differences in adolescent-parent adjustment observed between high and low socio-economic levels are not explained by differing

TABLE 6. *Comparison of Adolescent-Parent Adjustment of High, Medium, and Low Socio-Economic Level Families, with Broken Homes Held Constant*

	Broken Families						
Adjustment Quartile	High Socio-Economic Level		Medium Socio-Economic Level		Low Socio-Economic Level		Total
High quartile	8	(30%)	44	(20%)	2	(7%)	54
Middle 2 and 3	13	(50%)	100	(46%)	18	(60%)	131
Low quartile	5	(20%)	74	(34%)	10	(33%)	89
	26	100%	218	100%	30	100%	274

	Unbroken Families						
Adjustment Quartile	High Socio-Economic Level		Medium Socio-Economic Level		Low Socio-Economic Level		Total
High quartile	98	(38%)	176	(24%)	16	(13%)	290
Middle 2 and 3	119	(47%)	395	(53%)	51	(43%)	565
Low quartile	38	(15%)	173	(23%)	53	(44%)	264
	255	100%	744	100%	120	100%	1119

$X^2 = 56.7$.
Total X^2 is 63.8 with eight degrees of freedom; $P < .01$.

TABLE 7. *The Distribution of Adolescents from Small, Medium, and Large Families among High, Middle, and Low Adolescent-Parent Adjustment Quartiles*

Adjustment Quartile	"Only" Child		Two Children		3, 4, 5 Children		6 or More Children		Total
High quartile	54	(38%)	89	(32%)	157	(24%)	58	(17%)	358
Middle 2 and 3	66	(47%)	139	(50%)	339	(51%)	175	(49%)	719
Low quartile	21	(15%)	52	(18%)	169	(25%)	121	(34%)	363
	141	100%	280	100%	665	100%	354	100%	1440

$X^2 = 48.66$; $P < .01$.

distributions of small, medium, and large families at high and low socio-economic levels. Significant association is found only in medium and large families. For reasons not here apparent, socio-economic level becomes non-significant in small families.[30]

Employed Mothers

Since the working status of the mother was taken as one measure of socio-economic level, it was antici-pated that there would be a significant association between it and socio-economic level.[31] However, the literature of family relations has considered the working mother a factor of such importance that it appears necessary to demonstrate that the association between adolescent-parent adjustment and socio-economic level is not explained entirely by this factor. Since the employment status of mothers is also significantly associated with adolescent-parent adjustment,[32] it could explain the observed socio-economic differences. To

TABLE 8. *Comparison of Adolescent-Parent Adjustment of High, Medium, and Low Socio-Economic Level Families, with Size of Family Constant*

*Small Families***

Adjustment Quartile	High Socio-Economic Level		Medium Socio-Economic Level		Low Socio-Economic Level		Total
High quartile	75	(37%)	63	(31%)	0*		138
Middle 2 and 3	98	(48%)	103	(50%)	0*		201
Low quartile	31	(15%)	38	(19%)	1*		70
	204	100%	204	100%	1*		409

$X^2 = 2.1$.

*Medium Families***

Adjustment Quartile	High Socio-Economic Level		Medium Socio-Economic Level		Low Socio-Economic Level		Total
High quartile	34	(44%)	91	(23%)	1*		126
Middle 2 and 3	34	(44%)	200	(50%)	2*		236
Low quartile	10	(12%)	109	(27%)	1*		120
	78	100%	400	100%	4*		482

$X^2 = 18.5$.

*Large Families***

Adjustment Quartile	High Socio-Economic Level		Medium Socio-Economic Level		Low Socio-Economic Level		Total
High quartile	0*		64	(18%)	17	(12%)	81
Middle 2 and 3	1*		196	(54%)	68	(46%)	265
Low quartile	2*		100	(28%)	62	(42%)	164
	3*		360	100%	147	100%	510

$X^2 = 8.6$.
Total X^2 is 29.2 with six degrees of freedom; $P < .01$.

* Combined with medium group.
** Small families 1 and 2 children, Medium 3–4, Large 5 or more.

TABLE 9. *Comparison of Adolescent-Parent Adjustment of High, Medium, and Low Socio-Economic Level Families, with Employment of Mothers Constant*

	Employed Full-Time			
Adjustment Quartile	High Socio-Economic Level	Medium Socio-Economic Level	Low Socio-Economic Level	Total
High quartile	2*	32 (20%)	4 (10%)	38
Middle 2 and 3	1*	75 (50%)	22 (60%)	98
Low quartile	0*	45 (30%)	11 (30%)	56
	3*	152 100%	37 100%	192

$X^2 = 2.2$.
* Combined with medium group.

	Employed Part-Time			
Adjustment Quartile	High Socio-Economic Level	Medium Socio-Economic Level	Low Socio-Economic Level	Total
High quartile	13 (36%)	37 (32%)	4 (20%)	54
Middle 2 and 3	17 (48%)	60 (51%)	11 (55%)	88
Low quartile	6 (16%)	20 (17%)	5 (25%)	31
	36 100%	117 100%	20 100%	173

$X^2 = 1.4$.

	Not Employed			
Adjustment Quartile	High Socio-Economic Level	Medium Socio-Economic Level	Low Socio-Economic Level	Total
High quartile	94 (38%)	140 (21%)	12 (12%)	246
Middle 2 and 3	115 (46%)	355 (53%)	37 (39%)	507
Low quartile	37 (16%)	176 (26%)	48 (49%)	261
	246 100%	671 100%	97 100%	1014

$X^2 = 66.2$.
Total X^2 is 69.8 with ten degrees of freedom; $P < .01$.

check this possibility, employment status of mothers is held constant (shown in Table 9).

With employment status of the mother held constant, socio-economic differences in adolescent-parent adjustment remain above the 1% level of probability. We may, therefore, state with confidence that employment status of the mother does not explain the observed differences between the adolescent-parent adjustment of high and low socio-economic groups. We should point out, however, that socio-economic level is not an equally significant variable in homes where the mother is or is not employed. It is highly associated with adjustment where mothers are not employed, but shows no significant adjustment where mothers are employed part or full time.

Summary

Adolescents are, on the average, better adjusted to parents in high than in low socio-economic level families. This is shown by a comparison of mean adjustment scores of the two groups; by their distribution into high, middle, and low adjustment quartiles, and by an item analysis of the scale used to measure adjustment.

The higher scores of the high socio-economic group are not explained by the differential distribution of certain characteristics associated with both adolescent-parent adjustment and socio-economic level. These characteristics include proportion of broken homes, size of family, employment status of the mother, and rural or urban residence of the family. Significant socio-economic differences remain when each of the associated factors is held constant.

Conclusions

Socio-economic level of the family is a significant variable in the differential adjustment of adolescents to parents. It is not, however, the only significant sociological variable. Residence, size of family, broken homes, employment status of the mother, and age and

105899

sex of the adolescent are also significant factors.[33] Moreover, socio-economic level is not equally significant in all sub-groups considered in this study. Very small families, families with employed mothers, and broken families fail to show significant differences between socio-economic levels. Both the general finding that adolescent-parent adjustment is better at the high socio-economic level and the exceptions to that general finding noted above could provide a basis for further research.

NOTES

[1] C. B. Reuter, "The Sociology of Adolescence," *American Journal of Sociology,* 43 (1937), 414–427.

[2] Talcott Parsons, "Certain Primary Sources and Patterns of Aggression in the Social Structure of the Western World," *Psychiatry,* 10 (1947), 167–181.

[3] Robert K. Merton, "Social Structure and Anomie," *American Sociological Review,* 3 (1938), 672–682.

[4] Kingsley Davis, "The Sociology of Parent-Youth Conflict," *American Sociological Review,* 5 (1940), 523–535.

[5] Robert M. Dinkel, "Parent-Child Conflict in Minnesota Families," *American Sociological Review,* 8 (1943), 412–419.

[6] Arnold M. Green, "The Middle-Class Male Child and Neurosis," *American Sociological Review,* 11 (1946), 31–42.

[7] Ruth Cavan, *The Adolescent in the Family,* New York: D. Appleton-Century Co., 1934.

[8] Leland H. Stott, "Adolescent Dislikes Regarding Parental Behavior," *Pedagogical Seminary,* 42 (1937), 393–414.

[9] Residential findings of this study are reported in a paper by the writer in *Rural Sociology,* Dec., 1950.

[10] R. J. Havighurst and Hilda Taba, *Adolescent Character and Personality,* New York: John Wiley and Sons, Inc., 1949.

[11] The nearest is the adjustment of younger children reported in W. Allison Davis and R. J. Havighurst, *Father of the Man,* Boston: Houghton Mifflin Co., 1947.

[12] See the writer's master's thesis, "Factors Influencing Adolescent Adjustment to Parents," State College of Washington, Pullman, 1947.

[13] The hypotheses that each of these areas form a cluster of more highly correlated items than the scale as a whole was tested and rejected. Factor analysis found only one factor in the scale.

[14] Sewell gives a detailed description of the sigma method of weighting. See William H. Sewell, "The Construction and Standardization of a Measurement of Socio-Economic Status of Oklahoma Farm Families," *Oklahoma AES Technical Bulletin* 9, Stillwater, Oklahoma, 1940.

[15] This weighting procedure parallels quite closely the one used by E. A. Burgess and L. S. Cottrell, *Predicting Success or Failure in Marriage,* New York: Prentice-Hall, Inc., 1939.

[16] Detroit, Lansing, Battle Creek (fringe), Belding, Rockford, West Branch, Mesick, Elkton, Pickford, Onaway, Wakefield, Wayne, Lakeview, Stephenson, and Concord.

[17] The rural population was deliberately oversampled to make possible a comparison of various rural groups. Residence was held constant when socio-economic levels were compared.

[18] One girl was married, one was deaf, and another too retarded to be able to read well enough. Three omitted too many items, and the balance gave answers that contradicted themselves.

[19] Harold F. Kaufman, "Prestige Classes in a New York Rural Community," *AES Memoir 260,* Cornell University, Ithaca, 1944.

[20] Lloyd Warner, *Democracy in Jonesville,* New York: Harper and Brothers, 1949.

[21] A. B. Hollingshead, *Elmtown's Youth,* New York: John Wiley & Sons, Inc., 1949. After selecting his social classes by judges, he describes them in objective terms such as membership in organizations, education, etc. These could just as well have been combined into a statistical index which probably would have produced differences as significant as the judge method.

[22] All mother-adolescent items were included except five which closely paralleled items included. A larger number of items became prohibitive in terms of time and money.

[23] The lowest socio-economic group. This special check was considered desirable because sociologists have often been accused of imposing sets of values on groups who do not embrace them.

[24] Further methodological details are available in the writer's doctoral dissertation, "Adolescent Adjustment to Parents," Chapter 3, Michigan State College, East Lansing, 1950.

[25] A more detailed discussion of the residence factor is presented by the writer in *Rural Sociology,* December, 1950.

[26] A Chi-square value of 29.0 was obtained from a 2 by 2 table, which is significant, of course, above the 1% level.

[26a] All homes are considered broken in which the adolescent is not living with both biological parents.

[27] X^2 of 25.9 for a 2 by 3 table.

[28] The writer is indebted to Dr. Thomas C. McCormick for an examination of the mathematical assumptions of this use of Chi square.

[29] The Chi-square check of association between size of family and socio-economic level indicates that it is significant above the 1% level. A value of Chi-square of 568.4 is not often found for a 3 by 3 table. Note in Table 8 that there is only one low socio-economic level family with one or two children and only three high socio-economic level families with more than five children. A corrected coefficient of contingency of .733 was found between size of family and socio-economic status.

[30] One limitation of the sample is apparent here—virtually no low socio-economic families with small families. If such a sub-sample were available it might show significant differences.

[31] Above the 1% level of probability (X^2 of 57.7 for a 3 by 3 table). Notice in Table 9 that there are twelve times as many mothers employed full-time in the low as in the high socio-economic group.

[32] The association is significant above the 5% level of probability. This is not as close an association as the other variables considered in this study, or as close as is popularly supposed. Furthermore, the scores of adolescents from homes in which the mother is not employed outside the home average *lower* than those in which the mother is employed part-time. This finding will be discussed in greater detail in a forthcoming article in *Marriage and Family Living.*

[33] Age and sex are equated in the sampling process. Possible loading by either immigrant children or a particular religious group was also checked.

HOW TO READ A TABLE

W. Allen Wallis and Harry V. Roberts

*   *   *

Information can be packed into a table like sardines into a can, and if you cannot read a table, it is as if you had a can of sardines but no key. Ordinary reading ability is no more effective in reading a table than an ordinary can opener in opening a can of sardines, and if you go at it with a hammer and chisel you are likely to mutilate the contents.

We will try to extract information from Table 270 about the association of illiteracy with age, color, and sex. We urge that before you read further you study Table 270 and jot down your own conclusions in the sequence in which you reach them.

Example 270: Illiteracy

TABLE 270. *Illiteracy Rates, by Age, Color, and Sex, 1952*

Based on a sample of about 25,000. Persons unable both to read and to write in any language were classified as illiterate, except that literacy was assumed for all who had completed 6 or more years of school. Only the civilian, noninstitutional population 14 years of age and over is included.

Percent Illiterate

Age	White			Nonwhite			Both Colors		
(Years)	Male	Female	Both	Male	Female	Both	Male	Female	Both
14 to 24	1.2	0.5	0.8	7.2	1.4	3.9	1.8	0.6	1.2
25 to 34	0.8	0.6	0.7	9.7	3.8	6.4	1.6	0.9	1.2
35 to 44	1.2	0.5	0.8	7.5	5.9	6.6	1.7	1.0	1.3
45 to 54	2.2	1.4	1.8	12.8	10.4	11.5	3.2	2.3	2.7
55 to 64	3.6	3.4	3.5	19.4	16.9	18.1	4.7	4.4	4.5
65 and over	5.6	4.4	5.0	35.8	31.2	33.3	7.6	6.2	6.9
14 and over	2.1	1.5	1.8	12.7	8.2	10.2	3.0	2.1	2.5

Source: *Statistical Abstract: 1955*, Table 132, p. 115. Original source: Bureau of the Census, *Current Population Reports*, Series P-20, No. 45.

You will not extract any information from the table if you continue to divert your gaze from it in embarrassed bewilderment. Don't stare at it blankly, either—focus your eyes and pick out some detail that is meaningful, then another, then compare them, then look for similar comparisons, and soon you'll know what the table says.

There are at least two good reasons for learning to read tables. The first is that once the reading of tables is mastered (and this does not take long), the reader's time is greatly economized by reversing the usual procedure, that is, by studying the tables carefully and then just skimming the text to see if there is anything there that is not evident in the tables, or not in them at all. This not only saves time but often results in a better understanding: a verbal description of any but the simplest statistical relationship is usually hard to follow, and besides, authors sometimes misrepresent or overlook important facts in their own tables. A second

reason for learning to read tables is that users of research can better describe the data needed to answer their administrative or scientific problems if they can specify the types of tables needed, and this requires an understanding of tables. Research workers, in turn, can plan investigations more effectively if they visualize in advance the statistical tables needed to answer the general questions that motivate the research.

Consider, then, Table 270. By following a systematic procedure it is possible to grasp quickly the information presented. Here are the main steps:

(1) *Read the title carefully.* One of the most common mistakes in reading tables is to try to gather from a hit or miss perusal of the body of the table what the table is really about. A good title tells precisely what the table contains. In this case, the title shows that the table tells about illiteracy, in relation to age, color, and sex, in 1952, and that the data are presented as rates—percent illiterate.

(2) *Read the headnote or other explanation carefully.* In the headnote to Table 270 we get a more precise indication of the basis for classifying people as

illiterate. We see, in fact, that the rates are slightly too low because it was taken for granted that any person who had completed six or more years of school was literate; but it is reasonable to suppose that the error from this source is negligible. We note also that the mentally deficient, criminals, and others in institutions have been excluded, as have the armed forces, so that the data relate to people in everyday civilian life. Finally, we note that the data are based on a sample, so we make a mental note not to attach too much importance to any single figure, or difference between figures, without first looking up the sampling error.

Information of the kind given in the headnote of Table 270 is often not attached directly to the table, but must be sought elsewhere in the text. Those who prepare reports that include statistical tables should, but frequently do not, keep in mind not only the reader who reads straight through the report without putting it down, but also the user making a quick search for a specific piece of information.

(3) *Notice the source.* Is the original source likely to be reliable? In this case, the answer is definitely "yes," for the Bureau of the Census is one of the most competent statistical agencies in the world. The secondary source, the *Statistical Abstract,* is a model of its kind. But *you* are getting the data from a tertiary source, this book. What about its reliability? Unless you have checked some of our previous data against their sources, you really do not know about that, and even if you did it would be a mistake to put complete reliance on the data without verifying them.[1] Of course *we* assure you of our reliability; but we would not trust your infallibility, or even our own, no matter who gave *us* assurances.

(4) *Look at the footnotes.* Maybe some of them affect the data you will study. Sometimes a footnote applies to every figure in a row, column, or section, but not every figure to which it applies has a footnote symbol. This is the case with Table 269, in a sense. [This table is not included in the present selection, but the authors' observations on the use of footnotes are helpful.] The footnote indicates that some individuals are included in the total but not in any years-of-school class, which implies that some, and probably all, of the classes lack a few observations. The footnote, incidentally, would have been better if "a small number" had been specified more precisely, preferably as a percent of the total number.

(5) *Find out what units are used.* Reading thousands as millions or as units is not uncommon. Long tons can be confused with short tons or metric tons, meters with yards, degrees with radians (as in Example 82A) [here omitted], U. S. with Imperial gallons, nautical with statute miles, rates per 1,000 with rates per 100,000, "4-inch boards" with boards 4 inches wide,[2] fluid ounces with ounces avoirdupois, and so on. In Table 270 illiteracy is expressed in percent—incidence per 100—and age in years.

The foregoing steps are, in a sense, all for preliminary orientation before settling down to our real purpose—as a dog turns around two or three times before settling down for a nap. They do not take long, and ought to be habitual, but if you omit them you may suffer a rude awakening later—or never awaken at all.

(6) *Look at the over-all average.* The illiteracy rate for all ages, both colors, and both sexes—the whole population, in other words—is shown in the lower right hand corner of Table 270 as 2.5 percent, or one person in 40. This may surprise you, for probably not one in 400 and perhaps not even one in 4,000 of your acquaintances 14 years of age or older is illiterate. On a matter like this, for a country of 165 million people and three million square miles, neither one's own impressions nor the consensus of one's friends' impressions is valid.

(7) *See what variability there is.* It is quickly evident that there are percentages less than 1 and more than 30 in the table. There is, therefore, extraordinary variation in illiteracy among the 24 basic groups into which the population has been divided (two sexes, two colors, six age classes).

(8) *See how the average is associated with each of the main criteria of classification.*

(a) *Age.* Looking in the section for "both colors" and down the column for "both" sexes, we see that the illiteracy rate is essentially constant at about 1¼ percent from ages 14 to 44, but then rises sharply through the remainder of the age classes to a rate in the highest age class 5.7 percentage points larger than, and 5¾ times as large as, the rate in the lowest age class. (Avoid phrases such as "illiteracy increases with age," which suggest that given individuals change as they age.)

At this point, some competent table-readers, especially if they were particularly interested in the association between age and illiteracy, would pursue this path further. We shall, however, complete our survey of the gross associations with the three variables, then take up each in detail. Probably neither route has any general advantage over the other.

(b) *Sex.* In the "both colors" section, comparison of the entries at the bottoms of the "male" and "female" columns, which apply to all ages, shows that the illiteracy rate for males (3.0 percent) is over 40 percent larger than that for females (2.1 percent). In view of our finding about age, we make a mental note to consider the possibility that this is merely the association with age showing up again in the guise of a sex difference, through the medium of a difference in the age distributions of the sexes. Correspondingly, we make a note to check on the possibility that the apparent association with age is due to differences in the sex ratio at different ages. More generally, we recognize that the associations with age and sex may be *confounded*, that is, mixed together in what looks like an association with age and an association with sex.

The idea of confounding is important enough for a digression. Suppose illiteracy rates by sex and age were:

Age	Male	Female	Both Sexes
Young	1.0	1.0	1.0
Old	10.0	10.0	10.0

These hypothetical illiteracy rates are identical for young males and young females. They are also identical for old males and old females. But they differ greatly between the young and the old. In other words, there is a strong relation between age and illiteracy, but none at all between sex and illiteracy. Now suppose that the frequencies are as shown below:

Age	Male	Female
Young	100	300
Old	200	100

The over-all illiteracy rate for males would be . . .

$$\tfrac{1}{3} \times 1.0 + \tfrac{2}{3} \times 10.0 = 7.0;$$

for females it would be

$$\tfrac{3}{4} \times 1.0 + \tfrac{1}{4} \times 10.0 = 3.25.$$

Males show a higher over-all illiteracy rate, simply because relatively more of the males are old and the illiteracy rate is higher for the old of either sex. In such a case, the age and sex effects are said to be *confounded*. That is, what is really an age effect appears in the totals as a sex effect, because the age effect has had a different influence on the two sexes due to their different age distributions.

It is usual in statistics to refer to an association with, say, age, as an "age effect," or as the "effect of age," without intending the cause-and-effect implication that this term tends to carry in ordinary usage. All that is meant in statistics is association, and we will use the term "effect" that way.

(c) *Color.* To see the effect of color, we compare the entries at the bottoms of the "both" sexes columns in the "white" and "nonwhite" sections, and find the nonwhite rate (10.2 percent) to be 5⅔ times the white rate (1.8 percent). Again, however, we resolve to investigate possible confounding of all three effects.

The main effects, then, seem to be that *illiteracy rates are higher for older people, for males, and for nonwhites.*

(9) *Examine the consistency of the over-all effects and the interactions among them.*

(a) *Age.* The increase of illiteracy with age holds separately for whites and nonwhites. Some difference in detail does appear. For one thing, the nonwhite rate is not constant from ages 14 to 34, but is noticeably lower from 14 to 24. More conspicuous, the increase from the lowest to the highest age class is much larger for nonwhites than for whites: the differences are 29.4 per cent and 4.2 percent, and the ratios[3] 8.5 and 6.2. Thus, it appears that age has a greater effect on illiteracy for nonwhites than for whites. For the two sexes, on the other hand, age has about the same effect, as measured by the absolute change (5.8 percent for males and 5.6 percent for females) from the lowest to the highest age class; since females have a lower rate, this makes the ratio higher for females (10.3) than for males (4.2).

A still more careful study of the table would test whether these conclusions hold if we compare, say, the next-to-lowest age class with the next-to-highest (the conclusions are the same), thus guarding against aberrations in individual rates.

Before we italicize these conclusions derived from comparing the separate section totals, let us see whether they hold within sections, that is for each sex of a color, or for each color of a sex. Here, for the first time, we use the real core of the table, the rates for the 24 basic cells. Heretofore we have used only data combined by age, by sex, or by color, or by two of these, or (in step 6) by all three.

First, compare the males of the two colors. Then compare the females. Both comparisons confirm the conclusion that *the increases in illiteracy associated with increases in age are greater for nonwhites than for whites* and that *they are about the same for males as for females.* These statements are equivalent to saying that *the excess of nonwhite over white illiteracy rates is greater in the older age classes* and that *the difference between the sexes is not systematically related to age.*

(b) *Sex.* Similar detailed study leads to the conclusion that *the excess of the male over the female rate is higher for nonwhites than for whites.* Put the other way around, this says that *the difference between the colors is larger for males than for females.*

(c) *Color.* Our conclusions about the interaction between color and sex and between color and age have already been recorded in discussing age and sex.

(10) *Finally, look for things you weren't looking for—aberrations, anomalies, or irregularities.* The most interesting irregularity that we have noticed in Table 270 is in the age class 25–34. For white males this is below—in fact, one-third below—the rates for the preceding and following age classes. For the nonwhite

males, however, the rate is above that of the adjacent age classes by about one-third. (The white females also show a higher rate in this age class than in the adjacent ones, but only by 0.1, which might be almost all due to rounding the figures to the nearest tenth of a percent, and in any case is less than the necessary allowance for sampling error.) In attempting to form a plausible conjecture to explain this peculiarity, we first note that the period when this age class was at ages 6 to 8, and therefore learning to read and write, was 1924 to 1935. This suggests nothing to us, though it might to an expert on the subject matter. As a second stab, we note that during the period of World War II, 1942–45, this age class was 15 to 27 years old. It is, therefore, the group that provided the bulk of the armed forces. This lead seems worth investigating. Did the armed forces teach many illiterates to read and write? If so, did this affect white males more than nonwhite? Even so, why would the rate for nonwhite males be increased? Could it be that mortality among whites was higher for illiterates than for literates, but for nonwhites the reverse? We should be surprised if any of these is the explanation, but investigating them would probably lead us to the explanation. A possible explanation, of course, is that the aberration is due to sampling error, or even clerical or printing error, and that the search for substantive explanations would be in vain. But such anomalies are often worth pursuing; this is one of the secrets of serendipity, from which the most fruitful findings of research often result. We would certainly pursue these questions if we were investigating illiteracy instead of explaining how to read a table.

In summary, then, here is what can be read from Table 270, and in considerably less time than it has taken us to tell about it:

Illiteracy in 1952 among the civilian, noninstitutional population 14 years of age and older—

(i) Averaged 2.5 percent.
(ii) Varied greatly with age, color, and sex.
(iii) Was higher at the higher ages, for nonwhites, and for males, with
    (a) the age differences larger for nonwhites— that is the color differences larger at the higher ages;
    (b) the sex difference larger for nonwhites— that is, the color differences larger for males;
    (c) no interaction between age and sex.
(iv) Was, in the 25–34 year age class, anomalously lower for white males, but higher for colored males, than in the age classes just above and just below.

Example 277: Brains and Beauty at Berkeley

TABLE 277. *Mean Grades of College Women, by Appearance and Year in College*

Data on 643 women students of the University of California who had completed two or more years of college, classified by beauty of face. Grades averaged by scoring A as 3, B as 2, C as 1, D as 0, E or F as −1. Frequencies on which averages are based are shown in Table 280 [omitted].

Year	Homely	Plain	Good Looking	Beautiful	All Appearances
Junior	1.58	1.45	1.34	1.16	1.37
Senior	1.56	1.52	1.45	1.57	1.50
Graduate	1.67	1.70	1.70	1.53	1.68
All years	1.62	1.56	1.44	1.42	1.51

Source: S. J. Holmes and C. E. Hatch, "Personal Appearance as Related to Scholastic Records and Marriage Selection in College Women," *Human Biology*, Vol. 10 (1938), pp. 65–76. The means shown here have been recomputed from the original data, loaned by the authors, and in a few instances differ by one unit in the last decimal place from those given in the source.

Repeating the same steps as in reading Table 270, we find at stage 8 that grades are higher in later years in college and with poorer appearance (which, to repeat earlier warnings, does not necessarily mean that given coeds get better grades as they progress in college or regress in appearance). At stage 9, however, we find it necessary to introduce such strong qualifications to the appearance effect as almost to withdraw the finding. All we can say is that for juniors grades decrease with better appearance, but for seniors and graduate students there is no systematic relation. The main effect of appearance is partly a manifestation of the year-in-college effect, in conjunction with different distributions by appearance for the three college classes.

The mean for the plain, for example, is

$$\tfrac{68}{250} \times 1.45 + \tfrac{100}{250} \times 1.52 + \tfrac{82}{250} \times 1.70 = 1.56$$

and for the good looking it is

$$\tfrac{108}{236} \times 1.34 + \tfrac{84}{236} \times 1.45 + \tfrac{44}{236} \times 1.70 = 1.45$$

. . . The difference between these two means is partly due to the fact that the juniors, who have the lowest grades in both appearance groups, constitute 46 percent of the good looking and only 27 percent of the plain. Similarly, the graduates, who have the highest scores in both appearance groups, constitute 33 percent of the plain but only 19 percent of the good looking. Thus, the difference between these two appearance groups is partly due to the fact that the class effect operates differently in one than the other. The difference between the averages for the plain and good looking is not wholly due to the class effect, however, for among the plain the average for each class is as high as or higher than the average for the same class among the good looking.

Since the appearance effect is not present for the seniors or graduates, we conclude that its presence for all classes combined reflects partly the effect for the juniors and partly confounding of the class effect—that is, heavier representation in some appearance groups than in others of those classes which receive low grades. It would be possible for the appearance effect to work in one direction in all three classes, but in the opposite direction for all classes combined. For the data of Table 277 this is only barely possible, since no set of weights will result in a mean outside the range of the individual means. For the beautiful mean to exceed the homely mean, for example, virtually all of the beautiful and all of the homely would have to be seniors.

In interpreting data of this kind it is necessary to keep in mind selective factors that have determined whether individuals are available for such a sample.

SOCIAL CLASS AND PARENT-CHILD RELATIONSHIPS

Problem

Certain aspects of a society are often idealized. Individuals see some other part of society as more desirable than the one to which they belong, or they regard some previous period in history or their own childhood as more desirable than the present. Growing up on a farm is one common idealization. The relationship of the child with his family and the healthful hard work in the open air are contrasted favorably with conditions in the crowded urban scene. Similarly, the striving and achievement-oriented members of the middle class often idealize the children of the working class as happy-go-lucky and relatively free of the anxiety produced by the high demand for achievement which middle-class children usually experience (Davis, 1949).

Neither the article by Nye reprinted at the beginning of this problem, nor his study of "Rurality As a Variable" (Nye, 1950), find any support for these stereotypes. In fact, Nye's findings are almost the opposite. Both Nye (1950) and Sewell (1961) interpret such findings as showing the consequences of the rural or lower-class child's attempt to reconcile the culture and values of his own home and neighborhood with the different and "superior" values of the middle-class urban culture.

To retest Nye's original findings,* we will use the occupational classification of the father (coded in Box 24) as a way of determining social class (see Problem 2), and our rough measure of the child's rejection of his parents (coded in Box 54) as a way of determining the adequacy of parent-child relations.

The rejection-of-parents measure is derived from Questions 52 and 53 which ask how much the respondent would change in his own father and mother, with the answers ranging from "Nothing at all" (1) to "Just about everything" (6). To obtain the score for the rejection of parents (Box 54), the number of desired

---

* This is the first laboratory problem in which a specific research study is replicated. Consequently, in addition to reading the article by Nye which you will be replicating in simplified form, you will find it valuable to prepare an abstract of the Nye research. Use one of the Abstracting Forms from Appendix B for this purpose.

changes for each parent are added together. We assume that the greater the number of changes desired, the greater the respondent's rejection of his parents.

Hypothesis

In the light of Nye's findings and other material which you have read, state which of the three social-class groups (white-collar, farm, and blue-collar) you think has the highest, and which the lowest, rejection of parents. See Appendix B for more general information on writing a hypothesis.

Empirical Indicators for Problem 3

24. What was your father's occupation at the time you graduated from high school, or what was it before his retirement (please specify)?

_____

In addition please circle the answer category which best fits his occupation.

1 Professional (architect, chemist, doctor, etc.) or managerial position (department head, postmaster, police chief, etc.)
2 Proprietor, except farm (i.e., owner of a business)
3 Clerical or sales position
4 Farmer (owner-operator or renter)
5 Skilled workman or foreman (machinist, carpenter, etc.)
6 Semiskilled or unskilled workman (truck driver, factory worker, etc.)
7 Homemaker, or not employed outside the home
+ Don't know

52. If it were possible to change real parents into ideal parents, how much would you change in your MOTHER?
1 Nothing at all
2 One or two things
3 A few things
4 A fair number of things
5 A large number of things
6 Just about everything

53. If it were possible to change real parents into ideal parents, how much would you change in your FATHER?
1 Nothing at all
2 One or two things
3 A few things
4 A fair number of things
5 A large number of things
6 Just about everything

Data Analysis

1. *Sort* the code sheets into three social-class groups on the basis of the occupational classification of the father (coded in Box 24):

White-collar or middle class = 1, 2, & 3
Farm class   = 4
Blue-collar or working class = 5 & 6

2. *Tabulate* the rejection-of-parents score (coded in Box 54) for the code sheets in each social-class group on the Tabulation Form for Problem 3. You may tabulate either by sorting the code sheets into twelve piles on the basis of their rejection-of-parents scores and counting the number of cases in each pile, or by keeping a tally on Table 1 as you go along. To save time, divide up the tabulation with your partner.

3. *Add* the frequencies in each row and enter these in the "Total" column.

4. *Compute* the average rejection-of-parents score for each social-class group as follows:

(a) For each social class, multiply the number of cases in each rejection-of-parents category (listed in the "*f*" or "*frequency*" column) by the rejection-of-parents score (*x*) for that row and write this product in the *fx* column.
(b) Add the frequencies in each column to give the total number of cases (N) for each social class, and enter these totals at the bottom of each social-class column.
(c) Add the total *fx* scores and enter them at the bottom of each column.
(d) Compute the average or *mean* (M) for each social-class and for the total sample using the following formula:

$$M = \frac{\text{Total } fx}{N}$$

The first five or six people who have finished computing the means should enter them on the chart your instructor has put on the chalkboard.

Laboratory Report

1. The selection by Wallis and Roberts entitled "How to Read a Table" will be helpful in preparing this and other Laboratory Reports. Also reread the directions for writing Laboratory Reports in Appendix B before writing your Laboratory Report.

2. Summarize the finding verbally; that is, state what relationships are shown by your findings in this problem. Give special attention to the Discussion in your Laboratory Report. Be sure to discuss possible reasons for the differences you have found and/or the consequences of such differences. In addition to arguing from, or against, the references you have read, do not hesitate to advance your own reasoning.

3. Do not change your hypothesis to make it fit the findings. Hypotheses are often proven wrong by the evidence, and a reversal such as this is often the basis for a new understanding of the relationships. Speculate as to the possible reasons for any differences you have found.

REFERENCES

Davis, W. A. "Child Rearing in the Class Structure of American Society," in Marvin B. Sussman, ed. *Sourcebook in Marriage and the Family*. Boston: Houghton Mifflin, 1963. Pp. 225–231.

Nye, F. Ivan. "Adolescent-Parent Adjustment—Rurality as a Variable," *Rural Sociology*, 15 (1950), pp. 334–339.

Sewell, W. H. "Social Class and Child Personality," *Sociometry*, 24 (1961), pp. 340–356. Also in Robert F. Winch, Robert McCinnis, and Herbert R. Barringer, eds. *Selected Studies in Marriage and the Family*. Rev. ed. New York: Holt, Rinehart and Winston, 1962. Pp. 323–329.

SECTION/COURSE NO._____ DATE_____ NAME_____

Social Class and Rejection of Parents

Rejection of Parents (Box 54)	White-Collar (Box 24 = 1, 2, & 3)			Farm (Box 24 = 4)			Blue-Collar (Box 24 = 5 & 6)		
x	Tally	f	fx	Tally	f	fx	Tally	f	fx
1									
2									
3									
4									
5									
6									
7									
8									
9									
10									
11									
12									
TOTAL (N)									
MEAN (M)									
No answer			✕			✕			✕

SECTION/COURSE NO._____ DATE_____ NAME_____

Social Class and Parent-Child Relationships

HYPOTHESIS: _____

_____

_____

_____

_____

_____

_____

SAMPLE: _____

_____

_____

_____

_____

INDEPENDENT VARIABLE: _____

_____

_____

_____

_____

_____

DEPENDENT VARIABLE: _____

_____

_____

_____

OTHER FACTORS: _____

_____

_____

SUMMARY OF FINDINGS: _____

_____

_____

_____

_____

_____

_____

_____

_____

_____

_____

DISCUSSION: _____

_____

_____

_____

_____

_____

_____

_____

_____

_____

_____

_____

_____

_____

THE POWER TO MAKE DECISIONS

Robert O. Blood and Donald M. Wolfe

Introduction

The data presented in the tables and text come from a systematic probability-sample survey of families in the Detroit metropolitan area and from a comparable survey of farm families in southeastern Michigan. Structured and controlled interviews, lasting more than an hour each, were conducted with 731 urban and suburban wives and with 178 farm wives. Where comparable data are available, these data match very well the findings of the 1950 U.S. Census for the same geographical areas; the samples seem to be quite representative of the populations from which they were drawn. . . .

It may seem strange that in a study of marriage only one partner should be interviewed. However, many previous studies have shown a close correlation between what husbands and wives say about their marriages, making it possible to rely on one partner's responses. There are undoubtedly individual cases where the husband would have given a different picture from the one the wife gave us, but these differences tend to get lost in the shuffle when large numbers of cases are considered.

Wives, in general, probably look at marriage somewhat differently from husbands. Hence, it should be remembered that this is a wife's-eye view of marriage. But we assume that when we make comparisons between groups of wives—as between middle-class wives and working-class wives—the sex bias cancels out and the differences which emerge are real differences between families.

The selection of wives instead of husbands was largely a question of productivity. Wives are more easily located at home so that more interviews can be obtained from them. In addition, to the extent that wives invest more time and effort in family matters, they may provide more complete and useful data. Although unavailable at present, a comparable study based on interviews with husbands would nevertheless add valuable detail.

*　*　*

No change in the American family is mentioned more often than the shift from one-sided male authority to the sharing of power by husband and wife. Perhaps no change is more significant, either. The balance of power between husband and wife is a sensitive reflection of the roles they play in marriage—and, in turn, has many repercussions on other aspects of their relationship.

Power and Authority. Power may be defined as the potential ability of one partner to influence the other's behavior. Power is manifested in the ability to make decisions affecting the life of the family.

Authority is closely related to power. Authority is legitimate power, i.e., power held by one partner because both partners feel it is proper for him to do so. The family authority pattern is prescribed by the society at large in such forms as: "the man should be the head of the house"—or "husbands should not dictate to their wives."

Power, on the other hand, refers to the way in which husbands and wives actually deal with each other. Caspar Milquetoast, as a man, may be supposed to have considerable authority, but in practice he exercises very little power. Power and authority do not necessarily coincide.

Two Theories about the Sources of Power

The power to make decisions is influenced by the prescribed authority pattern. In a patriarchal system both the husband and the wife will ordinarily take for granted that the husband should make most of the decisions. He derives a measure of assertiveness from the social norm, and she, a corresponding measure of deference. But even in a tradition-bound society, there are variations between couples. Indeed, the whole conception of a hen-pecked husband implies a norm that is being violated.

The existence of such discrepancies suggests that there must be other sources of marital power beside authority. In the world at large, the illegitimate seizure of power usually rests on military might. But husbands and wives do not ordinarily point guns at each other. Even rolling pins and fists are more often preludes to the disintegration of marriage than the basis on which a balance of power is worked out.

The sources of power in so intimate a relationship as marriage must be sought in the comparative resources which the husband and wife bring to the marriage, rather than in brute force. A resource may be defined as anything that one partner may make available to the other, helping the latter satisfy his needs or attain his goals. The balance of power will be on the side of that partner who contributes the greater resources to the marriage.

Marriage itself may be thought of as an institution designed to meet certain vital needs of the participants. People get married because they believe that they will find sexual fulfilment, emotional response, companionship, and the new experience of parenthood, in living together. Both partners hope to attain these goals through the same marriage. Insofar as both partners contribute to each others' satisfaction in life, they build up a mutual respect that expresses itself naturally in mutual consultation. As one partner is able to contribute more than his share to the marriage, he acquires the basis for a more than fifty-fifty say in decisions. This is seldom a conscious process of weighing the balance. It is an automatic readjustment which occurs as the contributing partner discovers that he has a lot to offer to the marriage, while the receiving partner feels indebted for what has already been given and dependent upon what he hopes to receive in the future. Control over future resources is especially crucial, since decision-making involves the allocation of resources within the family. The partner who may provide or withhold resources is in a strategic position for influencing their disposition. Hence, power accrues spontaneously to the partner who has the greater resources at his disposal.

A second factor is closely related to resources. Anyone who is able to make a contribution is, almost by definition, a competent person—i.e., someone with special skills. To possess a skill enables the individual to make a contribution; in addition, it implies special competence in decision-making as such. Thus, a wife may not only depend on her husband for "bringing home the bacon" but recognize that in his work he becomes familiar with some of the complexities of life outside the home. Therefore, she may defer to his superior knowledge in decisions about politics, taxes, and cars.

The chief objective of this chapter is to look at the comparative competence of the two partners and their relative contributions to marriage, as explanations for the variations which occur between couples' balance of power. According to this hypothesis, Caspar is hen-pecked because he is incompetent and makes very little contribution to the life-satisfactions of his wife.

CULTURE OR COMPETENCE?

If authority patterns and personal resources both influence the balance of power, are they equally important? There are two different theories: according to one, families do what the culture tells them to do; the other states that they do what their own characteristics dictate. In a stable society, the two sources of power will coincide. American society, however, has not been stable. Everybody knows that the balance of power between men and women has been changing. Has it changed because our ideas about how men and women ought to treat each other have changed? Or has it changed because the comparative resources of American men and women have changed?

The answer is not likely to be completely one or the other—since changes in one are bound to affect the other sooner or later. If husbands become infected with democratic ideas and start giving their wives more freedom, the wives will gain more competence. On the other hand, if wives gain increased resources, old patriarchal notions are not likely to remain unaffected for very long.

Despite this interdependence of ideological and pragmatic sources of power, there may still be an important difference in their potency. Historical analyses may show that one changes first and the other follows after. Contemporary analysis may show patriarchal norms continuing to influence the balance of power under changing circumstances, or it may show families adapting rapidly to new conditions no matter what their ideological training.

The ideological theory will be tested first by looking for patriarchal subcultures in the Detroit area. If culture is more than just a rationalization of existing circumstances, Detroit families should be more traditional if they grew up on farms, or in "the old country," or in "the old days." This search will prove fruitless; the alternative pragmatic theory of the basis of power will have to be tested to show its usefulness. The evidence from Detroit in support of competence as the chief basis for power will be cumulatively impressive.

According to the resource theory, statements about patriarchal authority patterns or equalitarian ones are chiefly rationalizations of existing practice—like codifications of the common law. As people grow up under a husband-dominant family system, they come to take that balance of power for granted—and even to feel that it is right. Henceforward, the idea of patriarchy acquires momentum and influence in its own right, shaping generations to come until it is undermined by new conditions. At first, only the innovators in society see the handwriting on the wall and begin talking about new beliefs to fit new circumstances. For the rest of society, the old system hangs on by a kind of cultural lag, although increasingly paid only lip service. Finally, the social change is consolidated, and new ideas about marriage spread through the society to all but the most conservative.

From this analysis, it is clear that culture is not a sufficient explanation for power. It is not enough to say that wives used to be submissive to their husbands because they lived under a patriarchal system, or because that was the custom. The search must be pushed further into why the patriarchal system arose in the first place. The same search for "basic" causes will be necessary if we are to understand the modern pattern of decision-making.

The History of Power in American Marriages

The present is better understood if we look first at the past. In terms of the world-wide experience of the human race, we have clearly come from a patriarchal background. Murdock's (1949) comprehensive examination of 250 primitive and historic societies shows that far more societies have operated under husband-dominance than under any other system (such as wife-dominance or equality). There is similarly clear evidence on every hand that we Americans stem from patriarchal forebears, too. Why has patriarchy been so popular?

The dominance of men in marriage is often attributed to physical strength. While men do have more muscle power, any factor which operates purely in a biological fashion would be expected to have a universal effect. If superior musculature were the only reason for male dominance, we would expect men to dominate everywhere and in all times. The fact that they do not suggests that other factors must, at least, contribute to the picture.

Probably the most important of these additional factors is the economic role of men and women in different times and places (Ogburn and Nimkoff, 1955). For instance, hunting societies depend on the men for their food resources. The fact that men rather than women do the hunting reflects the great exertion required which only men can take. Meanwhile since women are childbearers and child-sucklers, they must stay behind by the fire (Scheinfeld, 1943). These are circumstances under which male dominance tends to prevail since the women depend on male prowess for sustenance. Under hoe culture, on the other hand, women have the necessary strength to perform productive work without having to stray far from home— hence they tend to assume a more influential role in the family. The domestication of large animals brings man back into the forefront because of the strength required to handle them and the wandering necessary to pasture them. The replacement of the hoe by the plow (whether drawn by horse, mule, or bullock) similarly enhances the role of the male.

That partner is most powerful who is the instrumental leader, who gets those things done which most urgently need doing if the family is to survive (Parsons and Bales, 1955). Such a leader is not only economically productive himself but functions as the organizer and administrator of other family members in the task of economic production.

OUR PATRIARCHAL FOREBEARS

Against this background it is possible to see why our American forebears were patriarchal. Under pioneer conditions, rugged masculinity was at a premium. Women had to be rugged, too, in order to endure the hardships of hunger and cold—but it was the men who wrested a living from the wilderness with axe and rifle. (Annie Oakley was a curiosity precisely because the rifle was so masculine a weapon.) A widow could hardly survive in the woods without grown sons to support her. It took a man to kill a bear, to fight off the Indians, to fell the trees and erect the cabin. (It is still men who build houses but the psychological impact is not the same when it is *other* men, and not the husband, who do the building.) In general, the more stark the conditions for survival, the more crucial the family decisions which must be made, so the more unchallenged the authority-figure is likely to be. Disobedience to the husband-father in the wilderness was like mutiny on a ship at sea, when all hands might be lost under inexperienced leadership.

As Americans shifted from hunting to agriculture, the conditions of life moderated, and the dominance of the male lost some of its stringent urgency. On the other hand, the farm homestead required the wife and children to pitch into many tasks of farming under the man's leadership. His position of economic leadership gave the man a dominant position in the family, which was strengthened by the periodic helpless dependence of the wife in childbirth and the obviously superior competence of the veteran farmer over his inexperienced children. The transition from forest to farm may have changed the precise basis of the man's authority but it hardly altered the extent of it.

Throughout the nineteenth century, a large share of Americans lived on farms. But even in the cities, marriage was still largely patriarchal. City life required the husband to go off to work away from home, but wives seldom followed. It was chiefly single women who worked in the early textile mills, according to Ogburn and Nimkoff. With few exceptions, factories in those days were noisier, dirtier, more dangerous, and less mechanized than they are now. Much of the work still required brute strength. So women—single or married—preferred not to work in them.

As for married women, the large number of children borne and cared for, and the lack of labor-saving devices made the housewife and mother too busy to work outside the home. Once again in the history of mankind, the man became the sole source of support for his dependents. And since the wife was one of these dependents, her position continued subordinate as before.

Not all city workers were factory hands. In small businesses, some wives did work with their husbands—but in a subordinate role comparable to the wife on the farm. The gradual increase in the professions required higher education which at first was closed to women, increasing the gap between educated husbands and their uneducated wives.

Through the Victorian era, the American family system remained patriarchal, challenged only by a few exceptionally educated and talented feminists. Since that time the picture has changed markedly.

THE RISE OF WOMEN

The employment of women in appreciable numbers began with World War I and continued into the booming 1920's. Not enough men were available to fill all the jobs needed by the nation. Moreover, industry was changing its environment and tasks, until women not only could tolerate them but were sometimes better suited to them than men. Large-scale business and industry required the development of extensive systems of communication and control whose letters and records were best typed by women. The increased economic productivity of the nation led to a corresponding rise in the standard of living, creating an opportunity for the American people to move beyond the mere necessities of life to cultural and recreational luxuries which made new demands on feminine talent. The same high standard of living made possible the purchase of labor-saving devices, ready-made clothes, and ready-to-eat foods, which freed the housewife from bondage to stove, sink, and needle. The productivity of the American economy required the development of advertising to create markets for consumer goods. This advertising succeeded so well that women with increased appetites for goods wanted to go to work so that they could raise the family level of living still further and faster. All these factors, accentuated by another world war and another period of prosperity, combined to create an intensified demand for women workers, and by women to work.

The result has been a dramatic rise in the proportion of married women employed outside the home. For single women, self-support has long since been taken for granted. The innovation is that it is no longer the wedding but the first pregnancy which brings this working span to a halt. Even then the halt is often temporary as an increasing number of middle-aged mothers go back to work to put their children through college or to fill the gap left by the departure of those children.

The productivity of the American economy has also made possible the luxury of the education of women (as in turn it has created a demand for educated women employees). Today more girls than boys graduate from high school, since the latter often drop out to go to work. Even at the college level there are now nearly half as many women as men enrolled.

The employment and education of women have given them resources which their grandmothers didn't have. The pay check of the working wife is a contribution to the family which would be expected to give her a greater interest in financial decisions—and greater respect from her husband. The participation of the wife in the outside world through her job gives her contacts with fellow workers which lessen her dependence on her husband for emotional support and increase the knowledge and skill she brings to decision making.

Such factors have produced a new generation of American wives who are more resourceful and competent than their grandmothers. They are no longer content to sit quietly by while their husbands make the decisions. This is not to say that there is necessarily exact equality between husbands and wives in contemporary America but that the predominance of the male has been so thoroughly undermined that we no longer live in a patriarchal system.

— The Contemporary Pattern of Power —

In order to measure the precise balance of power between husbands and wives one would have to assess their influence in all the family decisions which had ever been made—or at least all those which had been made over a considerable period of time. Such an exhaustive undertaking would exceed the capacities of husbands' and wives' memories.

Since a complete record of decisions is unobtainable, any study of marriage must rely on a sample of decisions to represent the larger whole. In this study, eight decisions were selected to provide an estimate of the relative balance of power between husband and wife.

The eight decisions are:

(1) What job the husband should take.
(2) What car to get.
(3) Whether or not to buy life insurance.
(4) Where to go on a vacation.
(5) What house or apartment to take.
(6) Whether or not the wife should go to work or quit work.
(7) What doctor to have when someone is sick.
(8) How much money the family can afford to spend per week on food.

These eight were selected because they are all relatively important (compared to deciding whether to go to a movie tonight). They are also questions which

nearly all couples have to face. (This is why no questions were asked relating to children.) Only three per cent of the couples at most answered any question in hypothetical terms (the three per cent who had never bought a car and the similar number who hadn't yet taken a vacation). The remaining criterion for these questions was that they should range from typically masculine to typically feminine decisions—but should always affect the family as a whole.

It was assumed in advance that contemporary husbands and wives would often talk things over in the process of arriving at a decision. Even a patriarchal husband may consult his wife as one source of opinion and one factor to be taken into consideration while he makes up his mind. The crucial question is not who takes part in the discussion but who makes the final decision. To get this information the lead-in statement to the battery of questions was as follows:

"In every family somebody has to decide such things as where the family will live and so on. Many couples talk such things over first, but the *final* decision often has to be made by the husband or the wife. For instance, who usually makes the final decision about . . . ?"

In order to provide comparable answers, the respondents were given a choice of "husband always," "husband more than wife," "husband and wife exactly the same," "wife more than husband," and "wife always" as response categories.

WHO DECIDES?

The wives' answer to the eight questions are shown in Table 1 with the items arranged in order of decreasing male participation.

Two decisions are primarily the husband's province (his job and the car), two the wife's (her work and the food), while all the others are joint decisions in the sense of having more "same" responses than anything else. Even the wife's working turns out to be a quite middling decision from the standpoint of the mean score, leaving only the food expenditures preponderantly in the wife's hands. Only the two male decisions are made more than half the time by a particular partner.

Sex Roles. The distribution of decisions by sex is not surprising. The husband's work is his chief role in life. From it he derives his greatest sense of well-being or malaise, and there he invests the greatest part of his energies. His work is so one-sidedly important to him that almost all the wives leave him alone for his final decision.

Automobiles are associated with the mechanical aptitude of males (Scheinfeld, 1943). Moreover, a large

TABLE 1. *Allocation of Power in Decision-Making Areas*

(731 Detroit Families)

Who Decides?	Decision							
	Husband's job	Car	Insur-ance	Vaca-tion	House	Wife's work	Doctor	Food
(5) Husband always	90%	56%	31%	12%	12%	26%	7%	10%
(4) Husband more than wife	4	12	11	6	6	5	3	2
(3) Husband and wife exactly the same	3	25	41	68	58	18	45	32
(2) Wife more than husband	0	2	4	4	10	9	11	11
(1) Wife always	1	3	10	7	13	39	31	41
N.A.	2	1	2	3	1	3	3	3
Total	100	99	99	100	100	100	100	99
Husband's mean power*	4.86	4.18	3.50	3.12	2.94	2.69	2.53	2.26

* The mean for each column is computed on the basis of the weights shown, e.g., "husband always" = 5.

proportion of the driving in the United States is done by males, giving them added interest in the choice of car.

At the other extreme, meal-planning is part of the wife's role in the division of labor . . . , giving to the wife the major responsibility for food expenditures.

The choice of doctor falls to the wife especially often where there are dependent children in the home, so that it is associated with her role as mother. However, it also reflects the general tendency of women to play a nurturant role for the sick and helpless.

The family vacation and the choice of house are most frequently joint decisions. Is this because they most clearly affect both partners equally?

The fact that insurance decisions are made somewhat more often by the husband may reflect the technical financial questions involved. If so, the financial training involved in his money-earning role gives him extra competence.

That the husband should be more involved in his wife's job decisions than she with his is understandable. For one thing, her work is seldom her major preoccupation in life the way it is for a man. Even if she works just as many hours a week, she does not usually make the same life-long commitment to the world of work. Nor is her pay check as indispensable to the family finances (if only because it is usually smaller). In such ways the choice whether to work or not is less vital to a woman than a man.

In addition, the wife's decisions about working have repercussions on the husband. If his wife goes to work, he will have to help out more around the house. If he is a business executive, he may prefer to have her concentrate her energy on entertaining prospective clients at home. As a small businessman or independent professional, he may need her services in his own enterprise. On the other hand, regardless of his own occupation, he may want her to work in order to help him buy a house or a business or pay for the children's education.

It may be, then, that the work role is so much the responsibility of the husband in marriage that even the wife's work is but an adjunct of his instrumental leadership, leaving this decision frequently in his hands.

THE BALANCE OF POWER

Whether families are patriarchal in general is far more important than whether they sometimes conform to patriarchal norms in a single area of decision-making. With eight questions so widely distributed between masculine and feminine roles, the Detroit families as a whole could not look very patriarchal when their answers to the whole battery of questions are totalled up. Even so, there might still be considerable variation between families, if in some the husbands consistently make the decisions while in others wives consistently do.

In actual practice, such consistency is rare. Less than one half of one per cent of the Detroit husbands make all eight decisions and a similarly small proportion of wives are all-powerful. Nevertheless such extremes do exist and exemplify the fact that it is possible to find all kinds of power-balances from the most patriarchal to the most matriarchal.

Given these eight particular questions, the aggregate balance of power falls slightly in the husband's direction. When the total scores for the eight questions, weighted as shown in Table 1, are converted into a ten-point scale reflecting the amount of influence exerted by the husband, the average score for all families is 5.09 (whereas a score of 4.00 is the equivalent of "husband and wife exactly the same").

Although families can be found varying all the way from one extreme to the other, most families bunch together around this mean score. Forty-six per cent of all the Detroit families have scores of four to six. Though slightly skewed to the husband's side in absolute terms, it seems preferable to label these as relatively equalitarian couples. This leaves twenty-two per cent with scores of seven or more who can be called relatively male-dominant and another twenty-two per cent with scores of three or less who are relatively female-dominant.[1] Even these extreme groups cluster close to the central group. This means that Detroit families, on the whole, are extraordinarily alike when it comes to the balance of decision-making.

The middle group of equalitarian marriages can be differentiated further according to whether they make most of their decisions jointly or whether they assign equal numbers of separate decisions to both partners. The former type is called "syncratic" and the latter "autonomic" (Herbst in Oeser and Hammond, 1954). Despite the fact that these four types (husband-dominant, syncratic, autonomic, and wife-dominant) are concentrated in the middle range of power, they still differ enough from each other to provide important distinctions between families in many respects.

The impression that the average Detroit marriage is properly labelled equalitarian is supported by answers to the question: "When you and your husband differ about something, do you usually give in and do it your husband's way, or does he usually come around to your point of view?" Thirty-four per cent say that they usually or always give in under these circumstances, twenty-four per cent say the husband does, but the remaining forty per cent (two per cent, no answer) give equalitarian responses. This forty per cent undoubtedly underestimates the proportion of equalitarian marriages because many wives made it entirely clear that they and their husbands agree on most things most of the time, leaving this question to apply only to marginal disagreements. When viewed against the relatively small margin of husband-winning over wife-winning cases, Detroit marriages have clearly moved a long way from nineteenth century patriarchalism.

The Sources of Power in Marriage

Having designated some marriages as relatively husband-dominant, let us search for the segments of the population in which the patriarchal tradition apparently still survives. Presumably it should be found intact among those families which have been less exposed to urban, industrial, and educational influences.

WHERE IS THE PATRIARCHAL FAMILY?

The groups which would be expected to be patriarchal are families now or formerly living on farms, immigrant families, old couples, uneducated couples, and Catholic marriages (because of the Catholic advocacy of the patriarchal ideal). However, none of these expectations is confirmed.

Farm Families? The typical number of decisions made by Michigan farm husbands is exactly the same as the score for city husbands. This does not necessarily mean that living on a farm no longer contributes to the husband's power. But it certainly means that its influence may be entirely nullified by other factors, at least on farms that are within the sphere of influence of a giant metropolis.

With no difference between the families living on farms and those living in the city, patriarchal survivals cannot be expected among people within the city who grew up on farms. The differences between migrants and Detroit-born families actually lie in the opposite direction from what was expected (with migrant wives making more rather than less of the decisions). This is probably due to their low social status rather than a reflection of any matriarchal cultural pattern.

Immigrant Families? A second place where patriarchal culture might survive is among immigrants from the old country. Families brought up under patriarchal norms would be expected to live by the ideals that they learned in their youth even after moving to a new country.

These expectations are refuted again. Immigrants turn out to be less patriarchal than native Americans (see Table 2). Again the differences which exist in this table are probably not a reflection of different ideas but of the relatively low-status position which immigrants hold in our society.

* * *

TABLE 2. *Husband's Power in Native-born and Foreign-born Families*

	Wife's Place of Birth	
	Native-Born	*Foreign-Born*
Husband's mean power*	5.24	4.94
Number of families	494	60

* Those interested in the statistical significance of differences between means of subsamples on this power index (assuming that the variance of the subsamples is the same as that of the total sample) may keep in mind that the probability is less than .05 of finding as great as .34, when the subsamples are around 200 cases each, or .69 when the subsamples are around 50 cases each, in size. (See Table A4 in Appendix A.) In all cross-tabulations, cases not ascertained on either variable have been omitted for the sake of simplicity.

Although society no longer insists upon a particular balance of power in marriage, the larger community still affects husband-wife relationships. Today, the more successful the husband is in the eyes of the community, the more dominant his part in marital decision-making.

Earlier it was suggested that the low social status of Southern farm migrants, foreign immigrants, and poorly educated husbands might account for their low power. Now it is desirable to look directly at indices of success in the community.

Occupation. Table 3 shows that, generally speaking, the higher the husband's occupational prestige, the greater his voice in marital decisions.[2] The major break comes between white-collar occupations and blue-collar occupations.

Why should the average white-collar husband have more say at home than blue-collar ones? Perhaps the prestige of white-collar work provides self-confidence in his own eyes and respect in the eyes of his wife. In addition, white-collar work involves reliance on the interpersonal skills of discussion and argument which are involved in decision-making. Moreover, husbands accustomed to responsible roles on the job would understandably be inclined to take responsibility in the home. As a result of such factors, white-collar husbands are extra-equipped with the knowledge and skills required for decision-making, and their wives correspondingly inclined to recognize their husband's competence along these lines.

Income. Because his work is his chief role in life,

occupational success is the crucial index of a man's competence. But the kind of job a man has is not the only measure of occupational achievement. After all, many men simply follow in their father's footsteps. The son of a professional man will usually be a white-collar worker too, and though this gives him prestige in the eyes of the community, it may not reflect an unusually competent personality.

A better measure of success on the job is how much money the husband earns. In part, this is simply a reflection of occupation. But extreme income differences go beyond this to sort out the most successful from the least successful workers.

Table 4 shows that the husband's earnings are an even more sensitive indicator of his power than his occupation. Partly this is because the families are now split into five groups instead of four. Mostly this is because smaller groups are separated out at both extremes. Husbands with less than $3,000 income are the least successful of the low-blue-collar workers, and those earning more than $10,000 the most successful of the high-white-collar workers (such as doctors and big businessmen).

Bringing home the bacon is a prime example of contributing a resource to marriage. That top-income-bracket husbands should be most influential in marriage reflects the magnitude of their contribution to the family exchequer. By contrast, where the total income of the family (rather than the husband's alone) is taken into consideration, the balance of power is altered in the wife's direction. As a result of the supplementary contribution of other family members (principally the wives themselves), the number of families in the $7–10,000 income bracket jumps from 84 to 131 while the husband's power falls drastically from 5.38 to 4.85. Above the $10,000 mark there are 78 multiple-income families compared to 48 one-income units, and the husband's power is reduced from 5.83 to 5.41. This comparison shows how the balance of power reflects the husband's resources alone only as long as other things are equal. So, high-income husbands are most powerful if their wives contribute no income.

Social Status. Income and occupation are interrelated variables. The husband's education is also related to the amount of power that he has. These are the

TABLE 3. *Husband's Power, by Occupational Status*

	Husband's Occupation			
	Blue Collar		White Collar	
	Low*	High	Low	High
Husband's mean power	5.07	4.98	5.36	5.52
Number of families	162	161	78	151

* Low-blue-collar jobs are semi-skilled, unskilled, and service. High-blue-collar: skilled workers and foremen. Low-white-collar: sales and clerical. High-white-collar: business and professional.

TABLE 4. *Husband's Power, by Income*

	Husband's Income				
	Under $3,000	$3,000 –4,999	$5,000 –6,999	$7,000 –9,999	$10,000+
Husband's mean power	4.58	5.00	5.25	5.38	5.83
Number of families	57	165	185	84	48

sorts of variables that sociologists often group together to summarize the social position or status of a family in the community. The Social Status Index used here is an aggregate of these three factors (occupation, income, and education) plus the prestige-ranking of the husband's ethnic or nationality background. The combined index gives a rough picture of a family's over-all prestige in the eyes of the community from the standpoint of these four characteristics.[3]

For the community as a whole, the husband's power is directly related to his social status: 4.39, 4.79, 5.00, 5.33, 5.56. However, the few white husbands in the lowest social status group differ sharply from their powerless Negro counterparts. Presumably these are old men . . . If this small group is dismissed as likely to be affected by factors other than status alone, the general conclusion . . . is that the higher the husband's social status, the greater his power.

Do high-status husbands exercise control equally over all eight decision areas? Examination of the relationship between social status and the eight separate decisions shows that high-status husbands make more decisions in only three areas: whether to buy life insurance, what house or apartment to get, and especially whether the wife should go to work or quit work. Actually what happens is not that more high-status husbands make these decisions unilaterally, but that fewer wives do. In other words, high-status husbands take a more active part rather than the wife making the decision by herself.

Are there any reasons why high-status husbands would want to control these particular areas? . . . High-status husbands are more apt to handle the money and bills. The reason for this appears to be that there is a larger increment of money involved beyond the level of daily necessities. At high-status levels, insurance correspondingly becomes more than burial insurance. As a major expenditure, it necessarily interests the husband. Such husbands are also making a major investment when it comes to choice of a house, whereas for low-status families one flat is about as good as another. Finally, the low-status wife more often feels she has a right to decide for herself whether she will go to work or not, whereas the high-status husband again takes more of an interest in these matters. This does not necessarily mean that high-status husbands are worried about a threat to their prestige if their wives go to work, but that they are concerned about the problems involved in the reorganization of their family life around a working wife. If such reasoning is sound, insurance, housing, and the wife's employment are all matters of special interest to the high-status husband.

In general then, social-status differences in decision-making lie in the more active sharing of responsibility by high-status husbands, whereas low-status men more often fail to take part in the decision-making process. This is the first of many signs which will appear of patterns of sharing in the middle class and of *apartheid* in the working class. The latter pattern often orients the husband outside the family, leaving the wife saddled with the burden of making family decisions unaided. In terms of the four kinds of decision-making, this means that middle-class families are more often syncratic (shared-equal), whereas working-class families tend to be more wife-dominant in their power structure.

* * *

THE COMPARATIVE RESOURCES OF HUSBAND AND WIFE

The social status of a family is largely determined by the husband as the representative of the family in the community. His occupation, his income, his education help to establish the family's prestige in the eyes of the community to a great extent, regardless of the wife's characteristics.

However, the balance of power is, after all, an interpersonal affair, and the wife's own characteristics cannot long be disregarded if we are to understand who makes the decisions. Wherever possible, it is desirable to compare the wife and the husband on the same characteristic, for then the comparative resourcefulness and competence of the two partners can be discovered. Once we know which partner has more education, more organizational experience, a higher status background, etc. we will know who tends to make most of the decisions.

Education. . . . We showed that the more education the husband had, the greater his power. However, for wives the relationship seems to be curvilinear. By putting the education of the husband and the wife together, it is possible to resolve this apparent contradiction.

The Detroit data shows that where the wife has at least five more years of schooling than the husband his power is only 4.29, but when the tables are reversed, his power is 5.68. The conclusion is clear that the more one partner's education exceeds that of the other, the larger his share in marital decision-making will be.

Such a relationship might be due simply to the fact that only comparatively high-status (and therefore powerful) husbands exceed their wives in education by five or more years, while it takes a comparatively low-status husband to be that much inferior to his wife. However, controlling by the husband's occupation does not wipe out the relationship (see Table 6). Instead, high-white-collar husbands continue to gain power if they exceed the wife's education, and to lose it if they fall short of the wife. And the same trends hold within

TABLE 6. *Husband's Power, by Comparative Education of Husband and Wife within Occupational Strata*

| Husband's Mean Power By Husband's Occupation | Comparative Education | | |
	Wife More	Equal	Husband More
High-white-collar	5.32 (31)	5.45 (42)	5.65 (78)
Low-white-collar	4.92 (12)	5.20 (30)	5.59 (37)
High-blue-collar	4.80 (117)	5.08 (84)	5.28 (82)
Low-blue-collar	4.79 (14)	5.44 (16)	4.88 (8)

the low-white-collar and the high-blue-collar groups, leaving only one low-blue-collar reversal.

Since comparative . education influences marital decision-making at all occupational levels, it proves to be a highly consistent resource for marital power.

Schooling trains people in verbal skills and knowledge which facilitate decision-making quite directly. In addition, schooling contributes to the effective participation of the individual in the community (through paid or voluntary participation) which in turn strengthens the power position of the individual. So whether directly or indirectly, the better-educated partner brings greater resources to the decision arena.

Organizational Participation. Activity in a formal organization provides the wife with a resource analogous to the husband's success on the job. Getting outside the home brings knowledge pertinent to settling household issues. Moreover, a person who has enough initiative to be active in the community seems also more likely to participate actively in family decision-making. By contrast, stay-at-home spouses may lack the personal and community-derived resources to play as active a role in making decisions.

Unfortunately, the questionnaire used in this study did not include information on the frequency with which husbands attend organizational meetings. However, it does yield the number of types of organizations both partners belong to.[4] Table 7 shows that the partner who belongs to more types of organizations—aside from a church—takes a more active part in family decisions. At the extremes, wives who belong to at least two more organizations depress the husband's power to 4.45 whereas the converse husbands raise it to 5.45. Presumably knowledge of the partners' comparative degree of activity in their organizations would yield an even better picture of the skills and resources they bring to the marriage.

TABLE 7. *Husband's Power, by Comparative Organizational Membership of Husband and Wife*

| | Comparative Organizational Membership | | |
	Wife More	Equal	Husband More
Husband's mean power	5.05	5.14	5.36
Number of families	85	216	250

Church membership was excluded from Table 7 because sociologists have traditionally viewed church membership as a conventional matter unlikely to signify much about the persons involved. The separate analysis of comparative church attendance in Table 8 suggests that separation is unnecessary—churches should be looked upon as another example of a formal organization. (Indeed labor unions with their much lower percentage of attendance at meetings are correspondingly less meaningful organizations to the rank and file.[5])

Table 8 shows that the more often the husband attends church, the more power he has. Churches are not unique in this respect. This is another example of the kind of influence attached to participation in any organization outside the home. Perhaps in a society where church-going is so much the norm, we should put it the other way around and say that individuals who attend *less* often than their partners tend to put themselves at a disadvantage and weaken their basis for participating in family decisions.

Work. Participation in organizations is in many ways the equivalent of holding a job. Both involve coming to the family from a point of independent leverage. Both involve outside contacts which bolster the resources in knowledge and interpersonal skill which the participating partner brings to the marriage. Working, of course, involves the additional contribution of money—the most tangible of all resources. For both reasons, we would expect the comparative work participation of the two partners to affect the balance of power.

TABLE 8. *Husband's Power, by Comparative Church Attendance of Husband and Wife (same church only)*

| | Comparative Frequency of Church Attendance | | |
	Wife More	Equal	Husband More
Husband's mean power	4.72	5.21	5.70
Number of families	99	370	20

TABLE 9. *Husband's Power, by Comparative Work Participation of Husband and Wife*

	Comparative Work Participation					
		Wife Not Employed			Wife Employed	
	Husband Overtime	Husband Full-Time	Husband None	Husband Overtime	Husband Full-Time	Husband None
Husband's mean power	5.62	5.28	4.88	4.50	4.46	2.67
Number of families	195	218	25	44	57	3

Table 9 shows that whichever partner works more gains power thereby. This is true not only for working wives versus non-working wives but even reflects the number of hours the husband works, with overtime husbands edging out husbands who work only a forty-hour week.

It is difficult to know where to place in this series the families in which neither partner is employed. In some respects, they might seem equivalent to couples where both partners work full time. However their equality in not working is tempered by the fact that many of these wives never worked. This may be why the husband's power is greater than that of two-income families.

Marital power reflects not only the current working relationship of the partners but the length of time the wife works after marriage. The more years the wife has worked since marriage, the more power she has (see Table 10). Only one-third of the wives who have ever worked since marriage are currently employed. Nevertheless, the number of years worked correlate with the wife's power regardless of whether she is still working.[6]

The relationship between the wife's employment and her power is complicated by the fact that more wives are employed in the wife-dominant, low-status segment of the community. Indeed this is one reason why low-status husbands on the whole have less power. However, controlling on social status and race shows that working wives have substantially more power on the average than non-working wives at all status levels. Indeed the comparative work participation of husband and wife is related far more closely to the balance of power in marriage than is the social status of the husband in the community taken by itself. This is not, however, to reject the importance of considering the husband's social position, for both his own community role and his wife's comparative resources contribute to the over-all balance of power in marriage.

The Power to Make Decisions

In summary, the power to make decisions stems primarily from the resources which the individual can provide to meet the needs of his marriage partner and to upgrade his decision-making skill. Because it is based on such tangible and relevant criteria, the balance of power may be said to be adapted to the interpersonal relationship of the two partners involved.

Contemporary married couples are freed from the "dead hand" of patriarchal tradition to work out their own destiny in the way best suited to them. This does not mean that they can work out their decision-making pattern in any fashion whatever, but that they are not bound by any "cake of custom" which arbitrarily installs one sex in power. Whereas in the past, custom often dictated that all families should be patriarchal, today the rise of women produces considerable variation between families (and even within families with the passage of time). With less sex-linked cultural norms, such variation incurs less penalty than it once would have. Indeed, the emerging norm may not be a particular pattern of male-dominance or equalitarianism but, rather, the idea of appropriateness. If a wife is working today, it is appropriate that she should have more voice in decisions, rather than be subjugated to an arbitrary standard.

Only at the wife-dominant extreme is there evidence of deviance from the norm today. It may be appropriate for the wife who is the sole support of her family to make most of the decisions, but it certainly is not normal for the marital roles to be reversed in this way. We will find throughout this study dissatisfaction associated with wife-dominance. This is not, however,

TABLE 10. *Husband's Power, by Length of Wife's Participation since Marriage*

	Wife's Work Participation in Years				
	0	Under 1	1–4	5–9	10+
Husband's mean power	5.80	5.65	4.97	4.66	4.29
Number of families	154	85	183	70	55

simply a reflection of breaking social rules. Rather, the circumstances which lead to the wife's dominance involve corresponding inadequacies and incompetencies on the husband's part. An inadequate husband is by definition unable to make a satisfactory marriage partner. So the dominant wife is not exultant over her "victory," but exercises power regretfully by default of her "no good" or incapacitated husband.

Within the range from husband-dominance to extreme equalitarianism, appropriateness appears to be linked with satisfaction. A wife who doesn't get to make many decisions does get to have her needs met by a resourceful husband, and the husband who "has to" share his power with his wife has the compensation of her greater contributions to the marriage.

Under these circumstances, power in American marriages is not a matter of brute coercion and unwilling defeat so much as a mutual recognition of individual skills in particular areas of competence and of the partners' dual stake in areas of joint concern. Given such a natural working out of particular decisions under varying circumstances, it is no wonder that most wives cannot say *why* they make decisions at home the way they do.[7] All they are aware of is that somehow their balance of power "just growed" and that it is right.

Only when American marriages are looked at *en masse* is it clear why power is patterned the way it is —and why it seems right to the couples involved. The answer lies in the tangible resources and skills which the two partners pool in marriage. Today's marriages have a variable balance of power which is not determined by the assignment of authority to one sex, but by the interplay of dynamic forces which affect the marriage from within and without.

NOTES

[1] The remaining 10 per cent are unknown because they failed to answer one or more of the eight decision questions.

[2] The generalization that husband's power is correlated with occupational status also holds within the Negro race (4.31, 4.60, no cases, and 5.00 respectively).

When controls for the wife's employment are instituted, there is one reversal at the blue-collar level among housewife families: 5.31, 5.16, 5.50, 5.68, while working-wife families show no difference at the blue-collar level: 4.22, 4.22, 4.77, 4.85.

[3] Income and education scores were assigned on the basis of the percentiles of the Detroit population falling at the various rank levels. Occupation scores used the percentile prestige ratings developed by the National Opinion Research Center. The ethnic scale was developed from ratings by 195 University of Michigan students from the Detroit area. The over-all score is a simple average of these four individual scores. Examples of scores are: $5,000 income, 61 points; factory worker, 26 points; 11 years of schooling, 42 points; Polish ancestry, 34 points. Such a family would have a Social Status Index of 40.75. (Further details are given in Lenski, 1954.)

[4] Most Detroiters belong to very few organizations aside from a church. Forty-two per cent of the wives and 19 per cent of the husbands belong to no non-church organizations at all, while 28 per cent and 40 per cent respectively belong to only one type (e.g., labor unions or lodges). Even this membership is often nominal, for almost a fourth of those women who belong to one or more organizations hadn't attended a single meeting in the three months prior to being interviewed.

[5] The median Detroit wife attends church every week, the typical husband about every two weeks.

[6] This generalization applies primarily to wives who work apart from their husbands. Gold and Slater (1958) find that young independent businessmen and professionals are more often patriarchal than junior corporation executives, despite the fact that the formers' wives often assist them in their work, whereas the latter do not. Apparently helping one's husband involves submission to his leadership and therefore should not be considered an independent resource for the wife in the same sense that working for someone else is.

[7] This question proved completely unworkable in early pretests of the questionnaire.

REFERENCES

Murdock, George P. *Social Structure*. New York: MacMillan, 1949.

Oeser, O. A., and Hammond, S. B. *Social Structure and Personality in a City*. New York: MacMillan, 1954.

Ogburn, William F., and Nimkoff, Meyer F. *Technology and the Changing Family*. Boston: Houghton Mifflin, 1955.

Parsons, Talcott, and Bales, Robert F. *Family, Socialization and Interaction Process*. Glencoe, Ill.: The Free Press, 1955.

Scheinfeld, Amram. *Women and Men*. New York: Harcourt, Brace, 1943.

WIFE'S EMPLOYMENT, SOCIAL CLASS, AND THE POWER STRUCTURE OF THE FAMILY

Problem

What determines the balance of power within a family? American middle-class culture tends to specify a norm of husband-wife equality. However, the position of husband and wife in the social structure may also affect their influence within the family. This laboratory problem is designed to test the idea that the wife's employment is one such structural factor. We suspect that social class affects the power structure within the family and, at the same time, that there are class differences in the extent to which the woman seeks employment outside the home. To untangle the *confounding** of the social-class and wife's employment variables, it will be necessary to repeat the test of the relationship between the wife's employment and her decision power separately for each social-class group. This procedure is known as *controlling for social class.*

* See p. 59 for an explanation of *confounding.*

We can also use these same data to determine whether our assumption about class differences in the wife's employment and in her decision power are correct.

This problem replicates the work of Blood and Wolfe, but since we do not have a measure of the frequency of the husband's employment, we will not repeat that part of the study. Our measure of decision power is very similar to that of Blood and Wolfe, except that it uses six instead of eight items, and the estimate of decision power is made by a child of the family (the respondent) rather than by the wife.

Hypothesis

State the relationship you expect to find between the wife's employment and her decision power, and also whether you think this relationship exists within white-collar, farm, and blue-collar families.

Empirical Indicators for Problem 4

24. What was your father's occupation at the time you graduated from high school, or what was it before his retirement (please specify)?

_____

In addition please circle the answer category which best fits his occupation.
1. Professional (architect, chemist, doctor, etc.) or managerial position (department head, postmaster, police chief, etc.)
2. Proprietor, except farm (i.e., owner of a business)
3. Clerical or sales position
4. Farmer (owner-operator or renter)
5. Skilled workman or foreman (machinist, carpenter, etc.)
6. Semiskilled or unskilled workman (truck driver, factory worker, etc.)
7. Homemaker, or not employed outside the home
+ Don't know

26. At what periods in your life was your mother employed FULL TIME for wages for one year or more (circle *all* the answers that apply)?
   0 Never
   a Preschool age
   b Elementary school age
   c Junior high school age
   d Senior high school age

27. At what periods in your life was your mother employed PART TIME for wages for one year or more (circle *all* the answers that apply)?
   0 Never
   a Preschool age
   b Elementary school age
   c Junior high school age
   d Senior high school age

VIII. THE LAST WORD

With regard to the following questions, which of your parents had the final say in your family during your last year in high school (if the problem never came up, guess which parent would have had the final say)?

A
THE FINAL SAY
1 = Mother always
2 = Mother more than father
3 = Father and mother exactly the same
4 = Father more than mother
5 = Father always

What car to get? _____	1 2 3 4 5	
Whether or not, or how much life insurance to buy? _____	1 2 3 4 5	
Where to go on a vacation? _____	1 2 3 4 5	
What house or apartment to take? _____	1 2 3 4 5	
Whether mother should go to work or quit working? _____	1 2 3 4 5	
Things concerning the children's activities (getting special privileges, discipline, etc.)? _____	1 2 3 4 5	

Data Analysis

A. WIFE'S EMPLOYMENT AND DECISION POWER

1. *Sort* the code sheets into three groups on the basis of the employment status of the wife. The three employment categories are based on the scores coded in Boxes 26 and 27, interpreted as follows:

> Never employed =
> 0 in both Box 26 and Box 27
> Full-time employment =
> 1 to 4 in Box 26; ignore Box 27
> Part-time employment =
> 0 in Box 26; 1 to 4 in Box 27

NOTE: This classification of the wife's employment is based on periods of work during the life of the respondent, and does not include cases in which the wife worked before the birth of the respondent.

2. *Tabulate* the Ultimate Power Index (UPI is coded in Box 115) for each employment category. This score is the average of "Which parent had the final say" on six specific decisions. UPI scores range from 1.0 to 5.0, with the low figures indicating more decisions by the wife. Record these data in Table 1.

3. *Compute* the average UPI in each employment category. Follow the directions given on page 62. However, in this case use the *upper* limit numbers for the X values. (Strictly speaking, the mid-point of the interval should be used, but our procedure simplifies the calculation and gives the *relative* positions just as accurately.) Complete Table 1.

B. CONTROLLING FOR SOCIAL CLASS

1. To save class time, your instructor will assign one-third of the class to do steps 2, 3, and 4 for the never employed mothers; one-third for the mothers with full-time employment; and the other third for the mothers with part-time employment.

2. *Sort* the employment group assigned to you into three social-class categories, according to the occupational classification of the father (coded in Box 24):

> White-collar = 1, 2, & 3
> Farm   = 4
> Blue-collar = 5 & 6

3. *Tabulate* the Ultimate Power Index scores for each of the three social-class groups (Table 2).

4. *Compute* the average Ultimate Power Index for the group you tabulated. The first five or six students who complete this step should enter their means on the chart your instructor has put on the chalkboard.

5. *Copy* the means for the groups tallied by the other sections of the class into the places needed to complete Table 2.

Laboratory Report

1. Reread Appendix B if you are not sure about how to write up your Laboratory Report.

2. Mention the precaution taken to control for social class under Other Factors.

3. Include in the Discussion of your report such things as the extent to which this replication supports the original study, the reasons underlying the findings, and the meaning and/or importance of the findings.

REFERENCES

Blood, R. O., Jr., and Hamblin, R. L. "The Effects of the Wife's Employment on the Family Power Structure," *Social Forces*, 36 (1958), 347–352.

Heer, David M. "Dominance and the Working Wife," *Social Forces*, 36 (1958), 341–347.

Hoffman, Lois W. "Effects of the Employment of Mothers on Parental Power Relations and the Division of Household tasks," *Marriage and Family Living*, 22 (1960), 27–35.

SECTION/COURSE NO._____ DATE_____ NAME_____

TABLE 1. *Ultimate Power Index by Wife's Employment*

Ultimate Power Index (Box 115)	Employment Status of Wife (Boxes 26 & 27)					
	Never Employed (Box 26 = 0) (Box 27 = 0)		Full-Time Employment (Box 26 = 1 to 4)		Part-Time Employment (Box 26 = 0) (Box 27 = 1 to 4)	
x	f	fx	f	fx	f	fx
1.0–2.0						
2.1–3.0						
3.1–3.5						
3.6–4.0						
4.1–4.5						
4.6–5.0						
TOTAL						
MEAN						
No answer						

TABLE 2. Ultimate Power Index by Wife's Employment and Social Class

Ultimate Power Index (Box 115)	White-Collar (Box 24: 1, 2, and 3)						Farm (Box 24: 4)						Blue-Collar (Box 24: 5 and 6)					
	Never Employed (Box 26 = 0) (Box 27 = 0)		Full-Time Employment (Box 26 = 1 to 4)		Part-Time Employment (Box 26 = 0) (Box 27 = 1 to 4)		Never Employed (Box 26 = 0) (Box 27 = 0)		Full-Time Employment (Box 26 = 1 to 4)		Part-Time Employment (Box 26 = 0) (Box 27 = 1 to 4)		Never Employed (Box 26 = 0) (Box 27 = 0)		Full-Time Employment (Box 26 = 1 to 4)		Part-Time Employment (Box 26 = 0) (Box 27 = 1 to 4)	
x	f	fx	f	fx	f	fx	f	fx	f	fx	f	fx	f	fx	f	fx	f	fx
1.0–2.0																		
2.1–3.0																		
3.1–3.5																		
3.6–4.0																		
4.1–4.5																		
4.6–5.0																		
TOTAL																		
MEAN																		
No answer																		

SECTION/COURSE NO._____ DATE_____ NAME_____

Wife's Employment, Social Class, and the Power Structure of the Family

HYPOTHESIS: _____

_____

_____

_____

_____

_____

SAMPLE: _____

_____

_____

_____

INDEPENDENT VARIABLE: _____

_____

_____

_____

_____

DEPENDENT VARIABLE: _____

_____

_____

_____

_____

OTHER FACTORS: _____

_____

_____

_____

SUMMARY OF FINDINGS: _____
_____
_____
_____
_____
_____
_____
_____
_____

DISCUSSION: _____
_____
_____
_____
_____
_____
_____
_____
_____
_____
_____
_____
_____

ATTITUDES OF CHILDREN TOWARD SUPPORTING AGED PARENTS*

Robert M. Dinkel

Introduction

How satisfactory it may be for aged parents to live with their children[1] depends in part upon the attitude of the younger generation toward their responsibility for the care of their elders.[2] Children who did not want to accept the obligation, but who did so anyway, because of family tradition, community opinion, or legal requirement might carry out the role with such little grace or with such manifest ill will as to make the parents aware of not being wanted or as to lead to friction and major conflicts.[3]

The attitude of children toward taking care of aged parents also has implications for the law of support, for its administration, for public housing for old people, and for the medical care of mentally deficient or bedridden cases. These implications are particularly noteworthy if the assumption is made that there should

be or eventually will be a definite relation between what the children want and what the law or its administration requires. If children do not believe they should extend home support to their aged parents, then the question of what substitutes the State should provide becomes pertinent.

Two general hypotheses have been advanced: (1) Catholics and Protestants, urban and rural residents, males and females, college and high-school students, and persons of various ages differ significantly in their attitude with regard to the responsibility of children, and (2) the attitude of children toward giving an aged parent a home varies with the degree of physical or psychological hardship that they would experience in the situation.

The Opinionaire

CONSTRUCTION

A hybrid instrument was devised by combining several features of the Likert and Thurstone methods. One hundred and sixty items were rated on a five-point scale from "very favorable" to "very unfavorable" by

Reprinted by permission of the author and the American Sociological Association from the *American Sociological Review*, 9 (1944), pp. 370–79.

* Paper No. 2137, Scientific Journal Series, Minnesota Agricultural Experiment Station. Assistance in the preparation of this material was furnished by the personnel of the Work Projects Administration, Official Project No. 265–1–71–236, Sub-Project No. 470.

14 social workers. Only those statements were retained that 10 or more of the judges had put in the same scale position. Sixty-six propositions passed this test. They were given weights from plus two to minus two according to the category in which they had been classified by the judges.

Two preliminary forms with 20 items each were chosen from 66 propositions. These two forms were so constructed that for every statement of a certain weight and subject matter in one there was a statement of the same weight and subject matter in the other.

They were given to 440 college students, using the Likert method of response. The first of the two forms was also given a second time with the instruction to answer by merely checking those statements with which there was agreement. The score for this type of response was the sum of the algebraic weights of the items that were checked.

Thirty of the 40 statements were found to have satisfactory discriminative value when tested by the Likert criterion. The two different methods of response correlated plus .86. This Pearsonian coefficient, based as it is on a small number of items, was considered sufficiently high to validate the simple-agreement type of response.

From the 30 statements of desired discriminative value, 20 were selected for the final form of the instrument. They were picked to give as well balanced an opinionaire as possible. Although the procedures used resulted in some tautology, there might be an appearance of greater duplication than is actually the case since the same subject matter may be found in positive and negative form and in both single and double weight.

RELIABILITY

The instrument was given twice to a group of 90 students in sociology at the University of Minnesota. The second administration came three weeks after the first. Anonymity was assured by having the students use numbers known only to themselves instead of names on their opinionaires. The Pearsonian coefficient on test and retest was plus .874.

VALIDITY

Validity has been largely assumed instead of proved. There are three main questions for which some answer would be desirable: (1) Do students have sufficient direct or indirect experience with the problem to have well-developed attitudes? (2) Does the opinionaire evoke the true opinions of the students? and (3) Do test scores assist one in predicting the degree of adjustment between the two generations when aged parents are taken into the home of one of the children?

Some fragmentary data were obtained on these questions. A group of 86 students in a beginning sociology class at the University of Minnesota were asked to write an essay on the subject of children supporting aged parents, citing whatever examples they could of their point-of-view. In 72 of the cases, the material was judged by the writer to be substantial and concrete, indicating sufficient background for the students to have a meaningful opinion on the problem. The essays were clasified in five groups, depending on the degree of belief in the responsibility of children. An analysis of the variance of test scores was then made. A probability of less than .001 was obtained that the distribution was due to chance factors. Finally, in a case-history study of 50 families, the writer observed some relation between test scores on the opinionaire and conflicts between parents and children.[4]

It should be noted that the scope of validity has not been extended to include a relation between test scores and support behavior; that is, between opinion and practice. The case histories of the 50 families indicated that there is not a high correlation between the two.

Description of the Sample

The sample was composed of 1,006 college and 318 high-school students. The college students were in attendance during the academic year 1939–1940 at the colleges of St. Thomas and St. Catherine and at the Universities of Wisconsin, Minnesota, and Notre Dame. The high-school group consisted of rural boys from many sections of the state of Minnesota who happened to be members in the summer of 1939 of the annual Farm Camp of the Y.M.C.A. and of seniors of the 1939–1940 class of University High School of Minneapolis and Jackson High School, Jackson, Minnesota.

About 200 of the college sample were students who attended summer classes in 1939 at the Universities of Wisconsin and Minnesota. These persons were considerably older than the others, ranging in age from 22 to 45 years. The other college students were from 16 to 22 years, with an average age of a little more than 19 years. The high-school students were between 16 and 19 years, with an average of 17 years.

In the college group there was an approximately equal number of Catholics and Protestants; also included were 24 persons of the Jewish faith and 50 persons who stated that they had no religion. The high-school students were predominantly Protestant; there being five of such affiliation to every Catholic.

The sex distribution was well balanced for the sample as a whole. Among the rural residents, however, there were two females to every male in the college group and just the reverse ratio in the high-school group.

Group Differences

One of the hypotheses is that Catholics and Protestants, urban and rural residents, males and females, college and high-school students, and persons of various ages differ significantly in their attitude toward the responsibility of children for the support of aged parents. The influence of these factors upon the opinion of students was determined by comparing average scores. Four factors were held constant while ascertaining the influence of the fifth by the method of sub-grouping. For example, the scores of 17-year-old Protestant males in their senior year of high school who had also lived all of their life in rural territory were grouped together in order to determine in part the influence of sex upon student opinion.[5]

RELIGIOUS AFFILIATION

Jewish, Catholic, and Protestant families are commonly supposed to differ in their degree of solidarity, traditionalism, authoritarianism, and related characteristics. These traits are probably correlated with opinion regarding family responsibility. Support of aged parents is, in fact, a form of family solidarity. That parents should be respected and assisted when in need is a provision of the traditional code of Christianity and Judaism. Finally, the more authoritarian the family system, the more the elders or patriarchs would be respected and provided for in case of need. Therefore, some association between religious affiliation and opinion regarding the obligation of children to give support is a reasonable hypothesis.

The order according to test score of the religious groups of the sample was Catholics, Jews, Protestants, and persons who professed having no religion. Catholics adhered most strongly and the persons of no religion the least to the belief that children should give support. The expected order was broken by the fact that the Jews instead of having the most favorable opinion toward the obligation of children had an average score between that of the Catholics and Protestants.

Differences between Catholic and Protestant college students in the extent of their acceptance of the individual statements of the opinionaire were large, averaging 17 percent and having a standard deviation of less than three percent. Differences between these two groups in average score (the algebraic sum of the weights of the statements agreed with) were tested by the standard error of the mean to determine their significance. Critical ratios for the four sex-residence subgroups shown in Table 1 range between 2.1 and 9.3 with only one being less than 4.0. Clearly, these ratios indicate differences that are not due to chance.

An analysis of the Catholic sample showed gradations of opinion among the students of different institutions that attest further to the existence of a definite association between religion and opinion. Women students at St. Catherine had a higher average score than the men at Notre Dame and St. Thomas. The Catholics in attendance at Minnesota and Wisconsin universities had an average score that was intermediate between that of the other Catholics and that of the Protestants at these two schools. That the students of St. Catherine should believe most strongly in the responsibility of children is believed to result from its imposing strict discipline and having the most rigid indoctrination of Catholic principles. That the Catholics at the state universities should have the lowest average score for persons of this faith follows from the secular character of these schools. In their cases, there is probably operating both a selective process that tends to attract Catholic students of weak religious belief in greater proportion than those of strong belief and a training process that modifies their original attitudes.

RESIDENCE

One of the widely used source books in the field of rural sociology states that the rural family is more integrated and has greater solidarity than the urban

TABLE 1. *Opinionaire Scores and Critical Ratios for Catholic and Protestant College Students According to Sex and Residence*[6]

Sub-Group	Number		Average Score*		Difference Between Averages	Critical Ratio
	Cath.	Prot.	Cath.	Prot.		
Male-urban	214	77	5.06	1.01	4.05	4.8
Female-urban	114	137	6.38	—.93	7.31	9.3
Male-rural	32	26	7.09	3.69	3.40	2.1
Female-rural	40	78	7.33	1.44	5.89	4.2

* The opinionaire has a theoretical range of 31 points, from minus 15 to plus 16.

TABLE 2. *Opinionaire Scores and Critical Ratios for Rural and Urban Residents According to Sex, Religion, and Educational Status*

Sub-Group	Number		Average Score		Difference Between Averages	Critical Ratio
	Urban	Rural	Urban	Rural		
College students						
Male-Catholic	214	32	5.06	7.09	2.03	1.9
Female-Catholic	114	40	6.38	7.33	.95	0.8
Male-Protestant	77	26	1.01	3.69	2.68	1.8
Female-Protestant	137	78	—.93	1.44	2.37	2.7
High-school students						
Male-Catholic*	18	22	1.14	8.18	7.04	3.5
Male-Protestant	28	107	—.86	5.62	6.48	4.8
Female-Protestant	33	59	—3.21	3.14	6.35	4.2

* Third-year students added to urban group to obtain a larger number of cases.

family. According to the authors, the bonds which hold the rural family together are quantitatively more numerous and qualitatively more intense than those holding the urban family together. From these and other distinctions that are drawn, the reader would infer that rural persons believe to a much greater degree than urban people that children should support aged and needy parents.[7]

In testing this hypothesis, residence was classified as rural or urban according to place of birth. This classification was found to be equivalent to predominant or continuous residence in rural or urban territory. About 70 percent of the college and nearly 100 percent of the high-school students had from birth continuous residence in one or the other type of place. Of the remaining 30 percent of the college students, 22 percent had lived from 75 to 95 percent of their years in the same type of place as that in which they had been born.

As shown in Table 2, rural residents uniformly had higher average scores than urban residents. Critical ratios for three sub-groups of high-school students were over 3.0 in every case, but for the college students, the ratios were only between 0.8 and 2.7. A single critical ratio of less than three ordinarily is not considered as indicative of a significant difference. When there are several random samples from the same universe, each might have a critical ratio of less than three, but the ratios when combined would be significant. Although the conditions of sampling used in this study do not permit a mathematical determination of the collective influence of these critical ratios, the consistency in the results points to a rural-urban difference in student opinion that is not due to chance factors.

The differences, nevertheless, between the rural and urban residents in the college sample are not nearly the size one would expect from the description of the rural family that has been referred to above. Through an analysis of the replies to individual statements of the opinionaire, it was found, for example,

that on the average the two residence groups differed only about five percent in the extent to which they agreed with the propositions.

Probably the true situation is that the two residence groups are not so different in their opinion as suggested by the authors that have been cited nor so similar as indicated by the test results. It is likely that these authors had in mind the rural societies of the past before the spread of modern means of communication and transportation. The opinions of college students, on the other hand, may not be representative of persons living in rural areas. The students usually are members of families belonging to the upper economic strata of rural society. By attending college, these individuals may have their opinions modified by mixing with persons from cities and by being in a social and intellectual atmosphere that tends to give higher prestige to urban values.

In making comparisons of test scores, furthermore, the several groups of the rural population were combined as if they were homogeneous in attitude. Recent studies, however, have indicated that village residents may be more similar in values to the urban than to the farm population. By not having given separate treatment to at least these two groups of rural people, the present analysis may have obscured sizeable differences between farmers and city residents in their opinion on the responsibility of children.

AGE AND EDUCATION

Social, as distinct from biological aging, was thought to be associated with test score. This type of aging does not take place year by year, but is more a matter of advancing from one social role or group to another. The age at which this is done is not fixed and uniform, but is only approximate. In age, therefore, the members of each group are not mutually exclusive.

Three age groups were recognized in the sample:

(1) the high-school group, ranging between 16 and 19 years, but concentrated largely in the 17 year-old category; (2) the regular college group, ranging between 16 and 22, but with the great majority being either 18 or 19 years old; and (3) the summer-session adults, who were between 23 and 45 years of age.

An analysis of the test scores within each of the groups confirmed the validity of the classification. The variation according to year of age was slight within the first two and irregular within the third. The smaller number of cases in the third plus the high degree of heterogeneity in their social and economic characteristics made it impracticable to attempt to account for their fluctuations in score. These cases, therefore, have not been used in the major comparisons of this study.

The factors of age and education are just about inseparable in comparing college and high-school students. The important fact, however, may not be two years of age nor two years of schooling *per se*, but that in going from one level to the other the students enter a different social group in membership and in values. The membership is different, because a process of selection takes place. Students with less than average intelligence or whose parents are in the lower economic strata, or who have little drive toward achievement tend to drop out in greater proportion than those who are at the other end of the distribution of these factors. Although it is difficult to characterize the values of the collegiate group since they vary so much from place to place and from one segment to another within the population of the same school, it may be held with some degree of fairness that they include a larger than average measure of sophistication, class consciousness, and irresponsibility.

The expected difference in opinion between the two groups, however, was not found in the sample. Differences in test scores were small and irregular.[8] While rural college students had lower average scores than rural high-school pupils, the relation was just the reverse for the urban groups. This negative finding may have been obtained for one or more of the following reasons: (1) no significant relationship exists; (2) additional factors would have to be controlled to demonstrate the correctness of the hypothesis; (3) the sample is not representative of the student groups tested; and (4) the true relationship is that indicated by the results and requires a different and more complex interpretation than the one that has been suggested.

SEX

Assuming that students either have insight into their future roles or are early conditioned according to them, more women than men students were ex-

pected to believe that children should support aged parents. This hypothesis followed from the fact that women usually are more dependent than men upon the family for economic security. One of the reasons for this greater vulnerability of women is that the care of children often makes it impossible for them to accept employment. When not tied down with this burden, women tend to experience greater difficulty than the other sex in obtaining a suitable position, because they have had less occupational training, because ordinarily they are discriminated against by employers in the recruiting of new workers, and because from early years they normally accumulate fewer years of job experience and job rights. In realization of these disabilities, a woman should be inclined to look to the family for the protection she often cannot earn for herself. A woman, furthermore, should find easier the acceptance of the status of dependency, since there is likely to be less reproach cast upon her than would be cast upon a man for failure to be self-supporting.

But the data do not bear out the hypothesis. Sometimes the males had a higher and sometimes a lower score.[9] Critical ratios were all between one-half and two-and-a-half. This lack of association may, of course, be due to an error in assuming that student opinion has been molded in accordance with future economic role as has been suggested above. Another explanation of the absence of a significant difference in opinion may be that some of the social factors in the situation balance the economic considerations. Two of these factors may in particular account for such a balance. First, women may experience greater trouble in adjusting to a common residence with children, because they are accustomed to being mistress of the household instead of having to take orders from a daughter or daughter-in-law. In the case of men, on the other hand, there is not a similar opportunity for their role to come into conflict with that of the son or son-in-law, except possibly in the farm family. Second, women may acquire greater insight than men into the difficulties of the two generations living together. This discernment may result from the fact that women spend more of their time in the home and in interaction with other family members than is common in the case of men.

SUMMARY

Religious affiliation and place of residence determine in part the extent to which students believe that children should support aged parents. Catholics more often than Protestants and rural more than urban residents believe in this obligation. In their acceptance of favorable statements, Catholics and Protestants differed on the average about 17 percent while rural and urban residents differed only about five percent. The

TABLE 3. *Percentage of Students by Religion and Residence Agreeing with Several Statements of Obligation of Children to Support Parents*

Statement	Protestant		Catholic	
	Urban	*Rural*	*Urban*	*Rural*
We should look to children to support aged parents	49	53	74	71
Aged parents should understand they have to stand on their own feet without help from children	20	13	9	4

factors of age, educational level, and sex, however, were not found to be related significantly to test score.

Replies of College Students to Individual Statements

The second general hypothesis of the study is that the attitude of children toward supporting an aged parent in their home depends upon the degree of physical and psychological hardship that would be experienced in the situation. This hypothesis has been tested by using the responses of the sample of college students to selected items of the opinionaire.

Several factors were controlled through verbal instructions in the administration of this instrument to the students. They were told to assume: (1) the children while able to give support would suffer a moderate degree of financial sacrifice by so doing; (2) if the children did not extend help, the parents would probably be able to get old age assistance, which would meet their subsistence needs although it would not provide them with the comforts to which they had been accustomed; and (3) the parents were in reasonably good mental and physical health, being neither senile nor bedridden.

The opinionaire statements described various degrees of difficulty that would be present in taking an aged parent into one's home. Although the items are not finely graded, they are able to indicate the range in the percentage of students accepting or rejecting the

obligation of children to give support as the circumstances vary from what might be considered normal to extreme hardship. The data are broken down by religious affiliation and residence since these two factors have been found to be significantly related to opinion.

Six of the 20 statements of the instrument are general in the sense that they do not specify either home care or financial aid as the method of giving support and make no mention of any difficulties that might be present in the situation. Two of these six statements, one positive and one negative, have been chosen as representative of this type of situation. The percentage of the college students agreeing with each of these two statements is shown in Table 3.

The statement that we should look to children to support aged parents puts the responsibility of the younger generation in the simplest of terms. No complications of unusual personality characteristics of the parents or unpleasant consequences to the home life of the children are introduced into the situation. About half of the Protestants and about three-fourths of the Catholics agreed with this statement.

An unequivocal rejection of the responsibility of children is made in the statement that aged parents should understand that they have to stand on their own feet without help from children. This idiomatic language puts the denial of an obligation in blunt terms that are almost harsh in their flat finality. There is scarcely any room for misunderstanding the attitude of a person who would so express himself. From four to

TABLE 4. *Percentage of Students Checking Each of Five Positive-Specific Statements According to Religion and Residence*

Statement	Protestant		Catholic	
	Urban	*Rural*	*Urban*	*Rural*
Children should overlook the trouble that aged parents might cause in the home	43	50	69	68
Children should put up with any inconvenience in their family life in order to help aged parents	23	31	44	48
Children should give a home even to aged parents who interfere a lot in family affairs	20	24	44	46
No matter how crabby, critical, and interfering aged parents are, children should give them a home	17	22	42	40
Children should be willing to give a home to an aged parent who is an extremely jealous busybody	16	19	33	33

20 percent of the college students agreed with this proposition.

Now see how these percentages change as different degrees of hardship are mentioned as part of the situation. From the remaining 14 statements, 11 were chosen for this analysis. They all refer to the specific method of helping parents by taking them into one's home. The first five presented below in Table 4 are positive in the sense that agreement with them indicates a favorable attitude toward assisting parents.

The statement that children should overlook the trouble that aged parents might cause in the home only suggests that there might be trouble. Since there is usually some friction in the interaction of family members, the situation is almost one that expresses no more than the normal degree of unpleasantness associated with taking parents into one's home. From 43 to 69 percent of the students agreed with this proposition. Since about the same percentage agreed with the general statement that we should look to children for the support of parents, the specific condition of the possibility of trouble does not greatly change the extent to which students believe in the obligation of the younger generation.

The second item in the group of five, that children should put up with any inconvenience in their family life in order to help aged parents, was agreed with by 23 to 48 percent of the students. The word, "inconvenience," suggests more a moderate degree of annoyance than a serious hardship. Nevertheless, from 20 to 25 percent fewer students agreed with this statement than the one just analyzed. Possibly, the qualifying adjective, "any," led many students to refuse to accept the proposition.

The next three statements represent situations involving a great deal of hardship to the children. If parents interfere a lot in family affairs, if they are very crabby, or critical, or if they are extremely jealous busy-bodies, they probably would endanger the happiness of their offspring. These three propositions were agreed with to about the same extent. From 19 to 33 percent of the students checked the one that had the lowest acceptance rate of the three. It is likely that these percentages indicate the minimum who believed that there should be responsibility for parents when the degree of difficulty was within limits that would be considered reasonable.

Thus, the belief of the college students in the responsibility of children dropped to 30 to 40 percent as the circumstances varied from those that might be considered approximately normal to those of extreme hardship. The high point was reached when 49 to 74 percent agreed that children should give support. The low point showed only from 16 to 33 percent continuing in this opinion.

The extent to which students reject the obligation of children also varies considerably with the particular circumstances of extending help. The negative statement which was the least agreed with was that aged parents should understand they have to stand on their own feet without help from children. As shown in Table 3, only four to 20 percent of the students checked their agreement with this item. That these percentages can be materially increased by reference to specific difficulties is demonstrated by the responses to the six statements described in Table 5.

The four conditions of the parents getting in the way, being unpleasant, being a nuisance, and being quarrelsome did not change substantially the percentage of students in agreement with the general negative statement that has been said to have been the least agreed with of this type. It would appear, therefore, that when students are of the general opinion that parents should not be supported it is because they believe that their elders would be unpleasant, quarrelsome, etc. How extreme, then, do the difficulties have to be before

TABLE 5. *Percentage of Students Checking Each of Six Negative-Specific Statements According to Religion and Residence*

Statement	Protestant		Catholic	
	Urban	Rural	Urban	Rural
Aged parents who keep getting in the way should not be given a home by their children	21	15	7	3
If aged parents are unpleasant, children should not give them a home	25	16	12	7
If aged parents are a nuisance in the home, children should refuse to take them in	24	23	15	4
Children should not give a home to aged parents who are quarrelsome	34	18	15	10
Aged parents who interfere with family affairs should be put out of your home	45	30	26	21
Children should not take care of aged parents if it makes for squabbling and turmoil all the time	67	64	40	32

a significantly greater percentage agrees that children should not have this responsibility?

There is a moderate increase in the extent of agreement with the negative side of the case when the condition is that of the parents interfering in family affairs. Then from 21 to 45 percent of the students believed that the parents should not be given a home. There was a very marked increase in the percentages when taking care of the parents was said to make for squabbling and turmoil all the time. From one to two-thirds of the students were then of the opinion that assistance should not be required of children. This appears to be the upper limit of student rejection of this obligation of the offspring when the circumstances are within reason.

SUMMARY

The hypothesis of this section has been that student opinion on the subject of children supporting parents varies according to the degree of hardship present in the situation. This hypothesis has been confirmed for the sample group. The sensitivity of opinion to this factor has been demonstrated for each of the several subgroups of college students. The number of students accepting the responsibility of offspring decreased about 36 percent and the number rejecting such obligation increased about 39 percent as the circumstances changed from those that might be considered normal to those of extreme hardship. Many more students accepted than rejected the obligation of children when the situation did not present unusual difficulties. The division of opinion was about even when the hardship was a severe one. Under extreme circumstances, the balance swung sharply to the side opposed to the support of parents.

Implications

The obligation of children to support aged and needy parents is apparently no longer well established in the mores. This fact has an important bearing upon the psychological security that parents obtain from the family which they rear. In the past, elders were fairly certain that come what might in the history of their personal relations with their offspring the latter would be willing to give assistance if it were necessary. Now, the children often take into consideration the nature of their personal relations with parents in order to come to a decision as to whether or not to help them. Parents, therefore, cannot be sure of obtaining support no matter how smooth their interaction with children happens to be at a particular time.

This change in family organization would be less significant if the States had universal pension laws as is the case in England. But the means test is still applied in this country so old age assistance is supposed to be given only to those persons whose children cannot afford to take care of them. Furthermore, the application of this test tends to stigmatize the recipient of the assistance to the extent that old people often feel that it is not respectable to take the money. The result is that parents who are in doubt about being helped by their children sometimes are equally uncertain about being able to qualify for assistance from the State or look upon it as an unacceptable alternative.

NOTES

[1] Children of aged parents include persons of adult status.

[2] For the purpose of this study, persons 65 years of age and over are considered aged. References in this study to parents usually are intended to be limited to aged parents who are in need of assistance. It is estimated that about 30 to 40 percent of aged parents are supported wholly or in part by their children. Usually, support is in the form of the parent or parents living in the home of a child.

[3] This statement is one of the important assumptions of this study. It provides a justification of a study of verbal responses apart from whether or not children are consistent in what they say should be done and what they actually do when faced with the problem.

[4] For an analysis of these conflicts, see Robert M. Dinkel, "Parent-Child Conflict in Minnesota Families," *American Sociological Review*, August, 1943, pp. 412–19.

[5] Only some of the comparisons made have been selected for presentation in table form in the following pages.

[6] Results for the high-school students have not been presented, because the number of Catholics in this part of the sample is very small. It should be noted, nevertheless, that the Catholic and Protestant high-school students differ in average score by only two and a half points.

[7] Sorokin, Zimmerman, and Galpin, *Systematic Sourcebook in Rural Sociology*, Volume 2, Chapter X, "The Family as the Basic Institution," pp. 3–41.

[8] The reader who is interested in the details may get them by re-arranging the data of Table 2.

[9] Again, a re-ordering of the facts of Table 2 will yield the details.

RELIGION AND FAMILY SOLIDARITY

Problem

The chaplain of Yale University recently said, "Never have our churches been so full and never have they had less influence." But theoretical considerations suggest that any institution as important as the church will influence many aspects of life, even if not always in the way church leaders envision. Empirical evidence on one of the interrelations between the religious system and the family system is presented in the study by Dinkel which you will be replicating in this laboratory problem, and more extensive evidence is reported in Lenski's *The Religious Factor* (1961). The specific factor studied in this problem is willingness to support aged parents. We are assuming that such willingness reflects family solidarity.

Because the major religious groups in the United States tend to differ in the average socioeconomic level of their members, however, differences among religious groups may reflect social class rather than religious influences on the family. Consequently, in this laboratory problem, as in several others, it will be necessary to control for the possibility of a confounding* of variables by dividing the sample into three social-class groups. With such a control, it will then be possible to discover whether religious affiliation makes a difference for family behavior, regardless of social class. This control also lets us use social class as an independent variable. That is, we can find out if there is greater family solidarity in farm, blue-collar, or white-collar families.

Hypothesis

From your reading and other knowledge, consider the various factors which tend to encourage or discourage familial solidarity in each religious group and in each social class, and formulate a hypothesis specifying differences in extent to which members of each religious group are willing to support aged parents.

Empirical Indicators for Problem 5

24. What was your father's occupation at the time you graduated from high school, or what was it before his retirement (please specify)?

_____

In addition please circle the answer category which best fits his occupation.
1 Professional (architect, chemist, doctor, etc.) or managerial position (department head, postmaster, police chief, etc.)
2 Proprietor, except farm (i.e., owner of a business)
3 Clerical or sales position
4 Farmer (owner-operator or renter)
5 Skilled workman or foreman (machinist, carpenter, etc.)

* See p. 59 for an explanation of confounding.

6 Semiskilled or unskilled workman (truck driver, factory worker, etc.)
7 Homemaker, or not employed outside the home
+ Don't know

36. What is your MOTHER'S religious preference?
1 Roman Catholic or Eastern Orthodox
2 Baptist
3 Lutheran
4 Methodist
5 Presbyterian
6 Other Protestant (please specify)_____
7 Jewish
8 Other (please specify)_____
9 None

87. Do you think that children should be responsible for looking after aged parents?
1 Strongly disagree
2 Disagree
3 Undecided
4 Agree
5 Strongly agree

Data Analysis

1. *Sort* the code sheets into three social-class groups on the basis of the father's occupation, as coded in Box 24:

White-collar = 1, 2, & 3
Farm = 4
Blue-collar = 5 & 6

2. Your instructor will divide your class into three sections and assign each group to do steps 3, 4, and 5 for one of the three social-class groups.

3. *Sort* the social-class group assigned to you on the basis of the religious preference of the mother, as recorded in Box 36. This is a nine-category code which must be simplified. There are various ways of doing this, depending upon the make-up of the sample and type of research problem.

If no one Protestant group predominates, the religious analysis can be simplified to a comparison of Catholics, Protestants, and Jews. Even if one Protestant denomination does predominate, your instructor may ask you to combine it with all the other Protestant groups to simplify the problem. In this case, divide your sample into three religious-preference groups as follows:

A. Catholic = 1
B. Jewish = 7
C. Combined
Protestant = 2, 3, 4, 5, & 6

However, if one Protestant denomination (e.g., the Lutherans) is prominent in your sample,* it may be interesting to consider the cases in that group separately from the rest of the Protestants. All other Protestants are treated as one group, in spite of known heterogeneity, because there are not enough cases to analyze each group separately. If you do separate out the prominent Protestant denomination, you will then have four religious-preference categories as follows:

A. Catholic = 1
B. Jewish = 7
C. Predominant
   Protestant (e.g.,
   Lutheran) = 3
D. Other Protestant = all other categories
                      except 8 & 9

3. *Tabulate* for each religious group the degree of agreement with the statement, "Children should be responsible for looking after aged parents," using the scores coded in Box 87. Record your results on the Tabulation Form. The *"Total"* column should be filled in by adding the totals of the other columns.

4. *Compute* the average or mean score denoting the extent to which members of each religious group are willing to support aged parents. Follow the directions for computing the mean given in Problem 3, page 62.

* Your instructor will determine this before the laboratory period.

The first five or six people completing this step should enter the following figures on the chalkboard: Means, Total fx's, and N's (on which each mean was based). If time permits, this data can be used to complete the section of the Tabulation Form entitled *"All Classes."*

Laboratory Report

In writing out this Laboratory Report give special attention to the Discussion. You may wish to refer again to the outline in Appendix B to see what should go into this section and also to reread the Wallis and Roberts article, "How to Read a Table," on pages 57–62. Be sure to include in your discussion possible reasons underlying the differences you have found.

REFERENCES

Lenski, Gerhard. "Socio-Religious Group Membership and Family Life," in *The Religious Factor*. New York: Doubleday, 1961. Pp. 213–220.

Streib, Gordon F. "Family Patterns in Retirement," *Journal of Social Issues,* 14 (1958), pp. 46–60. Also in Marvin B. Sussman, ed., *Sourcebook in Marriage and the Family*. Boston: Houghton Mifflin, 1963. Pp. 46–60.

SECTION/COURSE NO._____ DATE_____ NAME_____

Willingness to Care for Aged Parents by Religious Preference of Mother and Social Class

White-Collar Families (Box 24 = 1, 2 & 3)

Responsibility for Aged Parents (Box 87)	A Catholic (Box 36 = 1)		B Jewish (Box 36 = 7)		C Combined Protestant (Box 36 = 2, 3, 4, 5 & 6)		D Predominant Protestant (_____) (Box 36 =)		E Other (Box 36 =)		Total	
x	f	fx	f	fx	f	fx	f	fx	f	fx	f	fx
1												
2												
3												
4												
5												
TOTAL												
MEAN												
No answer												

Farm Families (Box 24 = 4)

Responsibility for Aged Parents (Box 87)	A Catholic (Box 36 = 1)		B Jewish (Box 36 = 7)		C Combined Protestant (Box 36 = 2, 3, 4, 5 & 6)		D Predominant Protestant (_____) (Box 36 =)		E Other (Box 36 =)		Total	
x	f	fx	f	fx	f	fx	f	fx	f	fx	f	fx
1												
2												
3												
4												
5												
TOTAL												
MEAN												
No answer												

Blue-Collar Families (Box 24 = 5 & 6)

Responsibility for Aged Parents (Box 87)	A Catholic (Box 36 = 1)		B Jewish (Box 36 = 7)		C Combined Protestant (Box 36 = 2, 3, 4, 5 & 6)		D Predominant Protestant (_____) (Box 36 =)		E Other (Box 36 =)		Total	
x	f	fx	f	fx	f	fx	f	fx	f	fx	f	fx
1												
2												
3												
4												
5												
TOTAL												
MEAN												
No answer												

All Classes

Responsibility for Aged Parents (Box 87)	A Catholic (Box 36 = 1)		B Jewish (Box 36 = 7)		C Combined Protestant (Box 36 = 2, 3, 4, 5 & 6)		D Predominant Protestant (_____) (Box 36 =)		E Other (Box 36 =)	
x	f	fx	f	fx	f	fx	f	fx	f	fx
Total for white-collar families										
Total for farm families										
Total for blue-collar families										
GRAND TOTAL										
MEAN										

SECTION/COURSE NO._____ DATE_____ NAME_____

Religion and Family Solidarity

HYPOTHESIS: _____

_____

_____

_____

_____

_____

SAMPLE: _____

_____

_____

_____

_____

INDEPENDENT VARIABLE: _____

_____

_____

_____

_____

DEPENDENT VARIABLE: _____

_____

_____

_____

_____

OTHER FACTORS: _____

_____

_____

_____

SUMMARY OF FINDINGS: _____

_____

_____

_____

_____

_____

_____

_____

_____

_____

DISCUSSION: _____

_____

_____

_____

_____

_____

_____

_____

_____

_____

_____

_____

_____

_____

_____

_____

YOUTH AND POLITICAL CHANGE*

Eleanor E. Maccoby, Richard E. Matthews, and Anton S. Morton

In each presidential election occurring in the mid-twentieth century, approximately one-ninth of the people eligible to vote are young people who are eligible to cast a presidential ballot for the first time, having had their twenty-first birthdays since the last presidential election. These young people are of great interest to social scientists and political practitioners alike, not only because they constitute a large enough group to carry considerable weight in any particular election outcome, but because it is possible that the political allegiances which they form early in their voting careers will be perpetuated for many years and thus have an impact upon a series of elections. We do not know a great deal about changes in the voting pattern of individual citizens, or groups of citizens, as they grow older and accumulate voting experience. Nor do we know

Reprinted by permission of the authors and the publisher from *Public Opinion Quarterly,* 18 (1954), pp. 23–29.

* This study was undertaken as a class project in a seminar on research methods in the Department of Social Relations at Harvard. The authors are indebted to Professor V. O. Key, for suggestions in the planning of the study and preparation of the report, and wish to thank the following seminar members, who participated actively in the planning, field work and coding for the study: Russell Davis, Elisha Greiffer, Mariam Lewin, Dr. Julius Prince, Mary Roseborough, Inge Schneier, Edward Tiryakian, and Benjamin Tregoe.

how many elements of the political ideology formed in late adolescence and early adulthood are retained for a life-time. It is a reasonable hypothesis, however, that young people, being less bound than older people by habit and old political ties, will be more responsive to the political pressures of the moment, so that they might play a greater role in mediating political change than their elders.

What do we already know concerning the political behavior of young people? With varying degrees of certainty, the following facts have been fairly well established:

1. A smaller percentage of young people go to the polls than do people in older age groups.[1]
2. In his choice of candidate, a young person tends to be similar to his parents.[2]
3. Despite the agreement with their parents, young people as a group have been more Democratic in party choice than older voters, at least since 1936.[3]

An interesting question is whether the young person's preference for the Democratic party means that he is less conservative in his ideology than older voters. In general, of course, there is a correlation between the liberal-conservative dimension and party choice, but the existing evidence does not point as strongly to a liberal ideology among the young as might be expected. Centers found a slight tendency for young people among the upper occupational groups to be more liberal, but among the laboring groups, the young were no more liberal than the old.[4] Lazarsfeld found greater conformity to one's group with increasing age, so that older Catholics were more strongly Democratic, old Protestants more strongly Republican, than younger people in the two religious groups. He suggested that increasing age brings about greater social conservatism, rather than greater political conservatism.[5]

In any case, an anomaly in the existing findings remains to be explained, and this is the fact that youth is consistently more Democratic than the older generations, while at the same time young people tend to follow in the political footsteps of their parents. Lubell has proposed an interesting hypothesis to explain this situation.[6] He points out that over the last two decades, children of immigrants have come of age; their parents were not eligible voters. Furthermore, the working-class urban masses, with their higher birthrate, have contributed disproportionately to each new crop of first-time voters. Possibly, young people vote proportionally just as their parents do, and it is the differential rates of population growth among the different social classes which explain the fact that young people as a whole have been consistently more Democratic than the older age groups. On the other hand, it is possible that young people tend to start their political careers with more "left" or liberal ideology, and become more conservative as they grow older and acquire a larger stake in the existing state of affairs. Possibly, both these factors operate jointly to produce a high proportion of Democrats among the young.

Some important questions to be answered by research, then, are: 1) To what extent do young people follow their parents' lead politically? 2) When they do differ from their parents in politics, do they move primarily in the Democratic direction, or are there counter-balancing changes in both directions? and 3) When the young person does take up a political position different from that of his parents, what are some of the psychological and sociological variables associated with the change? The present study has been focused upon these questions, in an effort to advance our understanding of the political behavior of young people.

The Study

The study was conducted in Cambridge, Massachusetts just after the presidential elections of November, 1952. Interviews were conducted with 339 people

aged 21–24 inclusive—a group eligible to vote in a presidential election for the first time in 1952. Originally, a probability sample of people within the desired age range was selected from the police lists of Cambridge, which are compiled in January of every year, and are intended to record the name, age and sex of every adult resident of Cambridge at the time of listing. In the course of interviewing, however, the list was found to be badly out of date and consequently the young people finally interviewed cannot be considered to be a representative sample of the young people of Cambridge.[7] However, the main objective of the study was not to produce descriptive statistics about Cambridge but to examine relationships between variables. For such purposes, the range of the sample is more important than its representativeness.

By way of background for the report which follows, it may be useful to present here the voting record for the city of Cambridge in the 1952 elections:

76 per cent of those eligible to vote cast a ballot in the presidential contest

41.8 per cent voted for Eisenhower (among those voting for one of the two major Presidential candidates)

35.5 per cent voted for Lodge, the Republican senatorial candidate

37.1 per cent voted for Harter, the Republican candidate for Governor.

It may be seen that even in a year in which the Republicans swept the country, and in which Eisenhower carried the state of Massachusetts (which has been Democratic for many years), Cambridge remained heavily Democratic. The margin for the Democrats was smaller than in previous years, however.

The following report must be interpreted, then, in the light of the fact that the study was conducted in a Democratic stronghold (predominantly working class), in a year which saw a major swing toward the Republican Party.

Political Preferences: Parent and Child

National poll data have consistently shown that youth are more Democratic than older age groups. This was true even in 1952 although Eisenhower carried a much larger proportion of the young vote than had earlier Republican candidates. It has not been clear, however, whether individuals change during their lifetime (switching from the Democratic to the Republican Party as they grow older), whether the ranks of the Democrats in the young age bracket are being swelled through the higher birth-rate in the lower Socio-Economic Status (SES) urban groups and by the arrival at

TABLE 1. *Relationship Between Party Choice of Young Voter and That of His Parents*

	Fathers		
Respondents	*Republican*	*Democrat*	*Independent*
Republican	60%	12%	30%
Democrat	26	81	35
Independent	14	7	35
Total	100%	100%	100%
N	58	192	17

	Mothers		
Respondents	*Republican*	*Democrat*	*Independent*
Republican	71%	9%	23%
Democrat	22	83	50
Independent	7	8	27
Total	100%	100%	100%
N	56	201	26

voting age of the children of immigrants, or whether both factors are operating.

If it is true that people change party allegiance in the Republican direction as they grow older, then it should follow that young people, as a group, would be more Democratic than their own parents. To check this, young voters were asked for their own party preferences and their choice of presidential candidates; they were also asked these two items of information about each of their parents.[8] Of course, there were some instances in which the young person had lost contact with a parent, or for some other reason did not know his parents' political preferences. Data are presented in Table 1 for the cases in which the young person could report the party choice of his parents.

As may be seen from Table 1, there is high agreement between the party choice of the young voter and that of his parents, but the agreement is higher when the parents are Democrats. This would suggest a slight shift on the part of the younger generation as a whole toward the Democratic Party, if there were as many Republican as Democratic parents.

In a Democratic stronghold like Cambridge, there are so many more sets of Democratic than Republican parents, that the small proportion of young people switching from Democratic to Republican Party allegiance more than offsets (numerically) the larger proportion of young people switching from the Republican allegiance of their parents into the Democratic party, so that over the sample as a whole, there were slightly fewer (not significantly) Democratic young people than Democratic parents. On the whole, however, the agreement of young people with the party choice of their parents is high: 74 per cent of those who can report their fathers' party preference prefer the same

party, and 76 per cent choose the same party as their mothers. In 86 per cent of the cases where the parents are both of the same party, son or daughter chooses that party.

Parenthetically, it should be noted that there is no evidence of the traditional "father dominance" in political matters. There are only 21 instances in the sample in which the father and mother disagree on their choices of political party, but when they do, the young person is slightly more likely (not significantly) to follow the mother's preference than the father's. When agreement with parents is studied according to the sex of the child, it appears that while the daughters are most responsive to the influence of the mother, sons are as likely to follow the mother as the father when parents disagree.

While we have seen considerable agreement between political preferences of the first-time voter and those of his parents, there exists a group of young people who choose a different party or a different presidential candidate than their parents, or both. What are the forces which might influence a young person to abandon the political orientation of his parents? The first step in studying this problem was to develop a score which would reflect the extent to which the young person had changed from the political position of his parents. This score is called the Index of Political Change. Six items of information were considered for the score: the respondent's party choice and presidential choice, his mother's party choice and presidential choice, and his father's party choice and presidential choice. Numerical values were assigned to each difference between the young person and either of his parents and these values were added, so that the highest score on political change would go to the young person

TABLE 2. *Relationship Between Amount of Parental Control and the Index of Political Change*

Index of political change by young voter	"In your case, when you were in your teens, did your family want to have quite a lot to say about your friends and the places you went and so on, or were you pretty much on your own?"		
	Parents had a lot to say	*About average amount to say*	*Parents left respondent on his own*
Major change in Republican direction	18%	7%	9%
Minor change in Republican direction	14	10	17
No change, family Republican	12 ⎱ 50*	9 ⎱ 69*	11
No change, family Democratic	38 ⎰	60 ⎰	45
Minor change in Democratic direction	7	7	9
Major change in Democratic direction	11	7	9
	100%	100%	100%
Number of cases	74	69	140

* The 19% difference between the "no change" groups in the first two columns is significant at the .05 level, using a two-tailed test.

who differed with both parents on both candidate and party choice. Differences on party choice were given twice as much weight as differences on candidate choice, on the assumption that party choice is a more pervasive indicator of political position than the preference for any particular candidate. Shifts away from the parents' political preferences were also labeled according to whether they were shifts away from a Democratic position and toward a Republican position, or vice versa.

What factors might produce a change on the part of the young person from the political orientation of his parents? The first hypothesis tested was one related to youthful rebellion. It has been popularly assumed that some young people are radical because they are throwing off the shackles of parental authority in their late adolescence. A reasonable assumption would be that the more rigid the control which the parents attempt to exercise over the teen-aged youth, the more he will feel the impulse to rebel and reject parental values when he is in a position to do so. An attempt was made in the current study to measure the strictness and rigidity of control exercised by the parents over the respondents when they were in their teens, and something about the reaction of the young person to his parents' effort at control.

As may be seen in Table 2, it is the children of the parents who attempt to exercise strictest control who most often change away from the political preference of their parents.

The highest conformity to parental political values is found among the group who were subject to moderate parental control. For the young person who is left rather completely on his own, conformity is less—presumably because his decisions are made more independently of family knowledge or influence. And conformity is also less for the rigidly-controlled group. Thus we see that maximum conformity by the young person to the political values of his family occurs when

his parents have been neither laissez faire nor authoritarian in their dealings with him—when they have taken an interest in him and attempted to guide him, but have used moderate pressure via persuasion rather than strong pressure by command or force.

Although there are too few cases to make a definitive test, it is interesting that the effects of parental training methods on political conformity seem greatest when the parents have a high level of interest in politics. Presumably, when parents do not consider politics important, their children will choose some other area of values in which to signify their loyalty or register their protest.

Among the strictest families, the change is largely toward being more Republican than the parents. This is unexpected, since "adolescent revolt" has been presumed to lead to leftward, rather than rightward, movement. It must be noted, however, that the strictest parental control was found at the lower SES levels, where the parents are heavily Democratic in political orientation. If the young person is to adopt a different set of political values than that of his parents, he *must* change toward the Republican party, unless he wants to go into the fringe parties, which very few young people do. (Only one member of our sample voted for the Progressive Party candidates.)

The fact that parental control is stricter in the low SES[9] group raises the question whether the relationship found in Table 2 could be an artifact of SES: that is, possibly both political change and strict control are found mostly at the lower SES levels, in which case of course the relationship between control and change would be difficult to interpret. Analysis shows that political change is slightly more common at the *upper* SES levels, so that the relationship in Table 2 is not an artifact of SES.[10]

It is true, however, that the relationship between the degree of parental control and the frequency of the young people's change away from parental politics is

TABLE 3. *Relationship Between Parental Control and Ideology, at the Low SES Level*

For low SES group only: *"In strikes and disputes between working people and employers, do you usually side with the workers or the employers?"*	*Believe parents interfere too much*	*Believe parents do not interfere too much*
Workers	47%	67%
Lean toward workers, reservations	21	17
Sometimes one, sometimes other	19	14
Lean toward employers, reservations	9	2
Employers	4	—
	100%	100%
Number of cases	43	64

found almost exclusively at the lower SES. That is, among the working-class group, young people changed most from their parents' political positions when parental control was strict and when the young people resented this fact. At the higher SES levels, this tends not to be the case.

It appears, then, that when young people at the lower SES level change away from the political preferences of their parents, the change is at least partly motivated by revolt against over-strict control. At the upper SES level, while there is as much or more change on the part of young people, it is *not* a function of the atmosphere in the home where they grew up, and other factors must be sought.

What about the *depth,* or generality, of the change away from parental politics which is engendered in the "revolt" group? Possibly, these young people simply give themselves a different party label from their parents, or choose a different presidential candidate, without changing any of the ideology which one would ordinarily expect to underlie political preferences. Possibly, on the other hand, the spirit of revolt goes much deeper, and takes the form of a basic shift in ideology (toward the right or left) which is then reflected in vote and party choice. Unfortunately, the study provided no measure of the ideology of the young voter's parents. The young voter himself, however, was asked three questions adapted from Centers' ideology questions,[11] and it is possible to compare the "revolt" group with the "non-revolt" group at a given SES level in their ideology (See Table 3).

There is a shift in the conservative direction among the young people who resent parental control, and who were shown earlier to be changing away from the party preference of their parents (changing largely in the direction of becoming more Republican). Two other ideology questions, one on public versus private ownership of power facilities and one on security versus individual initiative, both showed shifts in the same direction on the part of the "revolt" group, although the shifts were somewhat smaller. It appears likely,

then, that shifts away from parental political preferences on the part of young people who resent parental control are accompanied by (or perhaps preceded by) some changes in general politico-social attitudes.

Peer Group Influence

We have been examining parental influence on voting. What about the influence of the young person's peers: friends, fellow-workers, and spouse? As Table 4 shows, the young voter agrees on choice of party most highly with his spouse, next most highly with his friends, and least often with his fellow workers.

Seventy-seven per cent of the married young voters had the same party preference as their spouses; 64 per cent had the same party preference as the majority of their friends, and 46 per cent of those who worked agreed in party choice with the majority of their fellow-workers. In a heavily Democratic area like Cambridge, Republican young people cannot or do not surround themselves as easily with like-minded friends and fellow workers as do the Democrats, or else, possibly the young Republicans tend to assume that the people around them are Democrats unless they have positive knowledge to the contrary.

Of course, the amount of agreement on party choice does not tell anything about the extent and direction of influence. Possibly, the higher agreement with friends than fellow workers means that people have more freedom of choice as to friends than fellow workers, and that they tend to choose like-minded friends. Another possibility is that friends exert more influence upon each other—change one another's minds about politics more—than do members of work groups.

In an effort to trace lines of influence, the young voter was asked how much he talked about politics with his friends, fellow workers, and spouse. The amount of political discussion was fairly high with friends and spouse, lower with fellow workers, where we have seen that there is less agreement on party

TABLE 4. *Relationship Between Party Choice of Young Voter and That of His Friends, Fellow Workers, and Spouse**

	Young Voter's Party Choice		
	Republican	*Democrat*	*Independent*
Friends Mostly:			
Republican	52%	12%	24%
Democrat	28	74	52
Independent or 50–50	20	14	24
	100%	100%	100%
Number of cases**	71	203	29
Fellow Workers Mostly:			
Republican	35%	27%	42%
Democrat	42	52	25
Independent or 50–50	23	21	33
	100%	100%	100%
Number of cases**	48	132	24
Spouse:			
Republican	49%	4%	28%
Democrat	33	95	44
Independent	18	1	28
	100%	100%	100%
Number of cases**	33	103	18

* The young voter was asked the party preference of his spouse, and whether he thought his friends and fellow workers were mostly Republicans or mostly Democrats.

** The numbers of cases vary because only part of the sample were married, and a sizeable group of the sample (mostly women) were not working and therefore had no fellow workers. Almost all the sample had a group of friends whose political orientation they could discuss.

preference. When we relate the amount of discussion to the amount of agreement on politics, we find that people who prefer the same party as their fellow workers tend to talk politics with them quite a bit, while those who have a different political position than their fellow workers less often engage in political discussion at work. (This difference is significant at the .05 level.) The opposite situation tends to hold true within the home of young married couples: when they disagree on politics, they discuss them extensively, while with agreement, politics become a less central subject of discussion. Among friends discussion is as common when they are of a different party as when they are of the same party.

The findings on political discussion are interesting when viewed from the standpoint of group dynamics. A hypothesis among students of group dynamics[12] is that when a group is highly cohesive and a topic is central to the attainment of group goals, disagreement will produce discussion and mutual influence. If a group is not cohesive, and/or the topic is not central to its goals, disagreement will cut off discussion of the topic, or lead people to leave the group. Among the peer groups studied here it is reasonable to assume that the husband-wife team is the most cohesive, the group of friends the next most cohesive, and the work group the least cohesive in terms of the strength of the individ-

ual's desire for the approval of the group. The centrality of politics as a topic relevant to the functioning of the group is difficult to assess for these three groups, but we might expect that politics is least relevant to the work group, which has presumably been brought together for other reasons than agreement on politics, while friendships and marriage ties are presumably formed at least partly because of like-mindedness on a number of issues. Of course, if one views political alignment as an expression of membership in an economic interest group, one's political position *could* be viewed as central to the functions of his work group. In any case, our data suggest that the husband-wife team is a cohesive group and that political agreement is important to the smooth functioning of the group, so that disagreement produces discussion and mutual influence. On the other hand, the work group is either not cohesive or political views are irrelevant to the functions of the group, for disagreement on political matters cuts down discussion and thus prevents the work group from being a potent source of political influence. The friendship group occupies a position mid-way between the spouse and the work group in the extent of its probable influence in political matters.

We have seen that the younger voter less often agrees with his friends on politics than he does with his parents. It is interesting, however, that the friends

TABLE 5. *Influence of Friends, Related to Resentment of Parental Control*

Index of political change:	Resent Parental Control Friends' Party	
	Republican	Democratic
More Republican than parents	66%	25%
Same as parents, Republican	17	6
Same as parents, Democrat	17	50
More Democratic than parents	0	19
	100%	100%
Number of cases	18	52

Index of political change:	Do not Resent Parental Control Friends' Party	
	Republican	Democratic
More Republican than parents	33%	13%
Same as parents, Republican	38	4
Same as parents, Democrat	14	64
More Democratic than parents	15	17
	100%	100%
Number of cases	21	83

appear to exert more influence if the young person is resentful of parental control (See Table 5).

While the number of cases is small, there is evidence of interaction between home atmosphere and the influence of friends: once the psychological ground work for change is laid in over-strict home control, the young person becomes more responsive to the political orientation of his friends in his choice of party and candidate.

Social Mobility

A factor which might produce change away from the political orientation of the young voter's parents is social mobility. Presumably, if the young person moves up or down the socio-economic scale, he begins to take on the values of the group into which he has moved. Table 6 presents evidence bearing on this question. The upwardly-mobile young people (those having higher-level jobs than their fathers) are compared with the "charter members" of the class into which they move, and with the non-mobile people in the classes from which they came.[13] The question to be answered by the data is this: Are mobile young people politically more like the group from which they came or the group into which they have moved?

An important fact which is illustrated by this table is that the mobile young people seldom consider themselves Independents: they seem to make a definite party choice more often than non-mobile people. But apart from this, the upwardly-mobile people are more Republican than the class from which they came, and are similar to the class into which they have moved.

Similarly, when it comes to candidate choice, the upwardly-mobile group has adopted the behavior of its destination group: in fact, they chose Eisenhower more often than their peers, and considerably more often than their group of origin.

The downwardly-mobile group, on the other hand, presents quite a different picture. These people do not adapt themselves to the political preferences of their new social milieu—they are more like the class from which they originate than the class into which they move; in fact, if anything, they are more Republican than their class of origin. It appears, then, that those who move up the social scale seek to identify themselves with the political values of the higher group, but those who move down cling to the symbols of their former status. It should be noted that those in the downwardly-mobile group still have a chance of reaching the status from which they came: a young person of 21–24 years of age who has a poorer job than his father may yet achieve as good a job in later years. However, the young person who has already obtained a better job than his father is likely to remain at a higher status.

How deep do the changes of political orientation go among mobile young people? The study included only three questions on ideology, and therefore only an initial exploration of this question is possible; but analysis of the answers to these questions shows that the increasing Republicanism of the upwardly-mobile young people is by no means always accompanied by what might be considered appropriate ideological changes. For example, when asked where their sympathies usually lie in a strike, 73 per cent of the upwardly-mobile young people say they side with the workers, as compared with 71 per cent in the class

TABLE 6. *Social Mobility Related to Choice of Party and Candidate**

	Upwardly Mobile	*Non-Mobile, in Class Where Upward Mobiles Originated***	*Non-Mobile, in Class to Which Upward Mobiles Moved***
Party preference			
Republican definitely	18%	8%	21%
Republican leanings	5	—	—
Independent	9	18	28
Democratic leanings	12	1	8
Democratic definitely	56	73	43
	100%	100%	100%
Number of cases	82	73	73
Candidate choice			
Eisenhower	48%	28%	37%
Stevenson	52	72	63
	100%	100%	100%
Number of cases	82	72	72

	Downwardly Mobile	*Non-Mobile, in Class Where Downward Mobiles Originated***	*Non-Mobile, in Class to Which Downward Mobiles Moved***
Party preference			
Republican definitely	28%	21%	11%
Republican leanings	3	—	—
Independent	8	28	17
Democratic leanings	4	8	3
Democratic definitely	57	43	69
	100%	100%	100%
Number of cases	75	73	73
Candidate choice			
Eisenhower	46%	38%	27%
Stevenson	54	62	73
	100%	100%	100%
Number of cases	74	72	72

* Students are excluded from this table, since their mobility is still undetermined.
** For purposes of comparison, the non-mobile cases have been weighted to cancel out differences between them and the mobiles in socio-economic status. That is, for the first comparison, the non-mobiles have been weighted so as to have the same SES distribution as the mobile people at their point of *origin*. For the second comparison, the non-mobiles have been weighted so as to have the same SES distribution as the mobiles have in their *destination* class.

where they originated, and only 49 per cent in the class they have moved into. On the other hand, they are somewhat more likely than their class of origin (not quite significantly) to favor individual initiative instead of government-backed security. Downwardly-mobile young people, on the other hand, even though they do not take on the party labels and voting preferences of the lower group into which they move, do take on some of the ideology of this lower group: 69 per cent of downward mobiles side with the workers in a strike, as compared with 68 per cent of the group into which they have moved, and 43 per cent of the group from which they have come. Downwardly-mobile young people are also considerably more in favor of Govern-

ment ownership of large power facilities, and slightly more security-minded, than the class from which they came.

Lubell has assumed that most of the children of foreign-born parents, as they move up the economic scale, will take their Democratic party orientation with them. We see that while a good many of them become Republicans, they retain some of the ideology which might predispose them to return to the Democratic party. That is, their new party choice could be considered unstable at this age level, since it is not grounded in the system of beliefs most compatible with it, and either the party preference or the ideology should be subject to change on the basis of future

TABLE 7. *Relationship Between Education and the Index of Political Change*

	Education				
Index of Political Change	*College Graduates**	*Some College*	*High School plus Business or Vocational*	*High School Graduates*	*Some High School*
More Republican than parents	24%	32%	17%	27%	23%
No change, parents Republican	9⎫	24⎫	15⎫	14⎫	3⎫
No change, parents Democratic	33⎭ 42	28⎭ 52	46⎭ 61	44⎭ 58	69⎭ 72
More Democratic than parents	34	16	22	15	5
Total	100%	100%	100%	100%	100%
N	55	25	41	88	75

* Includes both graduates who have left college and those currently doing graduate work.

events. Similarly, the downwardly-mobile young people, while not currently changing their party and vote, are undergoing ideological changes which might predispose them to later shifts. A longitudinal study would be of the greatest value for following out the threads of change with mobility, as would a study conducted in a year when the general political swing was toward the Democrats instead of toward the Republicans.

Education and Ideology

We have seen that at the lower SES levels, political change is related to resentment of family authority, but that at the upper SES levels, this is not the case. Yet there is as much or more change away from parents' political positions among the upper-SES young people. What might be some of the sources of change in this group? One possible source is the better education of the high SES group. What is the relationship between education and political change? Table 7 shows the relationship is a positive one.

Of the college graduates in the sample, 58 per cent changed to some degree from the political position of their parents, while only 28 per cent of those who did not graduate from high school did so. Even when socio-economic status is held constant, the relationship appearing in Table 7 holds: at each class level, the better-educated young people change more.

The direction of the changes which occur with education are of some interest. At the lower education levels, the direction is clearly toward the Republicans, while among the college group more young people shift in the Democratic than the Republican direction. Of course, college students tend to come from the upper-income brackets, from parents of predominantly Republican preferences, so if they change, it must be in the Democratic direction. But it must be borne in mind that the college-educated young people include not only those from upper-SES families, but also include

a sizeable group of upwardly-mobile young people from lower-SES families. These upwardly-mobile young people, as we have seen earlier, tend to change in the Republican direction. It is therefore especially striking that there is as much shift in the Democratic direction (especially in a predominantly Republican year) as occurs among the college group. Is there a general tendency for college education to move people to the left politically? Previous findings on this point have not been conclusive. Newcomb's Bennington study showed students becoming more "liberal" during their years at college, but this study was done during the depression years.[14] Havemann and West, on the other hand, found that the people who had been out of college longest were the most heavily Republican.[15] Possibly, college exercises a temporary pro-Democratic influence, with graduates returning to the Republican fold as they grow older. It must be remembered, however, that the group studied by Havemann and West who had been out of college longest had been in college during conservative times. The people more recently out of college had gone through their intellectually formative years during depression and "New Deal" or "Fair Deal" years. The difference between the two groups may be due, therefore, to entirely different factors than age itself.

The data from the present study do not shed much light on the problem of change in college versus after college. It is true that much of the pro-Democratic shifts in our college group occur among young people who are *still in college*.[16] But those who remain in college are largely people who have chosen professional careers which require graduate work, and those who leave after a B.A. are largely those who choose to go into business. The greater Republican leanings of the latter group, then, need not reflect a growing conservatism after leaving college, but may reflect a difference in political viewpoints which exists throughout college between business-oriented and professionally-oriented students.

Regardless of the direction of change, college education is associated with change away from parental politics. How does education function to bring about political change? Presumably, in the course of obtaining an education, the young person is exposed to a wider variety of points of view and more information, so that he is able to make political choices on the basis of "rational" considerations, rather than simply on the basis of family tradition (or revolt against family tradition). If education actually functions this way, political change among the well educated should be accompanied by appropriate changes in ideology, while for the lesser educated, the relationship of ideology to change should not be so close. Examination of the replies to the limited number of ideology questions in this survey shows this is the case: among the college group, those who changed in the Republican direction are considerably more conservative on the items measured than those who remained Democrats, and those who changed in the Democratic direction are more liberal than those who remained Republicans. Among the groups with lesser education, the differences are by no means so clear: political change does not seem to be so consistently a function of ideology. Of course, we must not overlook the possibility that college educated people rationalize their ideologies *after* changing their party preferences, out of a need for consistency which is more compelling for them than for people of lesser education.

Summary and Conclusions

Just after the presidential elections in 1952, interviews were taken with 339 people aged 21–24 (people who had become old enough to vote in a presidential election for the first time in 1952). Their political preferences were compared with those of their parents and peer groups. The following findings emerged:

1. Agreement on candidate and party choice is highest between the young person and his family (parents and spouse), next highest with his friends, and least high with his fellow-workers. Findings on the amount of discussion of politics between the young person and each of these groups suggest that fellow-workers are not very influential in the formation of the young person's political opinions, while parents and spouse are of great importance.

2. Among the lower socio-economic groups, rejection of parental political values is associated with strict discipline in the home. The highest conformity to parents' politics occurs in the homes where the parents exercise moderate control over the young people—being neither authoritarian nor completely laissez faire.

3. Young people who are socially upwardly-mobile tend to adopt the political behavior of the group into which they have moved, becoming more Republican. Downwardly-mobile young people, on the other hand, are *not* similar to their new social milieu in their choice of candidate and party; rather, they remain as Republican, or more so, than the class from which they came.

4. The voting and party choice of mobile young people is not generally accompanied by appropriate ideology. The upwardly-mobile young people, while voting like their new social group, retain a good part of the ideology of the group from which they came. Downwardly-mobile young people take on some of the ideology of their new social class, while retaining the voting patterns of the group where they originated.

5. Young people who are well educated change away from the political orientation of their parents more often than poorly-educated young people. Among the better-educated, political change tends to be accompanied by appropriate changes in ideology, while for the poorly-educated, this is less often the case: in this group, political change appears to have a less "rational" basis.

NOTES

[1] Campbell, Angus, Gerald Gurin, and Warren E. Miller, "Political Issues and the Vote," *American Political Science Review*, Vol. XLVII (June, 1953), No. 2, p. 389. Lazarsfeld, Paul F., Bernard Berelson, and Hazel Gaudet, *The People's Choice*, New York: Harcourt, Brace, 1952, p. 44.

[2] Lazarsfeld, *op. cit.*, pp. 140ff.

[3] Cantril, Hadley, *Public Opinion, 1935–46*, Princeton: Princeton University Press, 1951, pp. 591, 602, 627, and 614. Campbell, *op. cit.*, p. 383.

[4] Centers, Richard, *The Psychology of Social Class*, Princeton: Princeton University Press, 1949, pp. 165 ff.

[5] Lazarsfeld, *op. cit.*, pp. 23 ff.

[6] Lubell, Samuel, *The Future of American Politics*, New York: Harper and Brothers, 1952.

[7] A sample of youth, as might be expected, is extremely mobile and difficult to locate for interviewing: 24% of the young people called upon had moved and could not be traced to a new address; 10% had been drafted; and a further sizeable group were not at home, after repeated callbacks. Comparisons with Census figures show that the group who were reached for interview include too many who are married, and too many at the upper end of the 21–24 age bracket.

[8] To determine party preference, the following question was asked: "In general which party do you like best, Republican or Democratic?" For candidate choice, the question was: "How did you vote for President in the election that's just past?" For the relatively small group who did not vote, this question was worded: "If you had voted in the last election, how do you think you would have voted for president?"

[9] For this study, SES level has been measured by rating the respondent's occupation on the Warner 7-point scale of occupational status. Students were not rated since their occupational status is not yet established. For a description of the scale see W. L. Warner, Marcia Meeker, and K. Fells, *Social Class in America*, Chicago; Science Research Associates, Inc., 1949.

[10] The proportion changing to some degree away from the parents' political position in each SES level is as follows:

SES Level	Per Cent Changing	No. of Cases
1,2,3 (upper)	50	47
4	45	69
5	39	45
6 and 7 (lower)	34	79
Students	51	33

[11] Centers, R., op. cit.

[12] Festinger, L., "Informal Social Communication," Psychological Review, Vol. 57 (1950), pp. 271–282.

[13] For married women, social mobility was measured by comparing the occupation of the young woman's husband with that of her father.

[14] Newcomb, T., Personality and Social Change, New York: Dryden Press, 1943.

[15] Havemann, E., and Patricia S. West, They Went to College, New York: Harcourt, Brace, 1952.

[16] Of the 48 young people with college educations who have left college, 16 became more Republican than their parents, 12 more Democratic. Among the 32 people still in college, 4 became more Republican, 11 more Democratic.

THE FAMILY AND POLITICAL BEHAVIOR

Problem

Political values and beliefs are, along with a religious system and other values, part of the social inheritance a child receives from his parents on the American scene at least, where political affiliations seem to be transmitted from parent to child. However, some individuals do move away from their parents' political affiliations. What accounts for these exceptions? One theory is that such shifts in political affiliation are not so much the result of an attraction to another political position as they are an act of rebellion, a sign of dissatisfaction with one's family, particularly with one's father.

Several of the questions in the Questionnaire on parental practices may show differences between the parental role behavior of fathers whose children have the same political affiliations and those whose children have adopted different political affiliations. For simplicity, we will use one *positive* practice, Instrumental Companionship (which reflects the amount of help the father gives the child), and one *negative* practice, Expressive Rejection (which reflects the amount of nagging and criticism which the child receives from the father).

Hypothesis

State what differences you expect to find in the amount of Instrumental Companionship and of Expressive Rejection between the fathers of children who have changed their political affiliation as compared to those whose children favor the same political party as their father.

Empirical Indicators for Problem 6

38. Which of the following comes closest to your FATHER'S political preference?

    1 Conservative Republican
    2 Liberal Republican
    3 Conservative Democrat
    4 Liberal Democrat
    5 Socialist

40. Which of the following comes closest to YOUR OWN political preference?

    1 Conservative Republican
    2 Liberal Republican
    3 Conservative Democrat
    4 Liberal Democrat
    5 Socialist

V. PARENT PRACTICES

During your last year in high school, how often did your father do each of the following?

For each item in this list, circle one answer number to show how often your FATHER engaged in this practice, . . . using the following rating scale:

0=Never
1=Sometimes
2=Frequently
3=Usually
4=Always or almost always

c Taught me things which I wanted to learn _____ 0 1 2 3 4

d Helped me with schoolwork when I didn't understand something _____ 0 1 2 3 4

    Box 60 = Sum of c and d

q Nagged at me _____ 0 1 2 3 4

r Scolded and yelled at me _____ 0 1 2 3 4

    Box 74 = Sum of q and r

Data Analysis

A. POLITICAL AFFILIATION OF FATHER AND CHILD

1. *Sort* the code sheets into three groups on the basis of the political affiliation of the father, using the scores in Box 38 (father's political preference), and combining them as follows:

> Republican = 1 & 2
> Democratic = 3 & 4
> Socialist = 5

2. *Sort* the Republicans into two groups, (a) those whose children have the same, and (b) those whose children have a different political affiliation from that of the father. The respondent's political affiliation is recorded in Box 40. See Table 1 of the Tabulation Form for a guide to these groups.

3. *Sort* the Democratic fathers and then the Socialist fathers as in Step 2. You should now have six groups of cases: (a) Republican fathers whose children are Republican; (b) Republican fathers whose children are different; (c) Democratic fathers whose children are also Democratic; (d) Democratic fathers whose children are different; (e) Socialist fathers whose children have the same affiliation; and (f) Socialist fathers whose children are different.

4. *Count* the number of cases in each group and enter on Table 1 of the Tabulation Form for Problem 6.

5. *Compute* the percentage of fathers whose children have changed their affiliation in each group of fathers. Use the table of percentages in Appendix D, and enter the scores on Table 1.

B. FATHER-CHILD RELATIONSHIPS AND CHANGE IN POLITICAL AFFILIATION

1. *Divide* the class into two groups. One half of the class will do the part of the analysis using the data for students with Republican fathers; the other half of the class will work with the data for students whose fathers are Democrats. We will omit the data for So-

cialist fathers since there are usually too few cases. It is important to do the analysis separately for Republicans and Democrats because social class is confounded with both political affiliation and father-child relationships.

2. *Tabulate* the Instrumental-Companionship scores (Box 60) on Table 2, and the Expressive-Rejection scores (Box 74) on Table 3. Do this separately for fathers whose children have maintained the same political affiliation and those whose children have adopted a different affiliation.

3. *Compute* the means for each group. See the instructions for computing means on page 62. The first five or six students who complete this step should enter their means on the chart on the chalkboard.

Laboratory Report

Reread the instructions in Appendix B on writing the Laboratory Report. Your laboratory report should be based on both the data you have tabulated and also the means from the tabulations done by the other half of the class.

REFERENCES

Davies, James C. *Human Nature and Politics*. New York: Wiley, 1963.

Hess, Robert D., and Torney, Judith V. *The Development of Political Attitudes in Children*. Chicago: Aldine, 1967.

Lipset, Seymour M. *Political Man: The Social Bases of Politics*. Garden City, N. Y.: Doubleday, 1960.

Middleton, Russell, and Putney, Snell. "Student Rebellion against Parental Political Beliefs," *Social Forces*, 41 (1963), pp. 337–383.

SECTION/COURSE NO._____ DATE_____ NAME_____

TABLE 1. *Political Affiliation of Father and Child*

Political Affiliation of Father and Child	Political Affiliation of Father					
	Republican (Box 38 = 1 & 2)		Democratic (Box 38 = 3 & 4)		Socialist (Box 38 = 5)	
	f	%	f	%	f	%
Same	(Box 40 = 1 & 2)		(Box 40 = 3 & 4)		(Box 40 = 5)	
Different	(Box 40 = 3, 4, & 5)		(Box 40 = 1, 2, & 5)		(Box 40 = 1,2,3, & 4)	
TOTAL		100%		100%		100%

TABLE 2. *Relationship between Father and Child's Political Affiliation by Instrumental Companionship of Father for Students Whose Fathers Are (check one): Democrats _____ or Republicans_____*

Instrumental Companionship of Father (Box 60)	Same Political Affiliation		Different Political Affiliation	
x	f	fx	f	fx
0				
1				
2				
3				
4				
5				
6				
7				
8				
TOTAL				
MEAN				
No answer		✕		✕

TABLE 3. *Relationship between Father and Child's Political Affiliation by Expressive Rejection of Father for Students Whose Fathers Are (check one): Democrats _____ or Republicans _____*

Expressive Rejection of Father (Box 74) x	Same Political Affiliation		Different Political Affiliation	
	f	fx	f	fx
0				
1				
2				
3				
4				
5				
6				
7				
8				
TOTAL				
MEAN				
No answer		✕		✕

SECTION/COURSE NO._____ DATE_____ NAME_____

The Family and Political Behavior

HYPOTHESIS: _____

_____

_____

_____

_____

_____

SAMPLE: _____

_____

_____

_____

INDEPENDENT VARIABLES: _____

_____

_____

_____

_____

DEPENDENT VARIABLES: _____

_____

_____

_____

_____

_____

OTHER FACTORS: _____

_____

_____

_____

SUMMARY OF FINDINGS: _____

_____

_____

_____

_____

_____

_____

_____

_____

_____

DISCUSSION: _____

_____

_____

_____

_____

_____

_____

_____

_____

_____

_____

_____

_____

_____

Part IV   INTERNAL PROCESSES

OF THE FAMILY SYSTEM

FAMILY SIZE AS A FACTOR IN THE MARITAL ADJUSTMENTS OF COLLEGE COUPLES

Harold T. Christensen and Robert E. Philbrick

It has been traditionally assumed that children and marital happiness go together, and are causally related. Popular support for this belief has been claimed in the fact that approximately three-fifths of all divorces are between childless couples, which seems to suggest that children hold a marriage together. What this line of reasoning fails to acknowledge is that: (1) divorce is concentrated in the early years of marriage, prior to the start of childbearing for many couples; (2) divorce alone is a rather poor criterion of maladjustment in marriage, it being well known that many unhappy couples remain together because of the expense, stigma, or inconveniences of a formal separation; and (3) though statistically associated, divorce and childlessness may not necessarily be causally related.[1]

Reported research on the relationship of family size to marital adjustment is contradictory. In the late twenties, Mowrer and Mowrer observed that in discordant marriages, such as those dealt with by marital

adjustment agencies, the chance for successful marriage decreases as number of children increases.[2] By way of contrast, Davis found greater happiness for wives with several children.[3] Popenoe also reported a positive relationship between number of children and happiness in marriage, with the happy couples of his educated sample averaging 2.04 children as against 1.67 for the unhappy.[4] No significant relationships in either direction were found by either Hamilton[5] or Bernard.[6]

Several studies have suggested, either explicitly or implicitly, that the problem cannot be solved without first taking into account the attitudes of couples toward children. Burgess and Cottrell found happiness in marriage to be associated with desire for children, whether couples had any at the time of the study or not. These authors also found that poorest adjustment was with couples who had children which they did not desire.[7] Terman found no correlations between presence of children and happiness in marriage, but suggested that this may be because opposing influences tend to balance each other out in a large sample and that the

Reprinted by permission of the authors and the American Sociological Association from the *American Sociological Review*, 17 (1952), pp. 306–312.

presence of children may actually affect any given marriage either way.[8] Landis and Landis reported that the happy and unhappy groups of their sample both tended to get larger as size of family decreased, and that childless couples fell at the two extremes of the happiness scale.[9] Locke, in comparing his happily married and divorced groups (with duration of marriage controlled) found the happily married to be significantly higher on desire for children, but there were no substantial differences regarding either childlessness or size of family.[10] Hill, in his study of the crises of separation and reunion incident to war, reported negative relationships between adjustment to crisis on the one hand and both actual and desired family size on the other.[11] Reed, in a careful study of 1444 "relatively fecund" Indianapolis couples, found an inverse relationship between marital adjustment and family size. He further discovered "an increase in marital adjustment with increasing success in controlling fertility according to the desires of the couple."[12]

Our Purdue study, to be reported below, was initiated to provide additional testing of this problem.

Sample and Procedure

The completed sample consisted of 346 married couples living within a student housing area at the university. At least one member of each married pair was a veteran and a student. The mean length of marriage was 4 years and 2 months; mean ages, 27.1 years for husbands and 25.6 for wives; mean cumulative education, 15.5 years for husbands and 13.3 for wives; mean number of children, 1.2 per family. The group was predominantly urban and Protestant. Only first marriages were considered.

The schedule was built in three separate sections: (1) background information concerning respondents, including number of children resulting from the marriage; (2) the Burgess-Cottrell-Wallin Marriage Adjustment Form; and (3) a group of questions designed to test the attitudes of couples regarding marriage and parenthood in the college setting.

Interviews were carefully conducted by field workers during July and August, 1950. Generally, two contacts were made with each family. During the first, the purpose of the study was explained, background information collected, and an appointment made for a second call at a time when both spouses would be present. At this second interview, parts two and three of the schedule were administered to each mate separately and without collaboration. Cooperation by respondents was high, as evidenced by the fact of only eight refusals.

Finally, data from the schedules were punched on IBM cards and analyzed statistically for significant relationships.

Testing the Central Problem

We were concerned first of all to know if family size is in any way related to marital adjustment in this college sample. To test this, adjustment scores were calculated for each spouse and related to number of children within the family. Results are shown in Table 1.

It will be noted that: (1) the average score of husbands was 23.0 and of wives, 28.0, neither of which is particularly high.[13] (2) With the exception of two-child families, wives show greater adjustment than do husbands.[14] This is particularly true with the childless group. (3) In general, the observed relationship between family size and the marital adjustments of both husbands and wives is a negative one. This is especially evident in the comparisons of childless mates with those having one or two children.

It is this last generalization that interests us most at this time. For wives, score differences between the childless and the one-child families were found to be statistically significant at the five per cent level of confidence, and between the childless and the two-child families, significant at the one per cent level. Other differences were not found to be significant. For husbands, none of the variations in score were found to be statistically significant. Nevertheless, it should be noted that their scores reflect a similar pattern to that of the wives. In this Purdue sample, therefore, marriage adjustment of wives is found to vary inversely with family size (up to two children) and the presumption of a similar relationship for husbands is raised.

As will be noted also, adjustment scores go up again with three children, suggesting a curvilinear relationship. We view this with caution, however, since the number of cases in the three-child category is small

TABLE 1. *Mean Marital Adjustment Scores of Husbands and Wives, by Number of Children in Present Family*[*]

Number of Children	Number of Cases	Marriage Adjustment Scores	
		Husbands	Wives
0	77	25.4	35.6
1	170	20.9	26.4
2	79	23.2	22.4
3	20	31.4	35.0
Total	346	23.0	28.0

[*] Since there were only three families with four or more children, the analysis has been limited to cases having three or fewer.

and score differences between this and the two-child group do not approach statistical significance.

Taking Values into Account

Perhaps number of children is not so important to marital adjustment as the way couples value the children they have, or do not have, in light of their circumstances. To test this possibility several questions were asked, each of which will be discussed in turn.

(1) *How many children do you desire during the course of your married life?*

Table 2 presents frequencies and marital adjustment scores arranged by ultimate number of children desired. It will be noted that more of the respondents wanted three children than any other number. No significant relationship was found between actual and desired number of children.[15]

In general, marital adjustment was found to increase with size of desired family—up to four children, at least. Statistically significant differences, at the five per cent level of confidence, were found between those desiring four children and those desiring only one or two offspring. This was true for both spouses. In addition, the difference in wives' scores between those desiring three and those desiring only one child was also found to be statistically significant.

This positive relationship between desire for children and marital adjustment, in the face of our earlier reported negative relationship between actual number of children and marital adjustment, suggests that some couples who want children eventually are, nevertheless, having them before they are ready. This failure in timing may result in partial maladjustment because of the disappointments and increased hardships frequently involved. Certain questions which follow bear upon this same point.

(2) *Were all of your children planned?*

For obvious reasons, this question was asked only of the couples having children. Husband and wife responses agreed in a remarkable manner, with only 14.4 per cent showing contradictory answers. The percentage of all parents saying that all of their children were planned was 34.4. This percentage differed by size of family, being 37.3 for parents with one child, 26.8 for parents with two children, and 23.0 for parents with three children. Thus, nearly two-thirds of these parents had "unplanned" children, with the proportion going up as size of family increased.

Table 3 compares adjustment scores according to the planned and unplanned status of children. It will be observed that, with one exception, scores are higher for couples in the "planned" group. As a further test, family size was disregarded, momentarily, so as to obtain larger numbers in the "planned" and "unplanned" categories for purposes of statistical manipulation. When the wives' scores of these combined groups were compared, the group with unplanned children was found to be lower, significant at the one per cent level of confidence. Similar comparisons between the husband groups showed non-significant differences but in the same direction as with the wives.

Another observation is that adjustment scores tend to increase with size of family in the "planned" husband and wife groups, but fail to do so in any uniform manner in the "unplanned" groups. We have already noted that "unplanned" families have the lower scores, and that the percentage of "unplanned" families increases with size of family. It would seem, therefore, that a major factor in the negative relationship between family size and marital adjustment, observed earlier in the paper, is the increasing presence of unplanned children as the family gets larger. If all children were planned, it may be that the relationship to marital adjustment would be a positive one as shown in the "planned" columns of Table 3.

TABLE 2. *Mean Marital Adjustment Scores of Husbands and Wives, by Number of Children Desired During Entire Marriage*

Number of Children Desired	Husbands		Wives	
	Number	Score	Number	Score
1	6	1.2	9	5.4
2	78	19.4	68	22.4
3	126	23.9	130	29.1
4	85	27.9	85	33.2
5 or more	23	24.4	24	29.9
Total*	318	23.4	316	27.9

* Twenty-eight husbands and 30 wives did not respond to query.

TABLE 3. *Mean Marriage Adjustment Scores of Husbands and Wives, by Planned and Unplanned Status of Children and by Size of Family*

Number of Children	Marriage Adjustment Scores			
	Children Planned		Children Unplanned	
	Husbands	Wives	Husbands	Wives
1	19.7	32.9	21.7	21.3
2	31.6	39.6	20.2	18.4
3	65.4	40.4	22.8	33.2

(3) *If starting over again, knowing what you now know, would you have fewer, the same number, or more children than you now have?*

A child may be unplanned but definitely welcomed at birth or at a later age in life. In other words parental attitudes may change with time. The above question was designed to discover how parents presently feel about the sizes of their families, after experience had operated.

Approximately sixty per cent of those answering said they would have the same number of children if doing it over again, compared with thirty per cent who said more and ten per cent who said fewer. Percentages differed by size of present family, as shown in Table 4. In general, percentages desiring fewer children increased with size of present family, while those desiring the same number or more decreased. This supports our earlier finding concerning parallel increases between unplanned children and family size, and is an evidence of internal consistency within the study.

Among the groups answering "fewer," "same," and "more," mean marriage adjustment scores were 10.0, 24.3, and 24.4 for husbands and 13.5, 28.2, and 29.8 for wives respectively. Statistical significance at the five per cent level of confidence was found between those desiring fewer children and all others combined, for both husbands and wives. This supports our earlier finding concerning lower adjustment scores for parents with unplanned children.

Exploring the Effects of College Attendance

Some of the questions made explicit reference to the college situation.

(4) *If starting over again, knowing what you now know, would you wait until after college to marry?*

About seventy-five per cent of all answering seemed satisfied; that is, they said that they would not wait if doing it over again. This compares with fifteen per cent who would wait and ten per cent who were

uncertain. Husbands and wives did not differ significantly in this respect.

Marital adjustment scores were 29.3, 10.5, and 2.6 for husbands and 33.4, 21.0, and 3.4 for wives respectively, according to the "would not wait," "uncertain," and "would wait" categories. For both spouses, scores between those who were either uncertain or would wait and those who would not wait were found to be significantly different at the one per cent level of confidence.

(5) *If starting over again, knowing what you now know, would you wait until after college to have children?*

Husbands and wives agreed rather closely in answering this, with about fifty eight per cent saying that they would not wait, twenty seven per cent saying that they would wait, and fifteen per cent remaining uncertain. Thus more spouses would wait to have children than to get married, if doing it over again, though in both cases the majority tended to endorse their past behavior.

For the "would not wait," "uncertain," and "would wait" categories, adjustment scores were 27.8, 18.3, and 14.7 for husbands and 32.4, 27.5, and 19.4 for wives respectively. Score differences between those who would and those who would not wait were found to be significant at the one per cent level of confidence, for both husbands and wives.

(6) *Does your and/or your spouse's attendance at college aid or disturb your marriage adjustment?*

Of the more than three hundred couples who answered, approximately twenty-eight per cent said that college attendance aids their marital adjustments, thirty-two per cent that it disturbs, and forty per cent that it has no effect. Husband and wife answers were not significantly different. Comparisons by present family size revealed some significant differences for the husbands, with the childless feeling that college is an aid to marriage adjustment more often than those with either one or two children.

TABLE 4. *Percentages of Spouses Desiring Fewer, Same Number, or More Children if Starting Over Again, by Size of Present Family*

| Children Desired as Compared with Present Number | Number Answering | | Number of Children in Present Family | | | | | | | |
| | | | 0 | | 1 | | 2 | | 3 | |
	Husband	Wife	H	W	H	W	H	W	H	W
Fewer	30	28			9.3	11.4	13.4	9.7	26.3	15.8
Same	167	167	35.5	30.8	58.0	56.3	69.0	77.8	57.9	73.7
More	89	80	64.5	69.2	32.7	32.3	17.6	12.5	15.8	10.5

Husbands who felt that college attendance aids marital adjustment had a mean adjustment score of 34.6, compared with 11.0 for those who felt that it disturbs. Similar figures for the wives were 28.7 and 15.8 respectively. For both spouses, differences were significant at the one per cent level of confidence.

(7) Does the presence of children in your family aid or disturb your marriage adjustment while in college?

About forty per cent of the answering parents indicated that children are an aid to marital adjustment, twenty per cent that they disturb, and forty per cent that they have no effect. Husband and wife answers were similar. Wives with one child tended more to regard the situation as aiding marriage adjustment, while those with two children regarded it more as a disturbing factor. This difference was significant at the two per cent level of confidence.

For the "aids" and "disturbs" categories, scores on marital adjustment were 27.2 and 8.2 for husbands, and 26.2 and 10.3 for wives respectively. In both instances, differences were significant at the one per cent level of confidence.

(8) Does the presence of children in your family aid or disturb the successful accomplishment of your college work?

Because of the extremely small number of wives attending college, only husband responses were analyzed for this question. Of those answering, about twenty-five per cent felt that children are an aid to college success, thirty-eight per cent that they disturb and thirty-seven per cent that they have no effect. Thus more fathers thought that children disturbed scholastic accomplishment than thought they aided it. A greater proportion of one-child fathers thought that the child's presence contributed to school success than did fathers with two or more offspring, but the difference was not significant.

Husbands who felt that children are an aid to college achievement had a mean marital adjustment score of 29.7, compared with 16.9 for those who felt that children disturb. The difference was significant at the one per cent level of confidence.

Summary and Theory

In this sample of Purdue students, we have found the relationship between family size and marital adjustment to be a negative one. This agrees with several other researchers; notably, the Mowrers, Hill, and

Reed, cited earlier in the paper. Each of these studies, including our own, has been of a highly selected segment of the population characterized by one or more specialized "problems"—the Mowrers were concerned with couples who appealed to social agencies for help; Hill limited his investigation to war-torn families; Reed's sample was from a large metropolitan center; and our own study involved a relatively young group engaged in the pursuit of higher education. Could it be that such things as family friction, war tension, urban living, and college competition create situations that make children undesirable to parents who might otherwise welcome them?

Our data give strong support to Reed's claim; namely, that marital adjustment increases according to the ability of couples to control fertility in line with their desires. In the present study, comparisons regarding marriage adjustment showed the following classes of individuals with significantly lower scores: (1) those desiring only one or two children; (2) those with unplanned children; (3) those desiring fewer children than now if they could start over again; (4) those who would wait until after college to marry if they could start over again; (5) those who would wait until after college to have children if they could start over again; and (6) those who felt that either college attendance or the presence of children disturbs either their marital adjustment or school performance. All of these give evidence of discontent or unmet desires.

It would seem that college attendance, when combined with marriage and parenthood, creates family tensions for some of the persons involved. We found the following factors to vary directly with size of family: (1) the proportion of parents having unplanned children; (2) the proportion of parents desiring fewer children if starting over again; (3) the proportion of husbands feeling that college attendance is a disturbing factor in marriage; and (4) the proportion of wives feeling that children disturb marriage adjustment while husband is still in school. Explanations given by respondents for their answers are revealing. Those persons who felt that college attendance is a disturbing factor in marital adjustment explained as follows: there are financial sacrifices and worries involved; living conditions are often unsatisfactory; school and lessons take too much time from home life; there is too little time for recreation; tensions from school are often transferred into the home; and the realization that the situation is temporary keeps one unsettled. Parents who felt that children are a disturbance to either marital adjustment or college performance listed the following reasons: they increase the economic demands; they complicate the housing situation; the added noise and distraction make studying difficult; and the added responsibility requires extra time, such as for night duty in case of infancy or illness, and for play "when daddy comes home."

Thus there is apparently no simple relationship between number of children and marital adjustment applying equally to all populations and all families. More important than sheer number is the value parents place on children, and this varies widely according to the personalities of the spouses and the circumstances that surround them. Insofar as family size is related to marital adjustment it is the discrepancy between expectation and realization that is important, and to determine this it is necessary first of all to take the values of people into account. In our own study, it has been evident that, for many students, the pressure of school work is sufficient to give children a negative value—at least during the college years. If pregnancies come anyway, unplanned, the result will likely be frustration and competing interests, which, in turn, may adversely affect the marriage relationship. It seems likely that other groups, in this highly competitive and insecure society of ours, are under similar pressure and in those groups we would also expect to find family size negatively related to marriage adjustment. Where pressure is less, or the desires of spouses regarding children are met, it seems likely that the relationship would be a positive one. And in addition to group variables in the values surrounding children there are the many personal differences which people hold. Therefore, as earlier suggested, the presence and number of children may affect any given marriage either way.

Students of measurement in marriage prediction and adjustment are coming to realize that their scale norms must be built in from the culture and class to which the tests will find application. An additional suggestion, based upon our research experience with this one factor of family size is that the individual values of the persons tested be taken into account so that the norms, insofar as is possible, will reflect the degree to which each person realizes his own goals.

NOTES

[1] For an enlightening elaboration, with statistical supports, see Paul H. Jacobson, "Differentials in Divorce by Duration of Marriage and Size of Family," *American Sociological Review*, 15 (April 1950), pp. 235–44. Among other things, Mr. Jacobson shows that divorce rate differentials between childless and parent-couples are not as great as are commonly supposed, and that the general trend is for these differences to diminish with duration of marriage, the two rates being practically identical after the thirtieth wedding anniversary. Though the chances for divorce are somewhat greater for marriages without children, it has not been substantiated that the presence of children acts as a deterrent to divorce; rather, (p. 244) "divorce and childlessness are probably concomitant results of more fundamental factors in the marital relationship."

[2] E. R. Mowrer and H. R. Mowrer, *Domestic Discord*, Chicago: University of Chicago Press, 1928, as cited by Lewis Terman, *et al.*, *Psychological Factors in Marital Happiness*, New York: McGraw-Hill, 1938, p. 173.

[3] Katherine Davis, *Factors in the Sex Life of Twenty-Two Hundred Women*, New York: Harper and Brothers, 1929, p. 47.

[4] Paul Popenoe, *Modern Marriage*, New York: The Macmillan Co., 1940, p. 268.

[5] G. V. Hamilton, *A Research in Marriage*, New York: Lear, 1948, p. 511.

[6] Jessie Bernard, "Factors in the Distribution of Success in Marriage," *American Journal of Sociology*, 40 (July 1934), p. 51.

[7] Ernest W. Burgess and Leonard S. Cottrell, *Predicting Success or Failure in Marriage*, New York: Prentice-Hall, 1939, p. 260.

[8] Lewis M. Terman, *Psychological Factors in Marital Happiness*, New York: McGraw-Hill, 1938, pp. 171–73.

[9] Judson T. Landis and Mary G. Landis, *Building a Successful Marriage*, New York: Prentice-Hall, 1948, p. 434.

[10] Harvey J. Locke, *Predicting Adjustment in Marriage: A Comparison of a Divorced and a Happily Married Group*, New York: Henry Holt and Co., 1951, pp. 158–70.

[11] Reuben Hill, *Families Under Stress*, New York: Harper and Brothers, 1949, pp. 126–28.

[12] Robert B. Reed, *Social and Psychological Factors Affecting Fertility*; VII, "The Interrelationship of Marital Adjustment, Fertility Control, and Size of Family," New York: Milbank Memorial Fund, 1948, pp. 383–425; quotation from page 423.

[13] The original prediction table shows these scores to be in the "somewhat adjusted" category, or a little above average. See Ernest W. Burgess and Harvey J. Locke, *The Family: From Institution to Companionship*, New York: American, 1945, p. 787.

[14] There were 199 wives with higher scores than their husbands and 137 husbands with higher scores than their wives, the average score differences being 23.3 and 20.6 respectively. Coefficients of $-.40\pm.03$ and $-.53\pm.03$ were found when the discrepancies between husband and wife scores were correlated with the scores of husbands and wives respectively. This suggests that when one spouse is well adjusted the mate will also tend to be well adjusted.

[15] Mean number of children desired by husbands was 3.42, and by wives, 3.44. Arranged by size of present families, means were 3.23, 3.17, 3.50, and 3.76; and 3.46, 3.10, 3.33, and 3.87, for husbands and wives and for the childless, one-child, two-child, and three-child groups respectively.

NUMBER OF CHILDREN AND MARITAL HAPPINESS

Problem

The traditional cultures of all known societies emphasize fertility. Fertility is valued as a goal in marriage, and children are seen as a source of personal happiness, as a source of helpful or necessary apprentices, as necessary for family continuity, as security in old age, and so on. However, in industrialized urban societies compulsory education and child labor laws have tended to convert children into financial liabilities.

Nevertheless, birth rates continue to be high, much higher than most demographers feel is desirable even in this country. Thus, uncontrolled fertility creates problems in the area of population growth.

Uncontrolled fertility may also create problems from a personal or individual viewpoint. Even the first child constitutes a sort of "crisis" (Blood and Wolfe, 1960, pp. 134–135; Dyer, 1963; LeMasters, 1957). Just as increases in the national population can cause strains for the society, increases in the size of the family group may put strains on the economic, physical, and emotional resources of the family, especially if the children are "unplanned." Christensen and Philbrick have found this to be so for a sample of relatively recently married college couples. Perhaps their findings apply only to couples in the somewhat difficult position of married college students. In this laboratory problem we will be able to retest their findings with a sample which represents primarily mature and stable marriages in which the husbands are probably near the peak of their success and earning capacity.

One difficulty in this problem is that both the independent and the dependent variables are confounded with social class. That is, many studies have shown that working-class and farm families tend to have greater numbers of children than do middle-class families (Peterson, 1961, pp. 218–222). Moreover, some other studies suggest that marital happiness is lower among members of the working class (Blood and Wolfe, 1960, p. 229; Komarovsky, 1962). Consequently, a relationship between the number of children and the marital happiness of the parents may occur because both factors are dependent on a third factor, that of social class. On the other hand, the relationship may exist, regardless of social class. This would be true if relatively large numbers of children in the family were one of the *causes* of the lower level of marital happiness of the working-class and farm families. But whatever the nature of the relationships among the three variables—number of children, marital happiness, and social class—it is clear that in investigating this issue you must use social class as a control variable.

Hypothesis

1. State what relationship you expect to find between the number of children in a family and the marital happiness of the parents.

2. Do you think this relationship holds equally well within working-class, middle-class, and farm families?

Empirical Indicators for Problem 7

11. Number of brothers:_____

12. Number of sisters:_____

13. Total number of children in your family (do not forget to count yourself!):_____

24. What was your father's occupation at the time you graduated from high school, or what was it before his retirement (please specify)?
_____

In addition please circle the answer category which best fits his occupation.
1 Professional (architect, chemist, doctor, etc.) or managerial position (department head, postmaster, police chief, etc.)
2 Proprietor, except farm (i.e., owner of a business)
3 Clerical or sales position
4 Farmer (owner-operator or renter)
5 Skilled workman or foreman (machinist, carpenter, etc.)
6 Semiskilled or unskilled workman (truck driver, factory worker, etc.)
7 Homemaker, or not employed outside the home
+ Don't know

55. How would you describe your parents' marriage?
1 Very unhappy
2 Unhappy
3 Not too happy
4 Just about average
5 A little happier than average
6 Very happy
7 Extremely happy

Data Analysis

1. *Sort* the code sheets into three social-class groups on the basis of the occupational status of the father, as coded in Box 24:

White-collar = 1, 2, & 3
Farm   = 4
Blue-collar = 5 & 6

2. *Subsort* each social class into three groups on the basis of the number of children in the family, as coded in Box 13:

Small family   = 1 or 2 children
Average family = 3 or 4 children
Large family   = 5 or more children

3. *Tabulate* the marital-happiness scores (as coded in Box 55) for each of the nine groups, and enter your results on the Tabulation Form.

4. *Compute* the mean or average marital-happiness scores for each number-of-children group within each social-class group. See page 62 for instructions on computing the mean.

5. *Compute* the mean marital-happiness scores for each social-class group by adding the three sums of values, adding the three N's, and dividing the combined fx's by the combined N's. See the formula at the bottom of Table 1.

Laboratory Report

1. See Appendix B for instructions on writing the Laboratory Report.

2. Under Findings report first on the social-class differences in the marital-happiness scores, and then describe the relationship which you have found between the number of children and marital happiness *within* each social class.

Additional Problem

Since religious ideology and rules may also affect family size, the religious factor should also be controlled. But this would make the problem too complex for one laboratory period. You may wish to speculate about the effect of religious differences upon the results, drawing on the data in Problem 5. If the composition and size of your sample permit, perhaps part of the class may wish to make a tabulation similar to the one designed for this problem, but holding religion instead of social class constant. They can then report their findings back to the class for discussion. The interrelations among religion, family size, and marital happiness would also make a good term paper topic.

REFERENCES

Blood, R. O., Jr., and Wolfe, D. M. *Husbands and Wives.* Glencoe, Ill.: Free Press, 1960.

Dyer, Everett D. "Parenthood as a Crisis: A Restudy," *Marriage and Family Living,* 25 (1963), pp. 196–201.

Komarovsky, Mirra. *Blue-Collar Marriage.* New York: Random House, 1962.

LeMasters, E. E. "Parenthood as Crisis," *Marriage and Family Living,* 19 (1957), pp. 352–355.

Petersen, William. *Population.* New York: Macmillan, 1961.

SECTION/COURSE NO._____ DATE_____ NAME_____

Number of Children and Marital Happiness of Parents by Social Class

Marital Happiness of Parents (Box 55)	White-Collar (Box 24 = 1, 2 &3) Number of Children (Box 13)						Farm (Box 24 = 4) Number of Children (Box 13)						Blue-Collar (Box 24 = 5 & 6) Number of Children (Box 13)					
	1–2		3–4		5 or More		1–2		3–4		5 or More		1–2		3–4		5 or More	
x	f	fx	f	fx	f	fx	f	fx	f	fx	f	fx	f	fx	f	fx	f	fx
1																		
2																		
3																		
4																		
5																		
6																		
7																		
TOTAL																		
MEAN																		
No answer		✕		✕		✕		✕		✕		✕		✕		✕		✕
COMBINED MEANS	Total fx = ___ + ___ + ___ = ___ / Total f = ___ + ___ + ___ = ___						Total fx = ___ + ___ + ___ = ___ / Total f = ___ + ___ + ___ = ___						Total fx = ___ + ___ + ___ = ___ / Total f = ___ + ___ + ___ = ___					

(Add totals in each number-of-children group within each social class)

SECTION/COURSE NO._____ DATE_____ NAME_____

Number of Children and Marital Happiness

HYPOTHESIS: _____

_____

_____

_____

_____

_____

SAMPLE: _____

_____

_____

_____

INDEPENDENT VARIABLE: _____

_____

_____

_____

_____

DEPENDENT VARIABLE: _____

_____

_____

_____

_____

_____

_____

OTHER FACTORS: _____

_____

_____

_____

SUMMARY OF FINDINGS: _____

_____

_____

_____

_____

_____

_____

_____

_____

_____

DISCUSSION: _____

_____

_____

_____

_____

_____

_____

_____

_____

_____

_____

_____

_____

_____

_____

CHILD ADJUSTMENT IN BROKEN AND IN UNHAPPY UNBROKEN HOMES*

F. Ivan Nye

A large number of research projects have shown differences in the adjustment of children in broken and unbroken homes. Regularly these comparisons favor the unbroken home. It is not known, however, whether children are better adjusted in homes psychologically broken, but legally and physically intact compared with legally broken homes. This problem has, with a few exceptions, escaped the attention of sociological research.

Dr. James Plant, psychiatrist, raised the question in 1944, with an article stating that legal divorce was preferable to separation without divorce insofar as the adjustment of the children is concerned.[1] Another suggestive statement is made by Paul Alexander more recently ". . . I would sit one day as the judge of the

juvenile court, the next day as the judge of the divorce court. When I would hear a divorce case, I had at my side the family record of the people, and believe it or not, in some years as high as 40 per cent of the people who came into court for divorce have *already been* in juvenile court with problems concerning their children."[2] This proportion is particularly high when the fact is considered that many divorced couples have no children.

More recently (1950), Goode gathered interview data from some four hundred divorcees who were mothers. His conclusions were necessarily tentative. He does, however, question the assumption that divorce leads to poorer adjustment in children. He summarizes in part:

When broken homes are classified into different types (widowed, separated, divorced), there is evidence that the separated home may lead to as many child problems or juvenile delinquency as divorce itself. Moreover, there is some question as to whether it is the divorce or the marital conflict that does the damage, and whether the different

Reprinted by permission of the author and the National Council on Family Relations from *Marriage and Family Living*, 19 (1957), pp. 356–361.

* Paper read before the Family Section of the American Sociological Society, Detroit, September, 1956. This report is from a larger study of specific and general parent-child adjustments. Supported in part, by grants from the College Committee on Research of the State College of Washington.

types of parent-child relationships might create the damage rather than the divorce or marital conflict. We found that almost all mothers worried about the effects of divorce on their children, but that almost all remarried mothers subsequently thought that their children's lives had improved after divorce. . . . Whether these mothers were correct is a matter for future research.[3]

More recently Judson Landis has compared the attitudes of college students from happy unbroken homes, and unhappy unbroken homes, and broken homes toward marriage and the family. In all cases he finds children from happy unbroken homes have the most positive attitudes. The attitudes of students from broken homes and unhappy unbroken homes are rather similar by some criteria, but by some the attitudes of those from broken homes were more positive than those from unhappy unbroken homes.[4]

The approach here employed is similar to that of Alexander, namely that the crucial factor in the adjustment of children is the socio-psychological success or failure of the family, not whether or not it is legally and physically broken. While it is still true that there is prejudice against divorce, there are also unfavorable attitudes toward quarreling and disunited families. While two parents may be able to provide more direct control than one, quarreling, bickering and competition between parents may make the home an unhappier place than it would be with one parent or a stepparent. The null hypothesis is tested that the adjustment of children in broken and unbroken but unhappy homes does not differ significantly.

Methodology

As part of a larger study of parent-child adjustment, data were gathered from a 25 per cent regular interval sample of three Washington high schools (N = 780). Respondents were boys and girls in grades 9, 10, 11, and 12. Data were gathered by anonymous questionnaires in the classroms under the general supervision of the writer. All the usual positive motivations were employed plus trap and interlocking questions.[5]

The home was considered broken if the adolescent did not ordinarily live with his original parents. The unhappy but unbroken families had to satisfy two criteria: they fell in the worst adjusted tercile based on a parental interaction score computed from the amount of parental quarreling, arguing, attempted domination by each parent, lack of mutual activities and interest, and an overall evaluation of happiness made by the student as reported by their children. If a family fell in the lowest tercile, the overall evaluation was again examined. If the marital happiness of *both* parents was rated average, unhappy, or very unhappy by the adolescent plus rated in the lower tercile by the interaction score, the family was included in the "unhappy unbroken" category. This category includes about one-sixth of the unbroken homes in the sample.

Unhappy Unbroken Families

It is always possible, of course, that some other variable associated with broken and unhappy unbroken homes might cause the differences in adjustment between children in the two categories. As a check on this possibility broken and unbroken homes have been compared with respect to a number of social characteristics.

It appears that boys drop out of high school in disproportionate numbers in both broken and unhappy unbroken homes. While there are 51 per cent girls in the sample as a whole, in broken homes of the children in school 56 per cent were girls, in the unbroken unhappy homes, 60 per cent were girls. The difference between 56 and 60 per cent is non-significant.

Other characteristics expressed in quantitative measures are shown in Table I. Qualitative characteristics were checked for significance of differences by chi-square.

Socio-economic level as measured by the occupation of the father is not significantly different for broken and unhappy unbroken homes. The same is true for aspiration level of the adolescent, and the qualitative characteristics of rural-urban residence, home ownership, type of house, unemployment of father, foreign birth of parents, birth in another state, education level of each parent, church attendance of adolescent and of fathers and mothers of adolescents, "shift" father works, employment of both parents at the same or alternate periods, and expectation of remaining in the community.

Some social structural differences were, however, found between broken and unhappy unbroken homes (see Table I). Some of these presumably favor adjustment in the broken, others in the unbroken unhappy homes. The younger fathers and mothers and the lower geographical mobility would favor adjustment in the unbroken unhappy homes. The smaller family in the broken category probably favors closer parent-child relationships. On the whole, it appears that the social characteristics of the two groups are similar and that where there are differences, some favor adjustment in each group. It appears improbable, therefore, that differences in adjustment found in this study can be explained by differing social characteristics of the two types of families, although the above is not, of course, a complete list of social characteristics.

Findings

The proportions of each group falling in the "poorest adjustment" categories are presented (see Table II).[6] The differences found by the employment of the several criteria of adjustment require that the null hypothesis be considered by areas of adjustment. In the areas of school adjustment, church attendance, and de-

TABLE I. *Some Social Characteristics of Broken and Unhappy Unbroken Homes*

	Unhappy Unbroken (Mean)	All Broken (Mean)	Standard** Error	Critical Ratio
Father's occupation level*	4.0	3.9	.18	.6
Child's aspiration level*	6.4	6.3	.22	.5
Family car value	3.4	3.8	.12	3.3
No. schools attended	2.9	3.6	.20	3.5
No. children in family	3.9	3.0	.22	4.2
Adolescent's age	15.7	15.9	.12	1.7
Mother's age	42.4	44.4	.65	3.1
Father's age	46.7	48.7	.72	2.8

* Empy's classification which is a combination of the North-Hatt and Smith scales is employed here. (Lamar T. Empy, "Relationship of Social Class and Family Authority Patterns to Occupational Choice of Washington High School Seniors," Unpublished doctoral dissertation, The State College of Washington, 1955.)

** The regular-interval sample obtained a proportionate sample from each classroom and from each row (front to back) within each classroom. To the extent that either classrooms or positions within the room are related to differences in behavior, the sampling error is reduced below that of a simple random sample. Since the sample is 25 per cent of the finite universe, the sampling error is further reduced, although in terms of a hypothetical universe it is unchanged. For the above reasons, the probability figures are on the conservative side, although differences from a simple random sample are believed to be slight.

TABLE II. *The Per Cent of Adolescents from Broken and Unhappy Unbroken Homes Who Fall into "Poorest Adjustment" Categories†*

Criteria of Adjustment	Happy Unbroken %	Unhappy Unbroken %	All Broken %	Divorced & Separated %	All other Broken %	Solo*** Mothers %
Psychosomatic illness	26	50**	33	31	38	43
Physical sensitivity	27	50**	30	31	28	31
Delinquency	23	48	36	39	29	33
Acceptance of parent (M)	31	42	35	35	33	17
Acceptance of parent (F)	20	55*	41	37	50	
Acceptance of child (M)	31	55*	42	44	39	27
Acceptance of child (F)	27	69**	42	40	49	
Discipline (M)	28	45*	31	30	35	20
Discipline (F)	21	46*	31	30	35	
Freedom & responsibility (M)	20	33	29	25	37	21
Freedom & responsibility (F)	24	41	32	28	41	
Money (M)	22	37	30	29	30	21
Money (F)	22	46	37	35	44	
Value agreement (M)	23	47**	25	26	23	17
Value agreement (F)	21	53**	33	34	29	
Appearance (M)	30	48*	34	31	40	35
Appearance (F)	26	59**	27	26	32	
Mutual recreation (M)	24	39	33	34	33	21
Mutual recreation (F)	24	52	42	42	44	
Occupation (F only)	19	47**	25	26	21	
Information & advice (M)	42	44	43	41	48	48
Information & advice (F)	26	56	48	46	56	
Disposition (M)	30	57**	34	36	29	28
Disposition (F)	29	75**	38	37	39	
Parental interaction	18	100	36	36	38	
School grades (D & F)	7	7	12	13	7	8
School teams (none)	77	81	85	84	88	81
Church attendance (never)	9	10	15	16	14	18
Delinquent companions	52	60	52	53	50	60
		(N=112)	(N=158)	(N=115)	(N=43)	(N=40)

† Per cents are based on the proportion from that category falling into the poorest adjustment *tercile* of the whole sample except in the cases of physical sensitivity, school teams, and delinquent companionship. In those the adjustment distribution was dichotomized.

* Difference significant at 5 per cent level between *Unhappy Unbroken* and *All Broken*.

** Difference significant at 1 per cent level between *Unhappy Unbroken* and *All Broken*.

*** "Solo" mothers is not an exclusive category. They are included in both the separated and divorced and "all other broken" categories.

linquent companionship the null hypothesis is tenable. With respect to neuroses as measured by psychosomatic illness and sensitivity concerning physical appearance it must be rejected. Likewise it must be rejected in the area of delinquent behavior. If the several measures of parent-child adjustment are considered together it must also be rejected, since thirteen of twenty-one measures show significant differences between the two groups, all in the same direction.

When comparisons are made separately by sex, the results remain essentially unchanged but show minor differences (see Table III).[7] For girls, differences favoring the broken home show some tendency to concentrate in the parent-child relationship. For boys, a slight tendency can be noted for more (than for girls) of the larger differences to be found outside the home, although a number of large differences in parent-child adjustment are present. All differences in excess of 11 per cent for both boys and girls favor the broken

homes with a single exception: attendance at church is higher for boys in the unhappy unbroken compared to the broken homes.

Stated positively it may be said that, *as a group*, adolescents in broken homes show less psychosomatic illness, less delinquent behavior, and better adjustment to parents than do children in unhappy unbroken homes. They do not differ significantly with respect to adjustment in school, church, or delinquent companions.

Divorce and Separation

A comparison of homes broken by divorce or separation with other broken homes generally reveals minor differences. A tabulation of differences of all sizes shows that in the "best adjustment" category nine measures favored the "other" broken, eighteen the

TABLE III. *The Per Cent of Boys and Girls from Broken and Unhappy Unbroken Homes Who Fall into "Best Adjusted" Categories*

	Boys			Girls		
Criteria of Adjustment	*Broken*	*Unhappy Unbroken*	*Difference*	*Broken*	*Unhappy Unbroken*	*Difference*
	%	%	%	%	%	%
Psychosomatic illness	51	16	35*	25	15	10
Physical sensitivity	73	64	9	68	41	27*
Delinquency	29	10	19*	19	15	4
Acceptance of parent (M)	13	18	5	30	27	3
Acceptance of parent (F)	15	22	7	21	9	12*
Acceptance of child (M)	15	9	6	41	24	17*
Acceptance of child (F)	20	9	11*	34	12	22*
Discipline (M)	29	16	13*	30	18	12*
Discipline (F)	31	13	18*	39	24	15*
Freedom & responsibility (M)	28	20	8	29	19	10
Freedom & responsibility (F)	25	11	14*	21	9	12*
Money (M)	32	24	8	48	37	11*
Money (F)	27	22	5	41	24	17*
Value agreement (M)	33	20	13*	34	25	9
Value agreement (F)	19	11	8	30	15	15*
Appearance (M)	35	13	22*	47	18	29*
Appearance (F)	19	9	10	43	12	31*
Mutual recreation (M)	19	16	3	45	28	17*
Mutual recreation (F)	16	13	3	37	21	16*
Occupation (F only)	26	27	1	40	21	19*
Information & advice (M)	14	18	4	37	27	10
Information & advice (F)	26	18	8	30	9	21*
Disposition (M)	35	24	11*	42	22	20*
Disposition (F)	24	9	15*	31	8	23*
Parental interaction	25	0	25	31	0	31
School grades (A students)	9	5	4	16	14	2
School teams (one or more)	29	38	9	4	6	2
Church attendance (regular)	37	30	7	48	57	9
Delinquent companions (none)	41	30	11*	53	46	7
	(N=70)	(N=45)		(N=88)	(N=67)	

* Difference is of the same magnitude as necessary to be significant at the 5 per cent level in Table II. Because of smaller sample size the difference is not necessarily significant in the above table.

divorced and separated, and one was the same. In the poorest adjustment category, eleven measures favored the "other" broken and seventeen the divorced and separated. Only a single difference is significant for a sample of this size. In the light of these data, it should be concluded that, contrary to folk knowledge, the adjustment of children in homes broken by divorce is not more difficult or unsuccessful than in homes broken otherwise.

Solo Parents

Our sample of solo parents is too small to warrant tests of significance; however, present data suggest that the adjustment of adolescents in "solo" parent homes is not much different from other broken homes by the criteria of delinquency, psychosomatic illness, school, or church adjustment. In the parent-child relationship, the adjustment is superior for "solo" mothers in each area except "appearance" and "mother as a source of information and advice." No evidence is found to suggest that there are more adjustment problems in families with "solo" parents than those in which the parent has remarried or in unhappy unbroken homes. No attempt was made to assess adjustment in homes in which the solo parent was the father because the number of cases (ten) was entirely too small.

Socio-Economic Level

Previous research has shown the importance of family analyses by socio-economic level. Consequently, the entire group was divided into upper, middle, and lower groups on the basis of the father's occupation.[8] The comparison of adjustment of children in broken and unhappy unbroken homes was analyzed separately within each category.

In the upper socio-economic category, of fifty-six comparisons made, thirty-two differed by at least 11 per cent. Of these, thirty-one favored the children in broken homes, one those in unbroken homes. In the middle socio-economic category, thirty-five differed by at least 11 per cent. Of these, thirty-four favored broken homes, one unhappy unbroken. In the lowest socio-economic level, twenty-six showed a difference as great as 11 per cent, with twenty-five favoring the broken home. Although slightly more of the differences are found in the middle category, the results appear conclusive that the differences found in the analysis of the total sample are reflected in the separate analyses by each socio-economic level.

Limitations of Present Research

Present findings are based on adolescent adjustment and on adolescent response. No generalizations are warranted to younger children from the present study. Additional research on the adjustment of younger children would seem to be indicated.

Present data were collected in a single western state from a primarily urban population. Generalizations to other areas of the United States should be made with caution.

Conclusions

The null hypothesis that the adjustment of adolescents in unhappy unbroken and in broken homes does not differ significantly is tenable in the areas of church, school, and delinquent companionship, but untenable in the areas of psychosomatic illness, delinquent behavior, and parent-child adjustment. In those areas, children show better adjustment in broken homes. Children of homes broken by divorce in terms of the overall adjustment picture do not have poorer adjustment than those from homes broken in other ways. Children living with solo parents differ from other broken homes and from unhappy unbroken homes in having superior adjustment to mothers.

The adjustment of parents individually and to their spouses is also much superior in the broken homes compared to the unhappy unbroken category. The proportion of dispositions of parents of each sex which is good is far higher in the broken homes category. Personal appearance is better on the average. Twenty-nine per cent of remarriages fell in the happiest "parent interaction" tercile compared to none in the unhappy unbroken homes. Present data suggest that disunited unhappy homes are related to poor adjustment in parents as well as in children.

Discussion

Present findings, taken in conjunction with previous research cited earlier, suggest that thinking concerning broken homes is in need of revision. Sociologists and psychologists have sometimes taken the position that there is little difference between a broken and an unhappy unbroken home, although there was little evidence on the basis of which either to accept or reject this position.

From the research evidence, it appears that this position must be abandoned. There are differences between the two categories of families with the differences favoring the "reconstructed" family including a step-parent, or the "partial" family composed of one parent and child or children. Failure to perceive the good adjustment both of children and spouses in many broken homes may stem from a concentration upon the tensions and adjustments which occur at the time of the break. After a period of adjustment, a new equilibrium is established, complicated, perhaps, by the necessity for each family member to play new and less clearly defined roles, but largely free of the unbearable conflicts of the previous unhappy marriage. The child is often relieved of a parent unable or unwilling to play the role of parent, and, if the remaining parent remarries, may receive one who can and will play the role satisfactorily.

There are, of course, some families which are broken which achieve no new equilibrium. The parents are unable or unwilling to bear the responsibilities of parents either in remarriage or as "solo" parents. *The family completely disintegrates*, the children become public charges and later contribute unduly to the population of juvenile detention homes, adult prisons, and state hospitals. *This* result, however, should be attributed to the personal irresponsibility or lack of ability of the parents, rather than to the fact that they decided not to live in the same house, and, in most cases, must be considered a continuation of a condition preceding rather than caused by the marital break.

NOTES

[1] James S. Plant, "The Psychiatrist Views Children of Divorced Parents," *Law and Contemporary Problems*, 10 (1944), pp. 807–18.

[2] Paul V. Alexander, "A Therapeutic Approach," *Conference on Divorce*, The Law School, University of Chicago, Conference Series Number 9 (February 29, 1952), p. 53.

[3] William J. Goode, *After Divorce*, Glencoe: The Free Press, 1956, pp. 329–30.

[4] Judson T. Landis, "A Comparison of Children of Divorced Parents and Children of Happy or Unhappy Non-Divorced Parents on Parent-Child Relationships, Dating Maturation, and Sex and Marriage Attitudes." Paper read before the National Council on Family Relations, Minneapolis, Minnesota, August 27, 1955. Landis concluded that while children in unhappy unbroken homes and divorced homes showed many similarities, "On the majority of items the children from unhappy homes had the poorest showing of all."

[5] The non-usable responses were of four types: (1) the overconformist, (2) those who wanted to shock the investigator, (3) the uninterested respondent, and (4) the non-reader. Overconformists were eliminated by the aid of "ringer" items–illness which everyone has had or delinquencies everyone has committed, the second group was eliminated by discarding the responses of the few who claimed to have committed "very often" every crime on our delinquency list, and the random marker was eliminated by interlocking questions. Approximately 1 per cent of the responses were discarded as invalid.

[6] The "best adjustment" categories were analyzed in similar manner. Space limitations preclude inclusion of these data, but findings parallel in opposite direction those shown in Table II.

[7] The "poorest adjustment" categories were analyzed in similar manner. Space limitations preclude inclusion of these data, but findings parallel in opposite direction those shown in Table III.

[8] Lamar T. Empy, "Relationship of Social Class and Family Authority Patterns to Occupational Choice of Washington High School Seniors," Unpublished doctoral dissertation, The State College of Washington, 1955.

MARITAL SUCCESS AND ANXIETY IN CHILDREN

Problem

Most social scientists agree that, at least in our culture, the best family environment for children is a home with two parents who are happily married. However, even if true, this ideal cannot be attained by all, and there has been considerable controversy over which of the possible alternatives is the most desirable. Should unhappily married parents maintain their marriage "for the sake of the children," or might the children be better off if the parents divorced and attempted to establish new, and hopefully more satisfactory, homes? The individual answer may vary, of course, but sociology, like all sciences, concentrates on attempting to determine what is generally true.

Hypothesis

In the light of the information presented in Nye's article, your textbook, and other reading you have done on the subject, state the differences you expect to find in the anxiety scores of children from broken homes, homes with unhappily married parents, and homes with happily married parents.

Empirical Indicators for Problem 8

7. At the time you finished high school, your parents were:
   1   Both living together
   2   Divorced
   3   Separated

4 Father was dead
5 Mother was dead
6 Temporarily living apart, for reasons other than marital problems (only if this situation had existed for one year or longer; otherwise circle 1 above)

55. How would you describe your parents' marriage?
1 Very unhappy
2 Unhappy
3 Not too happy
4 Just about average
5 A little happier than average
6 Very happy
7 Extremely happy

VII. YOUR OWN AND YOUR PARENTS' PERSONALITIES

Please rate yourself...on each of the following descriptions. Using the key below, circle one answer number...to show the degree to which the description fits YOU....

0 = Never
1 = Rarely
2 = Occasionally
3 = Sometimes
4 = Often
5 = Usually

Yourself

o Worries when there is little to worry about _____ 0 1 2 3 4 5

p Is tense and nervous _____ 0 1 2 3 4 5

Box 112 = Sum of o and p

Data Analysis

1. *Sort* the code sheets on the basis of the scores in Box 7 to distinguish the respondents from broken homes from those from unbroken homes.

Unbroken homes = 1 (Both living together)
Broken homes = 2 to 6 (All broken-home situations. These are the code sheets you clipped together and put aside in Problem 2. We are combining here divorced, separated, and widowed parents. There are undoubtedly many differences among these groups, but the number in each group is likely to be too small to consider them separately in a sample such as this.

2. *Subsort* the group of code sheets for respondents from unbroken homes to distinguish between the happily married and the less happily married parents, using the scores coded in Box 55:

Less happily married = 1 to 5 (From "very unhappy" to "a little happier than average")

Happily married = 6 & 7 ("Very happy" and "extremely happy")

Note that we consider the first group less happily married, and the second happily married, despite the wording of the actual answers to Question 55. This division is based on the fact that individuals generally tend to rate themselves as high as possible on questions such as this. As Kirkpatrick (1963) notes, if the respondent answers "average," it is ordinarily an indication that the marriage is *not* very happy.

3. *Tabulate* the anxiety score (Box 112) for each of the three groups. This Anxiety Index is a widely used measure, based on the number of "anxiety symptoms" checked (Levy, 1958).

4. *Compute* the average anxiety score of each group. Directions for computing the mean are given on page 62.

Laboratory Report

1. Follow the directions for writing the Laboratory Report given in Appendix B.

2. Be sure to include in the Discussion possible reasons underlying the differences you have found.

REFERENCES

Kirkpatrick, Clifford. *The Family as Process and Institution*. New York: Ronald Press, 1963.

Levy, N. "A Short Form of the Children's Manifest Anxiety Scale," *Child Development*, 29 (1958), pp. 153–154.

SECTION/COURSE NO._____ DATE_____ NAME_____

Anxiety of Child by Marital Success of Parent

Anxiety Index (Box 112)	Broken Homes (Box 7 = 2 to 6)		Unbroken Homes			
			Less Happily Married Parents (Box 55 = 1 to 5)		Happily Married Parents (Box 55 = 6 & 7)	
x	f	fx	f	fx	f	fx
0						
1						
2						
3						
4						
5						
6						
7						
8						
9						
10						
TOTAL						
MEAN						
No answer						

SECTION/COURSE NO._____ DATE_____ NAME_____

Marital Success and Anxiety in Children

HYPOTHESIS: _____

_____

_____

_____

_____

_____

SAMPLE: _____

_____

_____

_____

INDEPENDENT VARIABLE: _____

_____

_____

_____

_____

DEPENDENT VARIABLE: _____

_____

_____

_____

_____

_____

OTHER FACTORS: _____

_____

_____

_____

SUMMARY OF FINDINGS: _____

_____

_____

_____

_____

_____

_____

_____

_____

DISCUSSION: _____

_____

_____

_____

_____

_____

_____

_____

_____

_____

_____

_____

_____

MARITAL HAPPINESS OF PARENTS AND THEIR CHILDREN'S ATTITUDE TO MARRIAGE

Paul Wallin

Persons reared in present day urban America are exposed to a number of experiences which contribute to their conception of marriage, and influence their evaluation of marriage as a relatively desirable or undesirable status for themselves. Most of these experiences are vicarious: exposure to the representations of marriage in print, movies, the radio and television. Less vicarious is the learning of the risks of marital failure as epitomized by the divorce rate. But marriage is also very directly depicted and defined for the young by the marital relationship of their parents. It is in the home that they first and most continuously encounter marriage, not as a fiction or concept but as embodied in the behavior of their fathers and mothers with and toward one another. Apart from the picture of marriage which the child may build out of inferences from the parents' behavior one or both parents may wittingly attempt to indoctrinate the child with a conception of marriage as one of the great joys of adulthood or as a status to be warily approached if not altogether avoided.

Reprinted by permission of the author and the American Sociological Association from the *American Sociology Review,* 19 (1954), pp. 20–23.

For the majority of the young, one of the probable major effects of their vicarious learning about marriage is that it is made to appear a highly attractive and desirable status. ("And they lived happily ever after.") If this evaluation is not materially influenced by knowledge of the divorce rate it is still subject to some reality testing in that the child has intimate knowledge of the union of his parents, if of no other adults. To the extent that marriage as thus directly known is perceived as a highly satisfying experience the vicariously assimilated conception is reinforced or at least not contradicted. But insofar as the relationship of his parents is seen by the child as fraught with conflict and unhappiness his conception of marriage as a desirable goal may be challenged and his enthusiasm for marriage diminished.[1]

Favorableness of attitude to marriage is a variable of theoretical interest for a number of reasons. It may be important in accounting for individual differences in age at marriage. It may be associated with individual differences and sex differences in patterns of courtship and mate selection. And it may be related to marital success. If, as hypothesized above, favorableness of attitude to marriage varies with parental happiness, the former may be one of the intervening variables in the oft-noted correlation between the marital happiness of parents and that of their offspring.

The research reported below was concerned with testing the hypothesis of a positive association between the marital success of parents and the favorableness of their children's attitude to marriage. Since data were secured from men and women subjects it was also possible to test the widely-held assumption that in our society the unmarried female views marriage more favorably than does the male.

The Data

The data of the study were obtained with anonymous questionnaires filled out by students assembled in classes. The subjects rated their parents' marriage in answer to the question, "In your opinion, up to the time you were 12, were your parents on the average happy or unhappy in their marriage?" The response categories were: Very happy, happy, average, unhappy or very unhappy.[2]

Favorableness of attitude to marriage was measured with a Guttman scale developed by Richard J. Hill.[3] The nine items, which were tentatively concluded to be scalable for a sample of men and women, are presented here as ordered in the final scale. The scores given the various response categories are indicated in the parenthesis.

(1) If you marry to what extent will you miss the life you have had as a single person? Not at all (1), very little, to some extent or very much (0).

(2) In your opinion, to what extent will it trouble you to give up your personal freedom when you marry? Not at all (1), very little, to some extent, or very much (0).

(3) In your opinion, will adjustment to married life be difficult for you? Not at all (1), not too difficult, rather or very difficult (0).

(4) Do you ever have doubts as to whether you will enjoy living exclusively in marriage with one member of the opposite sex? Never (1), hardly, occasionally or frequently (0).

(5) In your opinion, to what extent will the responsibilities of married life be enjoyable to you? Very much so (1), fairly enjoyable, not too much or not at all (0).

(6) How happy do you think you will be if you marry? Very happy (1), happy, unhappy or very unhappy (0).

(7) Do you ever have doubts about your chance of having a successful marriage? Never or rarely (1), occasionally or frequently (0).

(8) Do you think you will find (or have found) a person who is a suitable marriage partner for you? Yes (1), no (0).

(9) Do you think it would be advisable for you always to remain single? Yes (0), no (1).

The subjects were scored on their responses to each of the nine questions. Their total scores ranging from zero to nine represent their positions on the continuum defined by the items as favorableness of attitude to marriage. These totals were then plotted against the subjects' ratings of their parents' marital happiness, the data for the men and women being separately analyzed.

The Sample Studied

The data of the study were secured from 394 women and 215 men by means of a questionnaire administered to classes in three colleges in the San Francisco Bay area.[4] The classes were for the most part in sociology or psychology. With few exceptions the subjects were undergraduate students. They ranged in age from sixteen to twenty-seven, the median age being 20. The sample was restricted to unmarried persons, whose parents were both living. The men and women were predominantly Protestant and of native-born parentage. The parents of about 55 per cent of the group had one or more years of college education.

The Findings

The findings for the men subjects are presented in Table 1. They are clearly consistent with the hypothesis that the happier the men conceive of their parents' marriage as being, the more favorable tends to be the men's attitude toward marriage. The mean favorableness score declines steadily from the "very happy" parents to those who are divorced.[5]

The results for the women are given in Table 2. We note first that they have a more favorable attitude to marriage than the men. The mean score of the women is 5.26 as compared with a mean of 4.11 for the men.[6] This difference obtains for each of the parental happiness categories. The data, therefore, support the assumption that the unmarried female is more positively oriented to marriage than the unmarried male.

The data of Table 2 suggest that the pattern of association between parental happiness and favorableness of attitude to marriage is not the same for women as for men. The striking difference is that in the case of the latter the relationship between the variables is linear, whereas in the case of the former it appears to be nonlinear. The mean scale score of the women de-

TABLE 1. *Marital Happiness of Men's Parents and Men's Scores on "Favorableness of Attitude to Marriage" Scale*

Scale Scores	Marital Happiness of Parents				
	Very Happy	Happy	Average to Very Unhappy*	Divorced	Total
(Low) 0	—	—	4	1	5
1	1	2	1	2	6
2	6	8	16	13	43
3	9	18	8	9	44
4	8	14	7	6	35
5	10	7	10	4	31
6	6	6	4	1	17
7	9	5	—	1	15
8	7	3	3	—	13
(High) 9	3	2	1	—	6
Total	59	65	54	37	215
Mean	5.15	4.25	3.56	3.03	4.11
Standard deviation	2.12	1.92	2.08	1.44	2.09

* Because of the small number of cases the categories average, unhappy and very unhappy have been combined.

TABLE 2. *Marital Happiness of Women's Parents and Women's Scores on "Favorableness of Attitude to Marriage" Scale*

Scale Scores	Marital Happiness of Parents				
	Very Happy	Happy	Average to Very Unhappy*	Divorced	Total
(Low) 0	—	1	—	—	1
1	5	2	4	2	13
2	10	4	14	3	31
3	16	14	14	10	54
4	19	16	19	7	61
5	22	20	5	4	51
6	27	10	8	7	52
7	29	15	4	5	53
8	25	9	5	9	48
(High) 9	17	7	3	3	30
Total	170	98	76	50	394
Mean	5.75	5.27	4.18	5.24	5.26
Standard deviation	2.17	2.07	2.09	2.28	2.22

* Because of the small number of cases the categories average, unhappy and very happy have been combined.

creases from 5.75 (for those who rate their parents' marriage "very happy") to 4.18 (for those rating their parents' marriage "average to very unhappy").[7] The mean score then rises to 5.24 for the women with divorced parents and this does not differ significantly from the mean scores of those who rate their parents' marriage "very happy" or "happy."

The relatively high mean score of women whose parents are divorced reflects the fact that a considerable proportion of the women in this group have scores near the upper limit of the scale. Thirty-four per cent score 7, 8, or 9. This contrasts sharply with the 2.7 per cent of the men having divorced parents who secure such high scores.

The finding of a sex difference in the pattern of association between parental happiness and favorableness of attitude to marriage must be regarded as tentative, because of the rather small number of men and women with divorced parents in the present study. Assuming, however, that the finding is sustained by subsequent research what explanation can be advanced for it?

The problem essentially is why, unlike the men subjects, a substantial proportion of the women with divorced parents confidently anticipate marriage as a source of happiness and satisfaction. One solution to the problem can be derived from the assumption that women to a greater extent than men look upon marriage as the essential framework of their adult life. Insofar as this is true it might be argued that, when led to take a dim view of marriage because of the decisive failure of their parents' matrimonial venture, men have greater tolerance than women for their pessimistic outlook. Generally speaking, the pessimism of the men relates to what they consider only a part of their future life; that of the women relates to what they consider their entire existence. The latter consequently are more highly motivated to reject the conception of marriage given to them by the experience of their parents. Some may even be convinced that having learned much from the marital failure of their parents they can look forward with all the greater certainty to marital happiness for themselves.

NOTES

[1] Even if it be assumed that the net effect of vicarious experience with marriage is negative the argument as to the impact of parental happiness or unhappiness would still hold. It would be expected that children reared by unhappily married parents would have an even more unfavorable attitude to matrimony than children whose parents were happily wed.

[2] The reliability and validity of marital happiness ratings are discussed at length in E. W. Burgess and L. S. Cottrell, *Predicting Success or Failure in Marriage*, New York: Prentice-Hall, Inc., 1939, chapter 3.

[3] "*Attitude Toward Marriage*," unpublished Master's thesis, Stanford University Library, 1951.

[4] San Francisco State College, Stanford University and University of California at Berkeley. Data were also obtained from students in four Negro educational institutions. These are not reported because the responses of the Negro women to the "attitude of marriage" items failed entirely to yield a scale and the responses of the men formed a scale with several non-scale types.

[5] The CR's of the differences between the various means are "very happy" and "happy," 2.47; "very happy" and "average to very unhappy," 4.03; "very happy" and "divorced," 5.82; "happy" and "divorced," 3.63; "happy" and "average to very unhappy," 1.62; "average to very unhappy" and "divorced," 1.44.

[6] The CR of the difference between the means is 6.35.

[7] CR of the difference between the means (a) for the categories "average to very unhappy" and "happy," 4.31; (b) for the categories "average to very unhappy" and "very happy," 7.17; (c) for the categories "average to very unhappy" and "divorced," 2.64; (d) for the categories "very happy" and "happy," 1.79.

PARENTS' MARITAL HAPPINESS AND CHILD'S ATTITUDE TOWARD MARRIAGE

Problem

Several studies have found that marital happiness or unhappiness tends to "run in families." All versions of the Burgess-Cottrell-Wallin type of marital prediction scale (Burgess and Cottrell, 1939; Burgess and Wallin, 1953) make use of this fact and include some estimate of the happiness of the parents' marriage in order to predict the success of the child's marriage.

There are many ways in which such a transmission of family patterns could operate. The present laboratory problem is concerned with only one factor, the effect of the happiness of the parental marriage upon the individual's motivation toward or interest in marriage.

Our Questionnaire used only two of the nine items reflecting attitudes toward marriage presented in the article you have read. To simplify the problem further, we sum the scores on these two items rather than developing the more complicated scales used in the reading for this problem. Nevertheless, the results should be comparable.

Since women are usually considered to be more interested in and more favorable toward marriage, we will analyze the results separately for each sex.

Hypothesis

State what relationship you expect to find between the happiness of the parents' marriage and the favorableness toward marriage of the men and women who are the children of these marriages.

Empirical Indicators for Problem 9

1. Sex (circle one answer number):
   1 Male
   2 Female

55. How would you describe your parents' marriage?
    1 Very unhappy
    2 Unhappy
    3 Not too happy
    4 Just about average

5   A little happier than average
6   Very happy
7   Extremely happy

84. (a) How difficult would you guess adjustment to married life will be for you?
   1   Not at all   difficult
   2   Not too   "
   3   Somewhat   "
   4   Considerably   "
   5   Very   "

(b) Do you ever have doubts about your chance of having a successful marriage?
   1   Never
   2   Rarely
   3   Occasionally
   4   Frequently
   5   Often
   6   Always or almost always

Box 84 = Sum of 84a and 84b

Data Analysis

A. SEX DIFFERENCES IN THE CHILD'S ATTITUDE TOWARD THE HAPPINESS OF THE PARENTS' MARRIAGE

1. *Sort* the code sheets into two groups by the sex of the respondent, using the scores coded in Box 1:

   Male   = 1
   Female = 2

2. *Subsort* the code sheets for each sex into three groups based on the happiness of the parents' marriage (coded in Box 55). Marriages are evaluated on a 7-point scale ranging from "very unhappy" to "extremely happy." Previous research has found that, for a question such as this, individuals tend to mark answers which are as high as possible on the scale because of the social desirability of positive answers (see the discussion of this variable on page 135, and in Kirkpatrick, 1963). On the basis of the scores in Box 55, sort the code sheets into three groups as follows:

   Unhappy marriages   = 1, 2, & 3
   Less happy marriages = 4 & 5
   Happy marriages   = 6 & 7

3. *Compute* the percentage of men and of women who regard their parents' marriage as happy or otherwise (use the percentage tables in Appendix D), and enter this information on Table 1. Is there any indication of a sex difference in the respondents' evaluation of their parents' marriages?

B. PARENTS' MARITAL HAPPINESS AND THE CHILD'S FAVORABLENESS TOWARD MARRIAGE

1. *Tabulate* the favorableness - toward - marriage scores (Box 84) for the three groups of men students on Table 2, and for the three groups of women students on Table 3.

2. *Compute* the mean favorableness-toward-marriage score for each group using the procedure outlined on page 62.

Laboratory Report

1. Follow the directions for writing the Laboratory Report given in Appendix B.

2. *Optional for the Discussion:* Assume that the respondents answered as truthfully *as they could*. Despite this, the methods used in this study to measure the independent and dependent variables could make the conclusions invalid. Explain why this might be so.

REFERENCES

Burgess, Ernest W., and Wallin, Paul. *Engagement and Marriage*. Philadelphia: Lippincott, 1953. Pp. 551–554.

Burgess, Ernest W., and Cottrell, Leonard S. *Predicting Success or Failure in Marriage*. New York: Prentice-Hall, 1939.

Kirkpatrick, Clifford. *The Family as Process and Institution*. New York: Ronald Press, 1963. Pp. 340–346. Also in Robert F. Winch, Robert McGinnis, and Herbert R. Barringer, eds. *Selected Studies in Marriage and the Family*. New York: Holt, Rinehart and Winston, 1962. Pp. 544–552.

Locke, Harvey J. *Predicting Adjustment in Marriage*. New York: Holt, 1951.

SECTION/COURSE NO._____ DATE_____ NAME_____

TABLE 1. *Marital Happiness of Parents by Sex of Child*

Marital Happiness of Parents (Box 55)	Men (Box 1 = 1)		Women (Box 1 = 2)		Total	
	f	%	f	%	f	%
Unhappy (1, 2, 3)						
Less happy (4 & 5)						
Happy (6 & 7)						
TOTAL		100%		100%		100%
No answer		✕		✕		✕

TABLE 2. *Child's Attitude toward Marriage by Marital Happiness of Parents for Men Students*

Attitude toward Marriage (Box 84)	Marital Happiness of Parents (Box 55)					
	Unhappy (Box 55 = 1 to 3)		Less Happy (Box 55 = 4 & 5)		Happy (Box 55 = 6 & 7)	
x	f	fx	f	fx	f	fx
2						
3						
4						
5						
6						
7						
8						
9						
10						
11						
TOTAL						
MEAN						
No answer		✕		✕		✕

TABLE 3. *Child's Attitude toward Marriage by Marital Happiness of Parents for Women Students*

Attitude toward Marriage (Box 84)	Marital Happiness of Parents (Box 55)					
	Unhappy (Box 55 = 1 to 3)		Less Happy (Box 55 = 4 & 5)		Happy (Box 55 = 6 & 7)	
x	f	fx	f	fx	f	fx
2						
3						
4						
5						
6						
7						
8						
9						
10						
11						
TOTAL						
MEAN						
No answer						

SECTION/COURSE NO._____ DATE_____ NAME_____

Parent's Marital Happiness and Child's Attitude Toward Marriage

HYPOTHESIS: _____

_____

_____

_____

_____

_____

SAMPLE: _____

_____

_____

_____

INDEPENDENT VARIABLES: _____

_____

_____

_____

_____

DEPENDENT VARIABLES: _____

_____

_____

_____

_____

OTHER FACTORS: _____

_____

_____

_____

_____

SUMMARY OF FINDINGS: _____

_____

_____

_____

_____

_____

_____

_____

_____

_____

DISCUSSION: _____

_____

_____

_____

_____

_____

_____

_____

_____

_____

_____

_____

_____

_____

Part V   DATING AND

MATE SELECTION

ADOLESCENT ROLE DEPRIVATION AND HIGH SCHOOL AGE MARRIAGE*

Lee G. Burchinal

One feature of the trend toward younger age at marriage in the United States has been the recent increase in high school marriages.[1] In view of the sociological pessimism regarding youthful marriage, the present research study was undertaken as an attempt to identify some factors associated with high school aged marriages.[2]

Theoretical Formulation

Aged-graded status placement in American society may be considered as the various levels of childhood, adolescence, and adulthood, although demarcation lines between levels are not clearly defined. Yet high school graduation, full-time employment, movement from home to a place of further study or employment are approximations of *rites de passage* from adolescence to young adulthood for American girls. For girls

who have not completed high school, marriage clearly confers adult status apart from or in addition to any other institutionalized means available to girls. As an adolescent, girls have school, community, family, dating and courtship roles, but marriage permits a new set of adult and marital roles. Girls who marry before the completion of high school, in effect, reject adolescent role behavior.

Rejection of the adolescent role would likely occur when girls feel some degree of role deprivation. Role deprivation may occur: (1) when present role satisfactions are less than present role expectations, or (2) when present role satisfactions are less than anticipated marital role satisfactions.

The major hypothesis of this study is: Role change is directly related to role deprivation. Marriage is taken as the index of role change. Two conditions considered in the context of interaction with one another have been identified for role deprivation. Operational conditions of the role deprivation are set forth in the hypotheses which follow:

1. Marriage is directly related to dissatisfaction with parental relations.

Reprinted by permission of the author and the National Council on Family Relations from *Marriage and Family Living,* 21 (1959), pp. 378–384.

* Published as Journal Paper No. J.-3520 of the Iowa Agricultural and Home Economics Experiment Station, Ames, Iowa. Project No. 1370. The writer gratefully acknowledges his appreciation to the Alumni Achievement Fund of Iowa State College whose grant made this research possible.

TABLE I. *Means, Direction of Differences and Tests of Significance for Married and Control Girls*

Variable	Means		Z *	P
	Married	Control		
FOR THE TOTAL GROUP				
Age at first date	13.98	14.38	1.52	.13
Age at first steady	14.90	15.47	2.40	<.02
Number of steadies	2.95	1.80	3.06	<.01
Number of steadies in love with	1.60	1.08	2.61	<.01
Fairness of discipline	3.81	3.81	.18	.86
Authority of mother	3.31	3.34	.10	.92
Authority of father	2.80	3.07	.62	.52
Acceptance of mother	6.22	5.50	1.26	.21
Acceptance of father	5.34	4.30	2.15	<.05
Number of friends married	2.71	2.10	2.53	.01
Edwards PPS scores (n = 37)				
Achievement	11.45	11.02	.40	
Deference	12.96	12.61	1.51	
Order	13.64	10.66	2.94	<.01
Exhibitionism	12.99	14.53	1.95	.05 < P < .10
Autonomy	10.91	12.10	1.39	
Affiliation	17.79	18.12	.39	
Intraception	17.06	16.23	.86	
Succorance	12.34	12.74	.43	
Dominance	10.02	11.18	1.65	
Abasement	19.47	18.33	1.26	
Nurriance	17.66	16.77	.92	
Change	16.66	17.28	.63	
Endurance	15.34	13.20	2.11	<.05
Heterosexuality	10.21	13.36	2.59	<.05
Aggression	11.29	11.34	.07	
	M > C**	M < C		
Date frequency at 14	29	10	2.85	<.01
15	27	13	2.06	<.05
16	14	10	.61	.54
Date seriousness at 14	31	12	2.74	<.01
15	29	10	2.88	<.001
16	28	3	4.32	<.001
FOR THE PREMARITALLY PREGNANT GROUP				
Age at first date	14.00	14.31	.33	.74
Age at first steady	14.87	15.87	1.36	.17
Number of steadies	2.68	1.73	1.83	.06
Number of steadies in love with	1.59	1.00	2.17	<.05
Fairness of discipline	3.71	4.05	.11	.91
Authority of mother	3.43	3.33	1.07	.28
Authority of father	3.00	3.60	.46	.65
Acceptance of mother	5.00	5.14	.32	.74
Acceptance of father	4.71	4.33	.34	.73
Number of friends married	2.86	1.71	2.48	<.05
Edwards PPS scores (n = 11)				
Achievement	9.82	11.27	.86	
Deference	12.27	14.09	1.38	
Order	12.36	10.45	1.09	
Exhibitionism	12.91	14.72	1.43	
Autonomy	12.64	12.00	.31	
Affiliation	17.72	18.45	.58	
Intraception	15.27	14.91	.22	
Succorance	12.91	13.64	.35	

TABLE I–Continued

Variable	Means		Z*	P
	Married	Control		
Dominance	9.18	10.91	1.01	
Abasement	21.72	19.18	1.92	.05 < P < .10
Nutriance	17.09	16.91	.07	
Change	17.63	17.91	.18	
Endurance	13.54	13.18	.80	
Heterosexuality	13.64	11.91	.80	
Aggression	11.09	10.45	.37	
	M>C	M<C	Z	P
Date frequency at 14	10	5	1.03	.31
15	10	8	.47	.64
16	3	5	.71	.47
Date seriousness at 14	8	7	.26	.40
15	10	5	1.29	.18
16	10	1	2.71	< .01

FOR THE PREMARITALLY NON-PREGNANT GROUP

Variable	Married	Control	Z*	P
Age at first date	13.97	14.97	2.14	< .05
Age at first steady	15.00	15.72	2.95	< .01
Number of steadies	3.00	1.86	2.45	< .02
Number of steadies in love with	1.61	1.17	1.60	.11
Fairness of discipline	3.71	3.80	.68	.50
Authority of mother	3.35	3.44	.20	.84
Authority of father	2.82	2.94	.39	.70
Acceptance of mother	7.00	5.80	2.54	< .01
Acceptance of father	5.38	4.23	1.46	.14
Number of friends married	2.61	2.33	.65	.52
Edwards PPS scores (n = 26)				
Achievement	12.17	10.93	.90	
Deference	13.28	12.01	1.53	
Order	14.13	10.78	2.79	.01
Exhibitionism	13.05	14.78	1.48	
Autonomy	10.20	12.17	2.34	< .05
Affiliation	17.86	18.02	.14	
Intraception	17.86	16.82	.84	
Succorance	12.13	12.40	.26	
Dominance	10.40	11.32	.78	
Abasement	18.56	18.02	.47	
Nutriance	17.94	16.75	1.29	
Change	16.28	17.06	.61	
Endurance	16.13	13.24	2.09	< .05
Heterosexuality	8.78	14.01	4.18	< .001
Aggression	11.20	11.75	.40	
	M>C	M<C	Z	P
Date frequency at 14	17	5	2.34	< .02
15	17	5	2.18	< .05
16	10	5	1.02	.31
Date seriousness at 14	21	5	2.94	< .001
15	18	5	2.34	< .02
16	16	2	2.25	< .05

* Z refers to the Wilcoxon signed-ranks test statistic in the case of continuous data or to the statistic used in the sign test in the case of greater or less than comparisons. (See Sidney Siegel, *Nonparametric Statistics for the Behavioral Sciences*, New York: McGraw-Hill, 1956, pp. 68–75 for the sign test and pp. 75–83 for the Wilcoxon matched-pairs signed-ranks test.) For the means on the Edwards test, t was used; all tests are two-tailed.

** The frequencies under M>C are those corresponding to comparisons in which married girls choose a response of greater dating frequency or seriousness than the control girls; M<C indicates the opposite condition. The remainder of the cases are included in tie situations or were omitted at the fifteen and sixteen age levels because the girls were married.

To test this hypothesis, the Stone fairness of discipline scale, the Nye parental acceptance scale, and the Landis-Stone parent authority scale were used to assess the girls' perceptions of their relations with their parents.[3] It was assumed that girls who expressed more favorable evaluation of their parents by the criteria of these scales were less likely to suffer from role deprivation in this area of their lives than girls who reported harshness or rigidity of discipline, authoritarian parental behavior, and who rejected their parents.

2. Marriage is the result of role deprivations arising from a set of intervening variables, the personality characteristics of the girls, which contributes to a desire for satisfactions expected from a change in roles.

Moss and Gingles found that married girls as compared with control girls were less well adjusted as measured by the Emotionality Scale of the Minnesota Personality Scale.[4] Martinson refers to the concept of "ego deficiency" as a summary index for the discrepancy between the "social" and "personal" adjustment of girls who married young and a control group of single girls.[5] The measures used by these researchers reflect obviously socially desirable responses on many test items which may partially invalidate the personality measures for uses to which they have been put.[6] Therefore, the adjustment concept approach was rejected as a criterion of personality assessment and the need-theory approach suggested by the studies of Winch was used.[7] The Edwards Personal Preference Schedule was selected as a test since it was designed to provide "quick and convenient measures of a number of relatively independent *normal* personality variables."[8] The pairing technique used for questions permits few obviously socially desirable responses to be apparent to the respondent.

Although not all fifteen need variables derived from the Edwards PPS are relevant to the purposes of this study, data for all needs are listed in Table I. Need variables selected for relevance to the girls' decisions to marry were deference, autonomy, succorance, change, endurance, and heterosexuality. Complete definitions of these need variables are provided in the Edwards Manual.

If the need measures obtained from the Edwards schedule have generality value, married girls were expected to score higher than control girls on deference, succorance, change, and heterosexuality, and to score lower on autonomy and endurance.

3. Marriage is directly related to the length and seriousness of the heterosexual involvement of the girls.

Married girls were expected to have begun dating and going steady earlier, had a larger number of steady dates, and been in love with a larger number of persons than the control girls. Since dating and courtship roles are generally directional, toward increasingly intimate physical involvements and psychological identification, the girls who eventually married while in high school were expected to have suffered a greater degree of role deprivation which only marital roles could fulfill.

Research Design and Field Procedures

Insofar as possible, an *ex post facto* research design was used in the present study. Efforts were made to match married girls with control girls on eleven characteristics. Unfortunately, the present design departed from the *ex post facto* model in one vital aspect. All the data in the present study were gathered *after* the girls had been married.

Data were obtained in nine Iowa communities and from eleven separate high schools during the spring of 1958. At each of the schools, a questionnaire containing matching and dating history items was administered to one or more classrooms of students which included one or more of the married girls who were attending school. For girls who had dropped from school, all data were obtained from home contacts.

Absolute matching was achieved for sixty pairs of married and unmarried girls on school attended, grade in school, and rural or urban socialization experience. Reasonably successful matching, though less precise, was achieved for the ages of the girls, the prestige levels of their fathers' occupations, their parents' educational levels, the religious affiliation of the girls, the presence or absence of both biological parents, and sizes of families of orientation. Details on matching data are available elsewhere and for purposes of brevity are not presented here.[9]

Results

Data are presented in Table I for the total group of girls and for two subgroups of girls, the premaritally pregnant and the premaritally non-pregnant girls. Twenty-three, or 39.6 per cent, of the fifty-eight girls for whom data were available on this factor were premaritally pregnant.

The hypotheses relating role deprivation and strained parent-adolescent relations or role deprivation arising from personality need characteristics of the girls were untenable. None of the mean differences on parent-adolescent relations supported the hypothesis. Taken as a whole, the personality needs comparisons listed in Table I also failed to support the hypothesis.

Only the hypothesis relative to the length and seriousness of heterosexual involvement received considerable support. Although five of the tests were not statistically significant, the data from the three groups of married and corresponding control girls showed a consistent pattern of differences. Married girls in the premaritally nonpregnant, pregnant, and total samples began to date and go steady at an earlier age, had a greater number of steady boyfriends, and were in love with a greater number of steadies or dates than the corresponding control girls.

In addition to the heterosexual involvement questions just cited, the girls were asked to check whether they dated less, about the same, or more frequently than other persons of their sex for ages fourteen, fifteen, and sixteen years. Also, they were asked to check whether they were not dating, dating around, or going steady at ages fourteen, fifteen, and sixteen. Again the bulk of the data supported the hypotheses although some differences in the patterns of dating activity were found for the premaritally and non-premaritally pregnant married girls.

One other factor which may produce role deprivation for adolescents might be the knowledge of marital life they gained from friends who married prior to graduation. The married and control girls were asked, "How many persons whom you have had as close friends have gotten married while they were still in high school?" For both subgroups, the married girls reported more close friends had married than the control girls, but the difference was minor for the non-premaritally pregnant group while it was larger and statistically significant for the premaritally pregnant group.

Apart from hypotheses relating to role deprivation and marriage, other data were available for analyses. Historically, high school marriages have been more common among girls of lower socio-economic backgrounds. The data in Table II show that this proposition was confirmed when the occupation prestige levels of the fathers of the married girls were compared with similar data for all girls who completed the original questionnaire.[10] The percentage of married girls from

TABLE II. *Percentages of Nonfarm Married and Unmarried Girls' Fathers by Levels of Occupational Prestige Scores*

North-Hatt Score Levels	Married	Unmarried	Difference
	n = 60	n = 315	
Less than 60	39.6	33.0	6.6
60–69	50.9	45.4	5.5
70 and over	9.5	21.6	−12.1
	Marshall's C = 1.48, P = .069		

farm homes, 8.6, and the percentage of unmarried farm girls who completed the questionnaires, 9.7, were very similar.

When the parents' educational levels were analyzed, further support was obtained for the hypothesis of greater frequency of young marriages among girls of lower socio-economic backgrounds. The mean educational level of the married girls' fathers was 9.7, for the fathers of all the other girls (n = 357) the mean was 10.9, t = 2.68, P < .01. Mothers of the married girls also had lower mean educational levels, 10.3, than the mothers of all the girls whose mean was 11.4 years of education, t = 3.75, P < .001.

The absence of one or both parents has been alleged to be a factor in various sorts of adolescent deviant behavior. This condition was tested for relationship with high school age marriage. Married and all unmarried girls were classified into a dichotomy: (1) families in which both biological parents were living together; and (2) other conditions in which one or both of the girls' original parents were not present in their homes during most of their lives. Eighty per cent of the married and 82.2 per cent of the unmarried girls came from "whole" homes, $X^2 = .69$, .30 < P < .50.

Discussion

One of the surprising features of the data was a complete lack of confirmation for the parent-adolescent relationship hypothesis. Moss and Gingles found that the early married girls in their *ex post facto* Nebraska study scored significantly and substantially lower on the Minnesota Family Relationship Scale than the control girls.[11] This raises the question of the validity of the present parent-relationship data for the hypothesis tested. The married girls in the present sample had been married from less than one month to twenty-seven months; the median length of marriage was 5.7 months. If the hypothesis was valid, could the comparatively short marriage experience of the girls be sufficient to cause a change in their evaluation of their relationship with their parents? Some data are available which may bear on this question. Almost half of the girls reported that their folks had been "against" their marriages, "tried to talk them out of it," or "wanted them to wait," but now their folks have "accepted it," or have "come around to our point of view." These data suggest that if strained parent-adolescent relations exist prior to marriage, the relations, from the girls' points of view, improve rapidly after a short time of marriage.

Some interesting results emerged from the analyses of the needs scores. One in particular was the direction of the differences in heterosexuality for the premaritally pregnant group and the reversal in the direction of these same scores for the non-premaritally pregnant group of girls. These data seemed to suggest that girls who were pregnant prior to marriage still have premarital heterosexuality interests. A mean of 14.34 is used as a norm for single women since this is reported by Edwards as the mean for the women in his test group. The mean for the premaritally pregnant girls, 13.64, approximated that of the norm group, but the mean for the non-premaritally pregnant group, 8.78, is considerably lower. If one assumes that the heterosexual need as measured in the Edwards PPS is a situational-response measurement subject to variation according to the degree that the heterosexual desires of the girls are satisfied, the non-premaritally pregnant girls who apparently had considerable dating experience and who freely selected marriage more likely had achieved considerable heterosexual satisfaction and, as the data show, have the lowest heterosexual scores. The premaritally pregnant girls, on the other hand, did not freely elect marriage: for the most part, it was forced upon them by their pregnancies. They may be resentful of the necessity of becoming married and probably still desire heterosexual satisfactions arising from dating roles rather than the heterosexual satisfactions arising from the dyadic marital roles. The feasibility of these speculations wait on pre- and post-marriage heterosexual need measurement. The fact that the PPS comparisons were based on small numbers of pairs probably needs no further elaboration.

The data seemed relatively clear on the relation of dating behavior to high school age marriage. Whereas the family relationship and personality needs data may have been greatly changed from what might have been obtained if these data had been obtained prior to marriage, the dating history data probably were not altered substantially by the intervening fact of marriage. Certainly early age of dating, going steady, or the tendency to fall in love with more dates and steadies are not the only or perhaps the major factors in high school marriages, but in the context of the generally nonsignificant results based on parent-adolescent and the needs scores of the girls, the dating history data take on added significance.

Results from the Nebraska and the present study are in conflict regarding the association of young age of marriage and socio-economic level of the family of orientation. Moss and Gingles found no differences in the mean educational levels of fathers or mothers for married and control girls. Married and control girls in the Nebraska study also did not differ greatly in the estimates of the ability of their families to send them to college.[12] In the Iowa study marked differences in mean educational levels for both parents and frequency distribution differences in the level of occupational prestige for fathers' jobs were found for comparisons between married girls and all other girls included in the

original questionnaire administration. An explanation of the differences in results for the two studies may lie in the fact that Moss and Gingles report data for girls who married prior to nineteen years of age while the Iowa data are based on girls who married prior to completion of high school. The modal age at marriage for women in Iowa in 1957 was eighteen years of age. One can safely assume that most of these marriages occurred after high school graduation and if socio-economic analyses were made for the ages up to and including this modal grouping, nonsignificant differences would be likely to be found.

Numerous questions were raised by this exploratory research project. Is it safe to assume high school marriage is deviation from the norms of the school age population? How much of a role change is anticipated by the girls? What were their expectations regarding marriage; that of their parents? What had been the role of their parents in their dating and courtship? What kinds of parental control and counsel were used? What kinds of parental behavior impede or expedite youthful marriages?

Husbands were virtually ignored in this study. What are the characteristics of men who marry high school-aged girls?[13] What was their role and that of the girls in reaching the decision to marry?

Finally, the writer recognizes that only crude role deprivation indices have been used. If role theory is used, future research might be designed to measure this concept directly.

Summary

High school age marriage was taken as an index of role change arising from adolescent role deprivation. Data related to adolescent role deprivation were obtained from a matched group of sixty married and control girls who were matched with varying degrees of success on eleven characteristics.

Little support was found for the hypothesis relating to parent-adolescent relationships and young age at marriage. Examination of the personality needs scores for the group of premaritally pregnant and the group of non-premaritally pregnant girls showed marked differences on the levels of heterosexuality needs. Otherwise only one theoretically meaningful difference emerged from the analysis of personality needs: the non-premaritally pregnant girls were less autonomous than the control girls. In general, married and control girls did not vary significantly on the needs scores. Girls who married prior to high school graduation, on the average, started dating and going steady at an early age, had more steady boyfriends, and felt that they had been in love with a larger number of dates and steadies than the control girls.

Married girls were found to have had a larger number of close friends who married while they were in school. Measures of socio-economic background such as fathers' occupations and parents' educational levels showed that married girls had lower family socio-economic levels than the norm group of 357 girls who also answered these items. However, married girls did not differ from unmarried girls in the proportion coming from families in which one or both parents were not present.

NOTES

[1] Although the view of decreasing age at marriage in the United States since 1900 is generally held, Thomas P. Monahan challenges the basis of the census reports. See *Pattern of Age at Marriage in the United States*, Philadelphia, Pennsylvania: Stephenson-Brothers, 225 South 15 Street, 1957.

For data relative to the increase in high school-aged marriages in Iowa, see Lee G. Burchinal and Loren Chancellor, "What about School-Age Marriages?", *Iowa Farm Science*, 12 (June, 1958), pp. 12–14.

[EDITOR'S NOTE: Since this article was written, Parke and Glick have published evidence which further documents the increase in teenage marriages during the period covered by Burchinal's research. However, their more recent data also indicate that "the marriage rate among very young women reached a peak perhaps ten to fifteen years ago and is now on the decline." See Robert Parke, Jr. and Paul C. Glick, "Prospective Changes in Marriage and the Family," *Journal of Marriage and the Family*, 29 (May), 1967, 249–256.]

[2] Ernest W. Burgess and Leonard S. Cottrell, *Predicting Success or Failure in Marriage*, New York: Prentice-Hall, 1939, pp. 115–17, p. 88; Lewis M. Terman, *Psychological Factors in Marital Happiness*, New York: McGraw-Hill, 1939, pp. 180–183; Harvey J. Locke, *Predicting Adjustment in Marriage*, New York: Holt, 1951, pp. 100–103.

[3] The fairness of discipline scale and its statistical properties were obtained from Dr. Stone. The authority scale may be found in Paul Landis and Carol Stone, *The Relationship of Parental Authority to Teenage Adjustments*, Bulletin 538, Washington Agricultural Experiment Station, Pullman, Washington, 1952. The acceptance-rejection of parents scale has been reported; see F. Ivan Nye, *Family Relationships and Delinquency*, New York: Wiley, 1958, pp. 76–77.

[4] J. Joel Moss and Ruby Gingles, "A Preliminary Report of a Longitudinal Study of Early Marriage in Nebraska," given at the Midwest Sociological Society meeting in Minneapolis, April 27, 1958.

[5] Floyd M. Martinson, "Ego Deficiency as a Factor in Marriage," *American Sociological Review*, 20 (April, 1955), pp. 161–164.

[6] See Albert Ellis, "The Value of Marriage Prediction Tests," *American Sociological Review*, 13 (December, 1948), pp. 710–718, for a critique of the weaknesses of direct questions in assessment of marital or interpersonal relations.

[7] Robert F. Winch, "The Theory of Complementary Needs in Mate-Selection: Final Results on the Test of the General Hypothesis," *American Sociological Review*, 20 (October, 1955), pp. 552–555.

[8] Allen L. Edwards, *The Edwards Personal Preference Schedule Manual*, New York: Psychological Corporation, 1953.

[9] Matching details will be sent upon request or are available in an unpublished Ph.D. dissertation; see Orlando Goering, "Sociological and Psychological Correlates of High School Marriage," Ames, Iowa; Iowa State College, 1959.

[10] Occupational prestige was defined by the North-Hatt scale; see C. C. North and Paul K. Hatt, "Jobs and Occupations: A Popular Evaluation," *Opinion News*, 9 (September 1, 1947), pp. 3–13.

[11] Moss and Gingles, *op. cit.*

[12] *Ibid.*

[13] Husband-wife age differences by ages of bride, residential propinquity, and degree of religious homogamy among other things have been reported for youthful marriages in Iowa in 1956; see Burchinal and Chancellor, *op. cit.* Economic and other post-marital data for the present sample of sixty couples will be forthcoming.

ROLE PRACTICE AND SEX AS DETERMINANTS
OF DATING PATTERNS

Problem

The status of male or female is a universal and clearly perceivable basis on which to assign and differentiate social roles. Moreover, the differences in reproductive functions fulfilled by men and women provide a biological basis for role differences on which all societies have built numerous elaborations. In this laboratory problem we will examine the way in which the status of male or female is associated with one aspect of performance of the dating role.

In addition to the behaviors ascribed by virtue of sex, the dating role is also influenced by many other factors, one of which is examined in this laboratory problem. This is the factor of *role practice*. The maxim "learn by doing" applies to social relationships as well as to technical skills. Almost every role must be practiced before it can be performed well, including the roles involved in the courtship process.

Burchinal shows that girls who married early tended to have started dating earlier than others. Apparently they started the courtship cycle early and, as a result, also finished the cycle (by marriage) early. Such a formulation is consistent with the idea put forward by Havighurst (1952) and Duvall (1962) that individual and family behavior develop through a relatively orderly sequence of social relationships which provide opportunities for learning the behavior appropriate to one's role. This reasoning, therefore, suggests that we may use the age at which a person starts dating as a factor which should, theoretically, influence the extent to which he or she is currently involved in the dating role.

Hypothesis

1. Are men or women students more advanced in dating status for their age?

2. What relationship do you expect to find between age at first date and present dating status?

Empirical Indicators for Problem 10

1. Sex (circle one answer number):
    1   Male
    2   Female

41. What is your present dating status?
    1   Not dating
    2   "Playing the field"
    3   Partly "playing the field"
    4   Often dating the same person
    5   Going steady
    6   Pinned
    7   Engaged
    8   Married

43. How old were you when you had your first real date?_____years

Data Analysis

1. *Sort* the code sheets into two groups on the basis of the sex of the respondent, as coded in Box 1:

> Male   = 1
>
> Female = 2

2. *Subsort* the code sheets for each sex into five groups on the basis of the age of the individual at the time of his first date which is recorded directly in Box 43:

> 13 or earlier
>
> 14
>
> 15
>
> 16
>
> 17 or later

3. *Tabulate* the present dating status for each age group, for men on Table 1, and for women on Table 2, using the scores for the present dating status coded in Box 41.

4. *Compute* the percentage in each dating-status group for each age and sex category. Use the percentage tables in Appendix D.

Laboratory Report

1. See Appendix B for general instructions on writing laboratory reports.

2. Include in your Discussion a consideration of what could account for the sex differences you find. Also discuss the implications of your findings in light of the fact that the age at which children start to date in American society has been declining.

REFERENCES

Duvall, Evelyn. *Family Development*. New York: Lippincott, 1962.

Havighurst, Robert J. *Developmental Tasks and Education*. New York: Longmans, Green, 1952.

Lowrie, Samuel H. "Factors Involved in the Frequency of Dating," *Marriage and Family Living*, 18 (1956), pp. 46–51.

SECTION/COURSE NO._____ DATE_____ NAME_____

TABLE 1. Dating Status of Men by Age at First Date

Dating Status (Box 41)	Age at First Date (Box 43)													
	13 or Earlier		14		15		16		17 or Later		Never	
	f	%	f	%	f	%	f	%	f	%	f	%
1												
2												
3												
4												
5												
6												
7												
8												
TOTAL		100%		100%		100%		100%		100%		100%
No answer		✕		✕		✕		✕		✕		✕

TABLE 2. Dating Status of Women by Age at First Date

Dating Status (Box 41)	13 or Earlier		14		15		16		17 or Over		Never	
	f	%	f	%	f	%	f	%	f	%	f	%
1												
2												
3												
4												
5												
6												
7												
8												
TOTAL		100%		100%		100%		100%		100%		100%
No answer		✕		✕		✕		✕		✕		✕

Age at First Date (Box 43)

SECTION/COURSE NO._____ DATE_____ NAME_____

Role Practice and Sex as Determinants of Dating Behavior

HYPOTHESIS: _____

_____

_____

_____

_____

_____

SAMPLE: _____

_____

_____

_____

INDEPENDENT VARIABLES: _____

_____

_____

_____

_____

DEPENDENT VARIABLE: _____

_____

_____

_____

_____

_____

OTHER FACTORS: _____

_____

_____

_____

SUMMARY OF FINDINGS: _____

_____

_____

_____

_____

_____

_____

_____

_____

_____

DISCUSSION: _____

_____

_____

_____

_____

_____

_____

_____

_____

_____

_____

_____

_____

CULTURAL FACTORS IN THE SELECTION OF MARRIAGE MATES[*]

August B. Hollingshead

The question of who marries whom is of perennial interest, but only during the last half-century has it become the subject of scientific research. Throughout American history there has always been a romantic theory of mate selection, supported by poets, dramatists, and the public at large. Social scientists, however —a group of jaundiced realists, by and large—have little faith in this pleasant myth as an explanation for the selection of marriage mates.[1] Their theories can be divided between (1) the homogamous and (2) the heterogamous.[2] The theory of homogamy postulates that "like attracts like"; the theory of heterogamy holds that "opposites attract each other."

Certain aspects of each theory have been investigated by psychologists and sociologists. The psychologists have confined their attention almost exclusively to individual physical[3] and psychological[4] characteristics. Sociologists have focused, in the main, upon factors external to the individual. As a consequence, sociological research has stressed such things as ethnic origin,[5] residential propinquity,[6] race,[7] religion,[8] socioeconomic status,[9] and social characteristics in general.[10] While all of these researches have used empirical data, only a few of them have attempted to measure the significant cultural factors that impinge upon mate selection against the background of the theories of homogamy and heterogamy. We shall attempt to do this in this paper.

My attack upon this problem will be to state the theoretical limits within which mate selection may take place, then turn to a body of data to determine how, and to what extent, specific factors influence the selection of marital partners.[11]

Viewed in the broadest theoretical perspective of democratic theory, the choice of marriage mates in our society might be conceived of as a process in which each unattached biologically mature adult has an equal opportunity to marry every other unattached biologically mature adult of the opposite sex. Viewed from the narrowest perspective of cultural determinism, biologically mature, single males or females have only

Reprinted by permission of the author and the American Sociological Association from the *American Sociological Review,* 15 (1950), pp. 619–627.

[*] Paper read at the annual meeting of the Eastern Sociological Society held in Boston, April 22–23, 1950. Grateful acknowledgement is made hereby to the Social Science Research Council for a grant-in-aid and to the Committee on Bursary Appointments, Yale University for their support of this project.

limited opportunity to select a marital partner. The first proposition assumes complete freedom of individual choice to select a mate; the second assumes that mates are selected for individuals by controls imposed on them by their culture. If the first assumption is valid we should find no association between cultural factors and who marries whom; if the second is descriptive of the mate selection process we should expect to find a strong association between one or several cultural factors and who marries whom. The second proposition, however, allows for individual choice within limits of cultural determinism; for example a Jew is expected to marry a Jew by the rules of his religion; moreover, he is more or less coerced by his culture to marry a Jewess of the same or a similar social status, but he has a choice as to the exact individual.

In the remainder of this paper I shall test five factors—race, age, religion, ethnic origin, and class—within the limits of the theories of homogamy and heterogamy and the abstract model I have outlined. The data utilized to measure the influence of these factors on the selection of marriage mates were assembled in New Haven, Connecticut, by a research team during the last year through the cooperation of the Departments of Vital Statistics of the State of Connecticut and the City of New Haven. All marriage license data on marriages in New Haven during 1948 were copied. Then parents, relatives, in some cases neighbors, were asked in February, 1949, to supply the addresses of each newly married couple. Addresses were obtained for 1,980 couples out of a total of 2,063 couples married in the city in 1948. Nine hundred and three couples, 45.8 per cent, had moved from the city, and 1,077, 54.4 per cent, were living in it in February, 1949. A 50 per cent random sample, drawn by Census Tracts from the 1,077 couples resident in New Haven, was interviewed with a schedule. The interview, which lasted from about an hour and a quarter to three hours, took place in the home of the couple, usually with both the husband and wife present, and occurred most generally in the evening or late afternoon.[12] In addition, twenty-eight census-like items such as age, occupation, birthplace, residence, and marital status, were available on all of the 1,980 couples.

The 523 interviewed couples were compared with the 1,457 non-interviewed couples, census item by census item, to determine if the interviewed group differed significantly from the non-interviewed group. No significance of difference was found at the 5 per cent level for any item, except where the husband and wife were both over 50 years of age.[13] Having satisfied ourselves that the interviewed group was representative of the total group, we proceeded with a measure of confidence to the analysis of our data.

Race

Our data show that the racial mores place the strongest, most explicit, and most precise limits on an individual as to whom he may or may not marry. Although inter-racial marriages are legal in Connecticut, they are extremely rare; none occurred in New Haven in 1948. Kennedy's analysis of New Haven marriages from 1870 through 1940 substantiates the rule that Negroes and whites marry very infrequently. Thus, we may conclude that a man's or woman's marital choice is effectively limited to his or her own race by the moral values ascribed to race in this culture. Race, thus, divides the community into two parts so far as marriage is concerned. Because there were no interracial marriages in 1948, and because of the small percentage of Negroes in New Haven, we will confine the rest of our discussion to whites.

Age

Age, like race, is a socio-biological factor that has a definite influence on marital choice. The effects of cultural usages and values on the selection of a marriage partner may be seen by a study of Table I. While there is a very strong association between the age of the husband and the age of the wife at all age levels, it is strongest when both partners are under 20 years of age. Men above 20 years of age tend to select wives who are in the same 5 year age group as they are, or a younger one. After age 20 the percentage of men who marry women younger than themselves increases until age 50. After 50 the marital partners tend to be nearer one another in age. Table I indicates further that controls relative to age rather effectively limit a man's choice to women of his age or younger, but that the woman cannot be too much younger or counter controls begin to operate. Evidence accumulated in the interviews shows it is widely believed that a young woman should not marry "an old man." The effects of this belief and practice are reflected in the lower left hand section of Table I. There we see that only 4 men above 45 years of age, out of a total of 144, married women under 30 years of age. The age-sanctions that impinge on a woman with reference to the age of a potential husband narrow her marital opportunities to men her age, or to slightly older men. This usage is reflected in the upper right corner of Table I, where marriages between older women and younger men are conspicuous by their absence. In short, differences in the customs relative to age and marital partners place greater restrictions on a woman's marital opportunities than a man's. Nevertheless, it is clear that the values ascribed

TABLE I. *Age of Husband and Wife by Five-Year Intervals for New Haven Marriages, 1948*

Age of Husband	Age of Wife								
	15–19	20–24	25–29	30–34	35–39	40–44	45–49	50 & Up	Total
15–19	42	10	3						55
20–24	153	504	51	10	1				719
25–29	52	271	184	22	7	2			538
30–34	5	52	87	69	13	5			231
35–39	1	12	27	29	21	2	3		105
40–44		1	9	18	17	8	2	1	56
45–49	1		3	6	16	16	7	1	49
50 & up			1	4	11	15	21	43	95
Total	254	850	365	168	86	47	33	45	1848

$X^2 = 2574.8905$ $P < .01$ $C = .76$ $\overline{C} = .80$

$C =$ The coefficient of contingency.

$\overline{C} =$ The corrected coefficient of contingency corrected for broad grouping by the formula given in Thomas. C. McCormick, *Elementary Social Statistics*, McGraw-Hill, 1941, p. 207.

to age restrict an individual's marital opportunities within narrow limits; and a woman's more than a man's.

Religion

The effects of religious rules on an individual's marital choices were very clear.[14] Next to race, religion is the most decisive factor in the segregation of males and females into categories that are approved or disapproved with respect to nuptiality. Ninety-one per cent of the marriages in this study involved partners from the same religious group. In the case of Jews, this percentage was 97.1, among Catholics it was 93.8 per cent; it fell to 74.4 per cent for Protestants. The differences in percentage, we believe, are a reflection of the relative intensity of in-group sanctions on the individual in the three religious groups. A striking point that emerged from our data is that the effects of religion on marital choice has not changed between the parental and present generation.[15] Table II shows that the number of Catholics who married Catholics, and Jews who married Jews, was almost the same in both generations. The number of Protestants who married Protestants dropped in the present generation, but not significantly in terms of the numbers involved.[16] The influence of religious affiliation on the selection of a marriage mate is obviously strongest in the Jewish group and weakest in the Protestant. This is reflected in the number of mixed marriages. On this point, we would remark that there is no consistent bias between sex and mixed Catholic-Protestant marriages; either partner is likely to be a Catholic or a Protestant. On the other hand, in Jewish-Gentile marriages it has been a Jewish male who has married a Gentile female.

I shall point out, in passing, that the very high as-

TABLE. II. *Religious Affiliation in the Parental and Present Generations*

A. Wife's Father and Mother*

Wife's Father	Wife's Mother		
	Catholic	Protestant	Jewish
Catholic	274	11	0
Protestant	9	75	0
Jewish	2	1	65
Total	285	87	65

$X^2 = 522.4592$ $P < .01$ $C = .74$

B. Husband's Father and Mother

Husband's Father	Husband's Mother		
	Catholic	Protestant	Jewish
Catholic	273	12	0
Protestant	14	70	0
Jewish	0	0	68
Total	287	82	68

$X^2 = 494.4359$ $P < .01$ $C = .73$

C. Husband and Wife

Husband	Wife		
	Catholic	Protestant	Jewish
Catholic	271	20	0
Protestant	17	61	0
Jewish	1	1	66
Total	289	82	66

$X^2 = 636.0297$ $P < .01$ $C = .77$

* The religious affiliation claimed by the interviewees is used here.

sociation we found between religion and marriage is not unique. Burgess and Wallin reported a coefficient of contingency of .75 for the 1,000 engaged couples they studied in Chicago;[17] our data revealed a coefficient of contingency of .77 in the present generation. This is not essentially different from theirs. Because religion is so effective a control in the selection of marriage mates I shall hold it constant and analyze other factors in terms of it.

Ethnic Origin

New Haven remained almost wholly Protestant religiously, and British ethnically, from its settlement in 1638 until the late 1830's. Between 1830 and 1880 Irish arrived by the hundreds; Germans and Scandinavians by the score. The Irish and a minority of the Germans were Catholic and they soon established themselves in this burgeoning railroad and manufacturing center. An expanding economy, coupled with political and economic unrest in Southern and Eastern Europe, resulted in the influx of thousands of Polish and Russian Jews, and tens of thousands of Italians between 1890 and 1914. After 1914, the stream of immigration became a trickle that has never again been allowed to run freely. Thus, today, New Haven is composed mainly of three large religious groups and seven European-derived ethnic stocks: British, Irish, German, Scandinavian, Italian, Polish, and Polish Jewish.[18] We cannot discuss how ethnicity is related to the selection of a marriage mate apart from religion, because religion and ethnic origin are so closely related. Observation of Table III will show that ethnicity within a religious group has been a very potent factor in influencing the mate selection process in both the parental and the present generations, but it was stronger a generation ago than it is now. Although ethnic lines are crossed within the Catholic and the Protestant faith more frequently in the present than in the parental generation, this is not true for the Jews. Furthermore, ethnic lines in both generations were crossed, for the most part, within religious groups. This means that the Catholics are becoming a mixture of Irish, Polish, and Italian as a result of intermarriage between these groups, but there is still a large block of unmixed Italian stock in New Haven and smaller blocks of Irish and Polish. The Protestants, on the other hand, select marriage partners mainly from the British segment of the city's population; a minority choose a partner from a Northwestern European group, and in some cases both partners will be of German or Scandinavian descent. Kennedy discovered this process in her study of New Haven mar-

TABLE III. *Intraethnic and Interethnic Marriages in the Present and Parental Generations by Religious Groups*

A. Catholic*		
Ethnic Derivation	Couple	Parents
Italian	119	302
Polish	11	56
Irish	21	75
Germany & Central Europe		19
British		4
Mixed	120	86
Total	271	542

B. Protestant		
Ethnic Derivation	Couple	Parents
British	18	61
Northwest Europe	3	20
Polish		2
Mixed	40	39
Total	61	122

C. Jewish		
Ethnic Derivation	Couple	Parents
Polish & Russian	66	129
German & Polish	0	3
Total	66	132

D. Mixed Religion		
Ethnic Derivation	Couple	Parents
British	3	26
Northwest Europe	1	13
Italian	0	9
Polish	2	11
Irish	1	8
Mixed	32	11
Total	39	78

* The religious affiliation claimed by the interviewees is used here.

riage records from 1870 to 1940, and developed her theory of the triple melting-pot in terms of it.[19]

Section D of Table III indicates that, in most cases, marriages across religious lines involve the mixing of ethnic stocks. This is true whether Catholics and Protestants marry, or Jews and Gentiles, because the members of each religious group came from such different parts of Europe. From the viewpoint of assimilation, marriages across religious lines are crucial if the triple melting-pot is to become a single melting-pot. But as Kennedy's and our data show, we are going to have three pots boiling merrily side by side with little fusion between them for an indefinite period. Furthermore, if the rules relative to mixed marriages in the Roman Catholic and Jewish churches were followed strictly there would be no mixing of the contents of one pot with those of another. To be sure, ethnic intermixture would occur, but within each respective religious group.

Class

Our discussion of the relationship between social class and marriage will be based on cases where the husband, the wife, and both parental families were *de facto* residents of New Haven.[20] The analysis of 1,008 marriages where the husband, the wife, and their families were residents of New Haven revealed that the class of residential area in which a man's or a woman's family home is located has a very marked influence on his or her marital opportunities. In 587 of these 1,008 marriages, or 58.2 per cent (see Table IV), both partners came from the same class of residential area. When those that involved a partner from an adjacent class area were added to the first group the figure was raised to 82.8 per cent of all marriages.

Careful study of the data presented in Table IV will reveal that the residential class in which a family has its home has a different effect on a woman's marital opportunities in comparison with a man's. While the modal, as well as the majority, of marriages at all levels united class equals, when class lines were crossed the man selected a woman from a lower class far more frequently than was true for women. For instance, if you look at Table IV you will see that 12 men from class I married women from lower ranking areas, and four of the twelve married girls from class V and class VI areas. On the other hand, 9 women from Class I areas married men from lower ranking areas, but 8 of the 9 came from a class II area and 1 from a class III area. No man from class IV, V, or VI areas married a woman from a class I area. If you follow down the successive class levels on Table IV you will see that this tendency is repeated all the way to class VI. It is clearest, however, in classes IV and V. In class IV, only 12 women from classes II and III combined married men from class IV. On the other hand, class IV men married 35 class V and 38 class VI women, for a total of 73. Fifty class V men married women from classes II, III, and IV, but 87 married class VI women. These figures reveal that the man has a wider range of choice than a woman, but he tends, when he goes outside of his own class, to marry a woman in a lower class. From whatever way we view Table IV, it is evident that the class position of a family is a factor that exerts a very important influence on the marriage choice of its children.

Now that we have seen the larger picture, we will look at it from the special perspective of a combination of religion and residential class. Because the number of cases where we knew both religion and class level was small in some residential areas, we have combined

TABLE V. *Residential Class of Husband and Wife by Religious Groups*

Residential Class of Husband	A. Catholic Residential Class of Wife	
	I–III	IV–VI
I–III	16	7
IV–VI	12	161
Total	28	168

$X^2 = 74.8413$ $P < .01$

Residential Class of Husband	B. Protestant Residential Class of Wife	
	I–III	IV–VI
I–III	12	4
IV–VI	1	18
Total	13	22

$X^2 = 18.0923$ $P < .01$

Residential Class of Husband	C. Jewish Residential Class of Wife	
	I–III	IV–VI
I–III	24	2
IV–VI	3	15
Total	27	17

$X^2 = 26.6687$ $P < .01$

TABLE IV. *Residential Class of Husband and Wife for Residents of New Haven*

Class of Husband	Class of Wife						Total
	I	II	III	IV	V	VI	
I	13	7	1	0	3	1	25
II	8	56	8	12	13	8	105
III	1	4	15	5	7	7	39
IV	0	8	4	55	35	38	140
V	0	12	8	30	252	87	389
VI	0	5	9	40	60	196	310
Total	22	92	45	142	370	337	1008

$X^2 = 1045.0605$ $P < .01$ $C = .71$ $\overline{C} = .77$

classes I through III, and classes IV through VI in Table V. Table V indicates very clearly that the class factor operates independently of religion, and with about equal force in each religious group. What is especially significant is that the effects of class position on who marries whom are so strong in each religious group.

Education operates in the same way as residence to sort potential marriage mates into horizontal status groups within the confines of religion. Within each religious group men with a particular amount of education married women with a comparable amount of education in very significant numbers. This tendency was strongest in the Jewish and weakest in the Catholic group. The strong association between the educational level of the husband and the wife, so evident in Table VI, is not a new development. We compared the education of husbands and wives in the parental generation by religious groups and found that for both the husband's parents and the wife's parents the association

held. Moreover, the coefficients of contingency for each set of parents by religion were almost the same, as the following tabulation shows:

Religion	Husband's Parents'	Wife's Parents'
Catholic	.57	.58
Protestant	.58	.59
Jewish	.59	.59

These coefficients indicate that education, along with religion, has influenced the mate selection process for at least two generations.

In summary, this paper has attempted to throw light on three questions: *first*, does a biologically mature unattached adult have an equal opportunity to marry an unattached mature adult of the opposite sex? *Second*, what restrictions are placed on his choice by society, and *third*, how effective are certain selected restrictions in limiting his choice? These questions become meaningful only when we relate them to the two propositions outlined in the introduction. There I set up a model with theoretical limits of absolute freedom of individual choice in the selection of a marital partner at one pole, and no choice at the other.

The data presented demonstrate that American culture, as it is reflected in the behavior of newly married couples in New Haven, places very definite restrictions on whom an individual may or may not marry. The racial mores were found to be the most explicit on this point. They divided the community into two pools of marriage mates and an individual fished for a mate only in his own racial pool. Religion divided the white race into three smaller pools. Persons in the Jewish pool in 97.1 per cent of the cases married within their own group; the percentage was 93.8 for Catholics and 74.4 for Protestants. Age further subdivided the potential pool of marriage mates into rather definite age grades, but the limits here were not so precise in the case of a man as of a woman. The ethnic origin of a person's family placed further restrictions on his marital choice. In addition, class position and education stratified the three religious pools into areas where an individual was most likely to find a mate. When all of these factors are combined they place narrow limits on an individual's choice of a marital partner. At the moment we cannot go beyond this point and assign a proportionate probable weight to each one.

In conclusion, I think the data we have presented strongly support the proposition that one's subculture, and one's race, age, and class positions in the society effectively determine the kind of a person one will marry, but not the exact individual. In a highly significant number of cases the person one marries is very similar culturally to one's self. Our data clearly support the theory of homogamy, rather than that of heterogamy, *but* a generalized theory of the precise influ-

TABLE VI. *Years of School Completed by Husband and Wife by Religion*

A. Catholic

Years of School Husband	Years of School—Wife		
	9 & less	10–12	13 & more
9 & less	35	19	1
10–12	33	128	27
13 & more	5	15	19
Total	73	162	47

$X^2 = 80.9784$ $P < .01$

B. Protestant

Years of School Husband	Years of School—Wife		
	9 & less	10–12	13 & more
9 & less	11	3	0
10–12	10	26	7
13 & more	3	6	16
Total	24	35	23

$X^2 = 38.9932$ $P < .01$

C. Jewish

Years of School Husband	Years of School—Wife		
	9 & less	10–12	13 & more
9 & less	0	0	0*
10–12	0	22	11
13 & more	0	8	26
Total	0	30	37

$X^2 = 12.6033$ $P < .01$

*The zero cells were not included in the X^2.

ence of cultural and individual factors on the selection of marriage mates remains to be formulated. This is an objective for sociologists to work toward.

NOTES

[1] For a discussion of this theory and some facts to refute it see A. B. Hollingshead, "Class and Kinship in a Middle Western Community," *American Sociological Review*, 14 (August, 1949), 469–475.

[2] E. W. Burgess and Paul Wallin, "Homogamy in Social Characteristics," *American Journal of Sociology*, 49 (September, 1943), 109–124.

[3] J. A. Harris, "Assortive Mating in Man," *Popular Science Monthly*, 80 (1912) 476–492. This is the earliest review in the literature that tries to give a scientific explanation of the question of who marries whom. The studies reviewed primarily dealt with physical characteristics: deafness, health, longevity, age, stature, cephalic index, hair and eye color.

[4] Harold E. Jones, "Homogamy in Intellectual Abilities," *American Journal of Sociology*, 35 (1929) 369–382; E. L. Kelly "Psychological Factors in Assortive Mating," *Psychological Bulletin*, 37 (1940), 493 and 576; Helen M. Richardson, "Studies of Mental Resemblance Between Husbands and Wives and Between Friends," *Psychological Bulletin*, 36 (1939) 104–120.

[5] Bessie B. Wessel, "Comparative Rates of Intermarriage Among Different Nationalities in the United States," *Eugenical News*, 15 (1930), 105–107; Bessie B. Wessel, *An Ethnic Survey of Woonsocket, R.I.*, Chicago: University of Chicago Press, 1931; James H. S. Bossard, "Nationality and Nativity as Factors in Marriage," *American Sociological Review*, 4 (December, 1939), 792–798; Ruby Jo Reeves, *Marriages in New Haven since 1870 Statistically Analyzed and Culturally Interpreted*, doctoral dissertation Yale University (unpublished), 1938; Ruby Jo Reeves Kennedy, "Single or Triple Melting-Pot? Intermarriage Trends in New Haven, 1870–1940," *American Journal of Sociology*, 39 (January, 1944), 331–339; Milton L. Barron, *Intermarriage in a New England Industrial Community*, Syracuse: Syracuse University Press, 1946. Barron has a good bibliography of studies in this area, pp. 355–366.

[6] James H. S. Bossard, "Residential Propinquity as a Factor in Marriage Selection," *American Journal of Sociology*, 38 (1932), 219–224; Maurice R. Davie and Ruby Jo Reeves, "Propinquity in Residence Before Marriage," *American Journal of Sociology*, 44 (1939), 510–517; Ruby Jo Reeves Kennedy, "Pre-Marital Residential Propinquity and Ethnic Endogamy," *American Journal of Sociology*, 48 (March, 1943), 580–584; John S. Ellsworth, Jr., "The Relationship of Population Density to Residential Propinquity as a Factor in Marriage Selection," *American Sociological Review*, 13 (August, 1948), 444–448.

[7] Romanzo Adams, *Interracial Marriage in Hawaii*, New York: The Macmillan Co., 1937; Otto Klineberg, *Characteristics of the American Negro*, New York: Harper & Bros., 1944, especially Part V where Negro-white intermarriage and the restrictions on it imposed by law are discussed; Ulysses G. Weatherly, "Race and Marriage," *American Journal of Soci-*

ology, 15 (1910), 433–453; Robert K. Merton, "Intermarriage and the Social Structure," *Psychiatry*, 4 (August, 1941), 371–374; Constantine Panunzio, "Intermarriage in Los Angeles, 1924–1933," *American Journal of Sociology*, 47 (March, 1942), 399–401.

[8] Reuben R. Resnick, "Some Sociological Aspects of Intermarriage of Jew and Non-Jew," *Social Forces*, 12 (October, 1933), 94–102; J. S. Slotkin, "Jewish-Gentile Intermarriage in Chicago," *American Sociological Review*, 7 (February, 1942), 34–39; Ruby Jo Reeves Kennedy, "Single or Triple Melting-Pot?" *op. cit.*

[9] Richard Centers, "Marital Selection and Occupational Strata," *American Journal of Sociology*, 54 (May, 1949), 530–535; Donald M. Marvin, "Occupational Propinquity as a Factor in Marriage Selection," *Publications of the American Statistical Association*, 16 (September, 1918), 131–156; Meyer F. Nimkoff, "Occupational Factors and Marriage," *American Journal of Sociology*, 49 (November, 1943), 248–254.

[10] Walter C. McKain, Jr., and C. Arnold Anderson, "Assortive Mating in Prosperity and Depression," *Sociology and Social Research*, 21 (May–June, 1937), 411–418; E. W. Burgess and Paul Wallin, "Homogamy in Social Characteristics," *American Journal of Sociology*, 49 (September, 1943), 109–124.

[11] For purposes of this paper we shall rely upon tests of significance and measures of association to tell us what cultural factors are of greater or lesser importance in the determination of who marries whom.

[12] Eighty-seven per cent of the interviewing was done by senior undergraduates and graduate students, 5 per cent by an assistant, and 8 per cent by the writer. Six per cent of the interviews were checked for reliability from one month to four months after the original interview.

[13] The principal reasons for this deviation were (1) twice as many older couples refused to be interviewed as those below fifty years of age, and (2) the age gap between interviewers and potential interviewees influenced the situation.

[14] R. J. R. Kennedy, "Single or Triple Melting-Pot? Intermarriage Trends in New Haven, 1870–1940," *op. cit.*

[15] Our discussion on this and subsequent points includes only white marriages where the religion of the couple and of their four parents was known. Moreover, the tabular materials include only white cases where the specific data called for by the table were complete. "Unknown" cases were eliminated in particular instances.

[16] The religious affiliation of marital partners in the present and parental generations was tested for significance; none was found; $X^2 = 6.7015$ with 8 degrees of freedom.

[17] E. W. Burgess and Paul Wallin, *op. cit.*, p. 115.

[18] We are excluding Negroes from our discussion.

[19] For a discussion of this theory see Ruby Jo Reeves Kennedy, "Single or Triple Melting Pot? Intermarriage Trends in New Haven, 1870–1940," *op. cit.*

[20] The index of class position used here was developed by Maurice R. Davie on the basis of the ecological analysis he had made of the city of New Haven. Davie has ranked the 22 natural ecological areas that are primarily residential into six classes. Class I is the best and Class VI the worst type of residential area. For a discussion of the project on which these ratings are made, see Maurice R. Davie, "The Patterns of Urban Growth," *Studies in the Science of Society*, G. P. Murdock, ed., New Haven, 1937, pp. 133–161.

SOCIAL-CLASS ENDOGAMY

Problem

"Who marries whom" is of perennial individual interest and also fulfills important functions for the society (Goode, 1959). In American society there are conflicting values concerning a desirable marriage, and conflicting functions which we expect to see fulfilled by a marital arrangement. On the one hand, we stress the importance of similarity of background and interests. This would imply marrying someone of one's own social class and religion. At the same time, we value individual choice and being in love, and we also approve of marrying upward in the social scale.

In this laboratory problem, we will determine the extent to which people in our sample marry within their own class and then check to see if our findings are similar to those of Hollingshead's study.

The socioeconomic-class position of women in our society is primarily based on that of the head of the household in which the woman resides: the father before marriage, and the husband after marriage. Therefore, in this study we will use the occupational classification of the respondent's maternal grandfather to determine the social-class status of the woman at the time of her marriage.

Hypothesis

From your reading and other observations, estimate the proportions of women from white-collar, farm, and blue-collar families who have married someone from the same class, from a higher class, and from a lower class.

Empirical Indicators for Problem 11

24. **What was your father's occupation at the time you graduated from high school, or what was it before his retirement (please specify)?**

_____

In addition please circle the answer category which best fits his occupation.
   1 Professional (architect, chemist, doctor, etc.) or managerial position (department head, postmaster, police chief, etc.)
   2 Proprietor, except farm (i.e., owner of a business)
   3 Clerical or sales position
   4 Farmer (owner-operator or renter)
   5 Skilled workman or foreman (machinist, carpenter, etc.)
   6 Semiskilled or unskilled workman (truck driver, factory worker, etc.)
   7 Homemaker, or not employed outside the home
   + Don't know

34. **What is your mother's father's occupation or what was it before his retirement (please specify)?**

_____

In addition please circle the answer category which best fits his occupation.
   1 Professional (architect, chemist, doctor, etc.) or managerial position (department head, postmaster, police chief, etc.)
   2 Proprietor, except farm (i.e., owner of a business)
   3 Clerical or sales position
   4 Farmer (owner-operator or renter)
   5 Skilled workman or foreman (machinist, carpenter, etc.)
   6 Semiskilled or unskilled workman (truck driver, factory worker, etc.)
   7 Homemaker, or not employed outside the home
   + Don't know

Data Analysis

1. _Sort_ the code sheets in your sample into three groups representing the social class of the wife. Use the occupational classification of the mother's father (Box 34), combined as follows, to give you the social class of the wife before marriage:

> White-collar = 1, 2, & 3
> Farm   = 4
> Blue-collar = 5 & 6

2. _Tabulate_ on Table 1 the occupational classification of the man each of these women married, using the scores coded in Box 24.

3. _Compute_ the percentages for each type of marriage, using the percentage tables in Appendix D.

4. _Circle_ the percentages for marriages in which the husband and wife are from the same social class.

Laboratory Report

This research (and also the research covered by Problem 12) brings out clearly the limitations of considering one factor a _cause_, and another a _consequence_, if the data are cross-sectional rather than experimental. In this case it is impossible to tell whether men seek women of the same socioeconomic status as marital partners, or the reverse, or, most likely, both. Consequently, the designation of the socioeconomic status of one or the other as "independent" is arbitrary.

Give special attention to the Discussion. Refer back to the outline in Appendix B to see what should go into this section. Be sure to include a discussion of the possible reasons underlying the differences found, and, if your hypothesis is not supported by your findings, discuss the reasons why.

REFERENCES

Goode, W. J. "The Theoretical Importance of Love," _American Sociological Review_, 24, (1959), pp. 38–47. Also reprinted in Marvin B. Sussman, ed. _Sourcebook in Marriage and the Family_. New York: Houghton Mifflin, 1963. Pp. 93–100.

Roth, J., and Peck, R. F. "Social Class and Social Mobility Factors Related to Marital Adjustment," _American Sociological Review_, 16 (1951), pp. 478–487. Also reprinted in Robert F. Winch, Robert McGinnis, and Herbert R. Barringer, eds. _Selected Studies in Marriage and the Family_. New York: Holt, Rinehart and Winston, 1962. Pp. 560–572.

Thomas, J. L. "The Factor of Religion in the Selection of Marriage Mates," _American Sociological Review_, 16 (1951), pp. 487–492. Also reprinted in Marvin B. Sussman, ed. _Sourcebook in Marriage and the Family_. New York: Houghton Mifflin, 1963. Pp. 108–111.

SECTION/COURSE NO._____ DATE_____ NAME_____

Social Class of Wife by Social Class of Husband

Social Class of Husband (Box 24)	Social Class of Wife (Box 34)					
	White-Collar (Box 34 = 1, 2, & 3)		Farm (Box 34 = 4)		Blue-Collar (Box 34 = 5 & 6)	
	f	%	f	%	f	%
White-collar (1, 2, & 3)						
Farm (4)						
Blue-collar (5 & 6)						
TOTAL		100%		100%		100%
No answer		✕		✕		✕

SECTION/COURSE NO._____ DATE_____ NAME_____

Social-Class Endogamy

HYPOTHESIS: _____

_____

_____

_____

_____

_____

SAMPLE: _____

_____

_____

_____

INDEPENDENT VARIABLE: _____

_____

_____

_____

_____

DEPENDENT VARIABLE: _____

_____

_____

_____

_____

_____

OTHER FACTORS: _____

_____

_____

_____

SUMMARY OF FINDINGS: _____

_____

_____

_____

_____

_____

_____

_____

_____

_____

DISCUSSION: _____

_____

_____

_____

_____

_____

_____

_____

_____

_____

_____

_____

_____

_____

A NEED-BASED THEORY OF MATE-SELECTION

Robert F. Winch

We can now set forth the three basic propositions of the theory of complementary needs in mate-selection:

1. *In mate-selection each individual seeks within his or her field of eligibles for that person who gives the greatest promise of providing him or her with maximum need-gratification.*
2. *There is a set of needs such that if person A behaves in a manner determined by a high degree of need X, A's behavior will prove gratifying to the need Y in a second person, B.*
3. *These two needs, X and Y, in the two persons, A and B, are said to be complementary if:*
   a. Type I complementariness: *X and Y are the same need, and the need is present to a low degree in B.*
   b. Type II complementariness: *X and Y are different needs. In this case specific predictions are made about selected pairs of needs. That is, taking account of the particular X, with respect to some Y's it is predicted that B will*

have a high degree and with respect to others that B will have a low degree.

An example of Type I complementariness: if one spouse, X, is high on the need to receive recognition, it would be predicted that the other spouse, Y, would be low on that need. An example of Type II complementariness: if one spouse is high on the need to be dominant, it would be predicted that the other would be high on the need to give deference. An obvious task in developing the theory is to be able to make the specific predictions involved in Type II complementariness. The types of complementary mating hypothesized in the next section constitute a bit of progress toward this goal.

. . . The degree to which the theory of complementary needs will be operative in any culture is contingent upon the degree to which the interpersonal relationship in marriage is evaluated as an important source of need-gratification. Where such meaning is given to marriage, as in America, it is consistent that there should be individual choice of mates and a long period of dating, courtship, and engagement during which to test personalities of potential mates. By contrast, in traditional China, where the congeniality

Reprinted by permission of the author and the publisher from Robert F. Winch, *The Modern Family,* revised edition, New York: Holt, Rinehart and Winston, 1963, pp. 585–603. Footnotes have been renumbered consecutively.

group of men was emphasized, marriages were arranged by the families—frequently between men and women who had never seen each other.

From these and previous observations it is hypothesized that mate-selection proceeds on the basis of complementary needs only under the following societal-cultural conditions:

1. The marital relationship must be culturally defined as a rich potential source of gratification.
2. The choice of mates must be voluntary (i.e., not arranged) and bilateral (i.e., both man and woman must possess at least the power of veto).
3. There must be provision for, and preferably encouragement of, premarital interaction between men and women in order to provide the opportunity for testing out personalities of a variety of potential mates.

It has been asserted that some needs are experienced unconsciously. This appears to be true of needs involved in social interaction. After some dating experience, for example, a boy will realize that with some girls he enjoys himself, can act "naturally," and so on, but that with others he feels strained or bored. It is for this reason that one needs to "test" a variety of personalities—to determine with what persons and with what types of persons one "feels comfortable" and with what persons and types one does not. Hence where the marital relationship is defined as potentially gratifying, as in this country, the practice of dating is functionally important in mate-selection.

The Status of the Theory

In one form or another the idea of complementary attraction can be traced back through the history of Western thought to Plato and Socrates.[1] In the present century the idea has appeared in the writings of Freudians and non-Freudians. A non-Freudian antecedent of the formulation is Durkheim, who saw attraction in friendship as based upon both similarity and complementariness of the personalities of friends. After remarking that we like those who think and feel as we do, he continues that since each of us lacks something, we are attracted to those who make up for our insufficiencies and make us feel less incomplete and with whom for this reason the relationship results in a "true exchange of services. One urges on, another consoles; this one advises, that one follows the advice, and it is this apportionment of functions or . . . this division of labor which determines the relations of friendship."[2]

Havelock Ellis, another non-Freudian, spoke of "a harmony, not necessarily an identity, or tastes and interests" as "essential to a complete marriage union,"[3] and Ohmann states that we are attracted to "those whom we need to complete ourselves."[4]

Among the followers of Freud are Flugel, who believes that one is attracted to a person upon whom one projects one's ego-ideal, and Benedek, who suggests that lovers exchange ego-ideals.[5] And asserting that in love there is compensation for not attaining the ego-ideal, Reik observes that we "jump into" rather than "fall in" love.[6]

Clinical corroboration of the principle of complementary mate-selection has been appearing in the literature for some years.[7] Of course the subjects of clinical study are not usually the most adjusted persons in the society, and for this reason the evidence might be thought of as supporting what we might call a "theory of complementary neuroses." Numerous writers of a psychoanalytic orientation have presented evidence in support of a complementary mate-selective process. For example, Mittelmann proposes five types of complementary relationship that he says he has seen in his practice:

1. A dominant and aggressive person married to a submissive and masochistic person.
2. An emotionally detached person married to one who craves affection.
3. A pair engaged in continuous rivalry for aggressive dominance.
4. A helpless and dependent person married to an endlessly supportive mate.
5. A person who vacillates between self-assertion and dependency married to one who vacillates between unsatisfied need for affection and giving support and help.[8]

In his unrestrained style Bergler tells us that "the neurosis of the woman complements the neurosis of the man she chooses, and vice versa." A masochistic woman, he says, is not conscious of her wish to be treated badly, nor is the "castrating" woman of her wish for an impotent man. Both will think of themselves as unlucky in mate-selection. "But 'luck' is not involved; unconscious choice is."[9]

In 1950 the author inaugurated a study to test the theory of complementary needs in mate-selection. The subjects of the study were 25 young couples who had been married less than two years and an average of one year. Husbands and wives were seen separately and simultaneously. They were given two interviews and a test. One interview was designed to elicit responses that would reveal the strengths and modes of expression of various needs. In the other interview they were asked to give an account of emotionally and developmentally meaningful experiences in their lives. The test was the Thematic Apperception Test.

Research on this kind of topic is difficult. The variables pertain to motivation. In laboratory experiments on motivation it is possible to deprive rats of food for a specified period, to interpret the deprivation as hunger drive, to present the animals with some task, and then to compare such performances with those made after eating, i.e., under conditions of "high drive" and "low drive." With respect to the kinds of needs conceived to be relevant to mate-selection such experimental manipulation of human subjects is hardly feasible in a democratic society. For this reason considerable time was spent in devising interview questions for the study of complementary needs, and hundreds of man-hours were devoted to the analysis of the responses of each subject. The outcomes of this intensive analysis were stated in both verbal and quantitative terms.

The central question of the quantitative analysis was whether or not the data supported the theory. The directions of 388 correlations were predicted in accordance with the concepts of Type I and Type II complementariness as set forth above. If nothing but chance was determining the rated levels of the needs in the pairs of spouses, it would be expected that approximately half of the correlations would come out in the predicted direction and half in the opposite direction; if some principle contrary to complementariness was operating, it would be expected that more than half of the correlations would take the sign opposite from that predicted. It turned out that 66 percent of the correlations showed the hypothesized sign, and the results were interpreted as supporting the theory of complementary needs in mate-selection.

Having been satisfied that the evidence pointed in the direction of the hypothesis, the writer then undertook the next step in the inquiry—to discover any new ideas in the data and thereby to refine the statement of the theory. To this end the writer undertook an intensive review of all the cases in a search for processes of mate-selection. Since this was not a hypothesis-oriented procedure but a hypothesis-seeking operation, whatever was found must be presented not as fact but as hypothesis.

Two principles, or dimensions, of mate-selection seemed to be running through most, but not all, of the cases. With respect to one of these dimensions it appeared that if one of the spouses was conspicuously nurturant, the other liked to receive nurturant care or, as it came to be called, the latter was high on receptivity. With respect to the other dimension it appeared that if one spouse was highly dominant, the other was likely to be submissive. Since most of the 25 couples showed both of these dimensions, it was possible to

cross-classify these couples in terms of the two dimensions. When this was done, a fourfold typology was derived with the following characteristics and nomenclature:

	Husband— Nurturant Wife— Receptive	Husband— Receptive Wife— Nurturant
Husband— Dominant Wife— Submissive	Ibsenian (from *A Doll's House*)	Master-and- Servant-Girl
Husband— Submissive Wife— Dominant	Thurberian	Mother-Son

Cases illustrating these four types and hypotheses concerning them appear in *Mate-Selection*, Chapters 7–11.[10]

The alert reader may have noticed something familiar about the dimensions underlying the four types of complementary mating: they are reminiscent of the parental functions—nurturance and control—that have constituted a major basis for the analysis of parent-child relations in Part V [of this book]. This suggests that the two dimensions are important not only in parent-child relations but also in marital and no doubt in other relationships that involve emotional gratification. It will also be noted that there are two types—Ibsenian and Mother-Son in which one spouse nurtures and dominates the other and thus, to use Ackerman's term,[11] "parentifies" the other. In the other two types there is not a clear-cut parent-child relationship.[12]

Immediately upon the recognition that the theory of complementary needs in mate-selection involves two dimensions whose names are similar to those of the two parental functions, there arises the question as to whether we have stumbled upon a tautology involving mate-selection and the parental functions and perhaps the function of emotional gratification as well. If we are using three different terms to refer to the same phenomenon, theoretical parsimony demands that we rid our system of the superfluous concepts. To illuminate this question let us make a few observations about mate-selection, emotional gratification, and the parental functions.

With respect to the hypothesized dimensions of mate-selection let us notice that they are presented as motives of the individual, which are subject to interindividual variation. The writer's research suggests that each individual may be seen as having some degree of need with respect to giving and/or receiving each of the parental functions. Furthermore, it has not been proposed that this formulation exhausts the motivational dimensions involved in mate-selection.

Let us turn to emotional gratification. Since in the setting under consideration mate-selection is based on love, and since love is defined as the positive emotion associated with experienced and/or anticipated gratifications coming from the behavior of the other (i.e., from the love-object), and since there is evidence that such love is based on the dimensions of complementariness, there is reason to think that nurturance-receptivity and dominance-submissiveness are dimensions relevant to the function of emotional gratification within the marital relationship. Does this mean, to use Ackerman's term, that according to the present formulation all the love involved in mate-selection—and indeed in marital interaction—implies or envisages the "parentifying" of one spouse by the other? Such is not the implication. It is true that two of the four types (Mother-Son and Ibsenian) involve parent-child relationships, but of course the other two do not. Moreover, the emotional gratification to be derived from the marital and from the parent-child relationships differ importantly from each other in that (1) the former includes but the latter prohibits sexual gratification, and (2) the kinds of behavior involved in nurturing and controlling vary greatly with the age of the object.

The parental functions are not, of course, individual motives but are social functions, i.e., activities and products of those activities that the family—because of its structure and its basic societal function —becomes obliged to carry out.

Tentatively, then, the answer to the question posed several paragraphs above is that the parental functions, the function of emotional gratification, and love-based mate-selection have in common the dimensions of nurturance and control. It is premature, however, to conclude that we are talking about only a single phenomenon because each of the three will undoubtedly be found to have elements not common to the others, and we are using the concepts of nurturance and control at two levels of analysis—the sociological and the psychological.

It had been hoped at the inception of the study that during the course of the research some procedure would be developed that would eliminate or reduce the requirement for clinical judgments, and which would therefore be more reliable and less time-consuming. In this effort the project was not successful. Because of the difficulty and expense of gathering and analyzing the data it seems unlikely that the study will ever be replicated—a likelihood that the writer views sadly.[13]

The Case of Bill and Mary Carter[14]

After having spent several years in military service Bill Carter is finishing college. Mary, his wife, is out of college and is teaching school. Bill is a tall, slender chap of twenty-two. He does not appear to be very athletic. The interviewer reports him as mild, shy, and lacking in fire. Bill says that he looks tough (which hardly conforms with the interviewer's impression), but that really he isn't. He sees himself as "quiet but not withdrawn." He has few friends. In a group he likes to stand back, and he engages in no behavior that will bring him the group's spontaneous attention. On the other hand, he likes to receive recognition for any achievements. As the foregoing suggests, Bill has something of a "problem" with respect to the matter of self-expression. A clue as to why Bill has difficulty in expressing himself is seen in his statement that "I have a mild temper—too mild sometimes. I'm inclined to criticize myself and I don't assert myself enough to other people."

It appears that Bill inhibits himself in what he says to others because he fears that what he will say will be hostile, and he fears to express hostility to other people. There is evidence, moreover, that these fears have resulted in a repression of his anger and hostility, and hence that his inhibition in expression functions at an unconscious level. Customarily such a pattern suggests that the person has learned that angry outbursts will bring upon him dire and painful consequences. In Bill's case this interpretation is corroborated by a story he told in the Thematic Apperception Test.[15] In this picture a young woman has her hand on the arm of a young man who seems about to leave her. Bill said: "She is trying to stop him from doing something of a violent nature. . . . She's trying to dissuade him from doing that because it would hurt him more than it would hurt the other person."

Although our information about Bill is not sufficiently comprehensive to give us a completely satisfactory explanation of how his personality developed, some light will be shed by considering his childhood and the nature of his relations with his parents.

Bill's recollection of his mother as she appeared in his childhood is that she was attractive and demonstrative. She was given to strenuous exertion and self-sacrifice on behalf of her children. (Bill has a younger sister.) Bill feels that the exertions and the self-sacrifice were somewhat exaggerated and were used by his mother as a basis for demanding the love and affection of her children. His mother was a very dominant person and apparently controlled Bill and his sister, and his father as well. Bill thinks that his mother felt "unloved," especially during menopause, and that his father did not satisfy her sexually. Although in childhood he felt closer to his mother than to his father, he has come to regard her as possessive and demanding, and now prefers his father.

Bill describes his father as intelligent, objective, quiet, considerate, deliberate, yielding, and as filled with self-pity when his mother "imposes on" him. Early in their marriage there was considerable friction between Bill's parents; they only spoke to each other for two of the first five weeks they were married. Bill admires his father's composure but changes his mind when he sees what "happens to" his father because of it. By this Bill is apparently referring to his mother's behavior in "imposing on" his father and his father's behavior in submitting and in showing self-pity.

Bill is a conformist. Like many other people, he appears to use conformity as a technique for obtaining recognition from figures in authority. At one time in his boyhood Bill's parents suggested that it would be helpful to the family if he would earn his spending money. Shortly thereafter he started selling newspapers. He built up an impressive record and worked so hard at this endeavor that his parents subsequently admonished him against overwork. When asked for his earliest memories, Bill recounted two incidents (one from the sixth grade, and the other from the first grade), when his teachers registered marked approval of his performance in the classroom. Currently he is quite gratified when his professors compliment him on his work and ability.

Bill's consistent pattern of seeking recognition from persons of authority, plus the (for him) strongly ambivalent feelings toward his mother, suggest that in early childhood he greatly desired her approval and affection. While overtly and superficially demonstrative and affectionate, however, Bill's mother appears to have been incapable of giving him the kind of affectionate approval he sought. For this reason we may suspect that she continually frustrated him and that he tried harder and harder to earn her love.

His report that his mother felt "unloved" and that she "demanded" affection from her children suggests that she was very sensitive to any expression of criticism or hostility. To achieve her acceptance, therefore, Bill undoubtedly learned to inhibit, and indeed to repress, his expressions of hostility. As we shall see, the nature of Bill's interaction with Mary, his wife, demonstrates quite conclusively that Bill has strong unconscious feelings of hostility. It seems probable that he has possessed such feelings most of his life. Today he seldom criticizes anyone or even entertains consciously hostile thoughts. As not infrequently happens, Bill has gone to the extremity of unconsciously directing his hostility toward himself. Accordingly, he has been inhibited in his quest for recognition by a fear of competing with others and of the possibility of incurring their hostility. In high school Bill generally received good grades, but once he nearly failed a civics course; on this occasion he became very depressed and considered suicide. He tends to regard any criticism of himself as warranted and to assume the blame for anything that goes wrong.[16]

In summary form our interpretation of the developmental dynamics in Bill's case is as follows. In childhood he greatly desired his mother's approval, love, and recognition. This she did not (and probably could not) give. From these circumstances flowed two important consequences: one concerns his striving behavior, and the other, his hostility. He tried harder and harder to earn her love through his accomplishments, and subsequently generalized this drive so that it related to other figures of authority. He inhibited his tendency to express hostility, repressed it into unconsciousness, and ultimately directed it toward himself. These dynamic trends resulted in the Bill we now see: earnest and hard working but noncompetitive; shy, diffident, nonhostile in thought and nonaggressive in speech and manner; self-abasing and self-blaming when "blame" is in order.

Mary, Bill's wife, is a very different sort of person. She is of medium height and weight, has dark hair, is generally attractive and very neatly groomed. She speaks energetically and vivaciously, almost dramatically. She laughs frequently and gives the impression of being secure—almost oversecure—in her beliefs. Having a quite good opinion of herself and her abilities, Mary has never been one to assume blame without due cause. She is a somewhat hostile person and generally expresses it when aroused. She is a person who "gets things off her chest."

From childhood Mary's need for recognition has been high. She studied music and greatly enjoyed performing in recitals. She was successful in dramatics in school. She enjoys working in organizations and likes positions of authority and responsibility. She has considerable need to dominate and derives gratification for this need from her work with children. Among the attractions of teaching is the obligation (as she sees it) to impart a philosophy to the children—to make them stand up and take it on the chin when they do something wrong, to teach them not to be prejudiced against each other's race and religion. For her, the role of teacher is definitely one of superordination and giving directions.

Mary describes her mother as talented, intelligent, hyperactive, dominating, and very adequate in providing for her children's physical needs. Her mother was decidedly less adequate in providing her children with sympathetic understanding. (Mary has two sisters: one older, and one younger than herself.) When Mary was a child, she liked her mother better than her father, and it is clear that Mary has formed a similar identification with her. Mary says: "When I was a kid, I just wanted to be another Mama . . . like my mother." Despite the identification there is much evidence that Mary feels quite hostile toward her mother. Her mother now "drives her to a frazzle." As in the case of Bill, it appears that her mother frustrated her affectional needs. Mary's position in the family was quite different from Bill's, however, for she was the second of three girls, and she regarded both her sisters as more talented than herself. In this situation there was undoubtedly less incentive than in Bill's case to seek the mother's approval through quiet achievement. Instead, Mary adjusted by becoming hyperactive, noisy, talkative, and generally engaging in behavior that seemed unsubtly designed to get attention.

As Mary describes the situation, her father was a relatively meaningless figure during Mary's childhood. Her father is vocationally quite successful but has been very submissive to her mother. She sees her father as easygoing, for otherwise "no one could live with Mother without being ready for an institution." Although Mary thinks of her mother as having been the preferred parent in childhood, she has shifted her preference to her father. The shift apparently began to take place as her father took more notice of her during adolescence. Mary sees herself as the most tomboyish of the three girls, regards herself as her father's son-substitute, and currently as her father's favorite. Today she seems to have quite a strong attachment to him, but still is critical of him for "allowing Mother to walk over him."

Dynamically, Mary seems somewhat less complicated than Bill. Like Bill she has a strong need for recognition, but unlike him she expresses the need much more directly. In both cases it appears that the strength of the need resulted from experiences with frustrating mothers. The differences in the attending circumstances, however, can be seen as leading to the quite different outcomes. Bill identified with his quiet, submissive father; Mary, with her hyperactive, dominating mother. Bill's younger sister apparently did not overshadow Bill with her achievements; both of Mary's sisters were more talented.

We may anticipate the discussion of cultural and psychic definitions of the ideal mate[17] by noting that both Bill and Mary had fantasies of their ideal mates that were quite different from the persons whom they actually married. Bill's early conception of the ideal mate was a girl who would be "blonde and real sweet and quiet." In early adolescence Mary conceived of her ideal as looking "like a movie star practically," but "after tussling with a few who were extremely good-looking and therefore had women falling all over them and were quite spoiled, I suddenly decided that I didn't like that at all. It dawned on me that all these years my mother had been implanting in me the real values you find in a man; he didn't have to be good-looking." From these remarks we can see that neither Bill nor Mary satisfied the other's preconception in appearance, and Mary is certainly not the "real sweet and quiet" type Bill once had in mind. Why did these two get married to each other, and how do they interact with each other? Perhaps we can answer these questions better if we tackle the latter first.

Bill started dating late in his high school career and dated a good deal while in military service. Before meeting Mary he went consistently with only one girl whom he characterized as "a very cute kid but she didn't have any brains . . . she wouldn't even consider college. I couldn't even think of life with her—I would have been miserable. I didn't think I could marry her."

Mary had dated a number of men and was engaged to two before she met Bill. The first of the two was a handsome man in a military uniform who was in a special entertainment unit. Mary remarked: "He liked me in my more glamorous moments, and I'm not glamorous that often. . . . I was too natural and down to earth for him." Mary met the second man at college. He was tall and "sophisticated," although not good-looking. They were engaged after knowing each other for about two months. They planned an early wedding, but in this case the boy decided that he was not in love. One of the things that Mary liked about Bill was that he loved her as she was "naturally." This appears to have two principal meanings: with Bill she did not feel called upon to appear glamorous, and she did not have to inhibit her highly expressive nature.

Mary is clearly more dominant than Bill. In contrast to his wife, who likes positions of responsibility and authority, Bill has no desire to hold office in an organization, and if he were to hold an office, he would prefer not to be president. When Bill got out of the service, he had a negative attitude toward religion and he liked to visit bars. Since meeting Mary, he has taken over her value system; he now goes to church and likes it, and he seldom drinks. She has taught him bridge and an interest in classical music. He concedes that she has had more influence on him than he has had on her.

One of the things that attracted Bill to Mary was the fact that she was outspoken, free in her criticism, and able to express hostility, whereas he could not. Since meeting his wife, however, he has learned to express a bit of his hostility, or, as he phrased it, he has "learned to roar a little." Further evidence that Bill recognizes Mary's influence on him in this regard is that he believes that she "re-created my enthusiasm." The most obvious construction on the latter remark is that she has demonstrated to his satisfaction that he need not inhibit so completely his impulses to express hostility. (From his life history, however, it seems doubtful that he has behaved very "enthusiastically" since early childhood, when he began to repress his hostility.)

In most activities it appears that Mary is the more capable. She regards herself as his superior in all intellectual areas except physics, in which she has no interest and which is his specialty. She believes that she excels him in all card games except gin rummy. They spend considerable time playing cards with each other, and she states that she gives him no quarter in these games because he is old enough to take defeat. Bill regards Mary as his superior in many ways—from card-playing to the way in which she handles people. He had an opportunity to observe her with her pupils at school one day and remarked: "We never had teachers like that when I was in school."

Mary dislikes being alone, and apparently her need of people is the need for an audience. Here Bill fits very adequately into her scheme of things. Bill expresses his admiration of her fire and enthusiasm; he is an attentive audience as she tells of her daily exploits. From time to time he gives her advice when she encounters problems in her work. She is not particularly cognizant of his function as an adviser, however, and it is his respectful attention during their daily conversations rather than his advice that provides her with gratification.

In his relationship with his wife, Bill continues his struggle for recognition. In view of her ability and dominance, he is limited in the techniques he can use to achieve recognition from her. This, however, is not a novel situation for Bill, since for most of his life he has been seeking recognition from persons whom he looks up to—his mother, his grade school teachers, his professors, and so on. There are two techniques he has hit upon with his wife. One is that of being generous and thoughtful with numerous gifts and remembrances; the other is assuming the role of attentive listener.

Now, let us analyze the couple in terms of complementary needs. Since it is clear that both spouses have a high need for recognition, it may appear at first that their needs are mutually contradictory rather than complementary. As soon as we take into account differences in modes of expression and in related needs, however, we can see that their need-patterns are complementary. Bill implements his need for recognition by means of a strong need to achieve as well as to provide Mary with attentions. Mary applauds his capacity for

hard work and registers appreciation of the wide variety of attentions with which he showers her. He does not express his need for recognition in an overt, exhibitionistic fashion. If he did, he would be in competition with her dramatic style of expression. Mary implements her need for recognition by trying to dominate, by seeking deference, and by being the center of attention. Bill is self-abasing and has little need to dominate, and he gives Mary considerable deference for her many talents.

Since any normal life involves interaction with other persons besides one's spouse, we must take account of outside sources of gratification. Bill gets gratification from his work and the achievement it represents, and from professors who compliment him on the quality of his work. Through her general ability and her success in her profession Mary receives recognition from her superiors on the job, as well as from the children in her classroom.

Both Bill and Mary have a good deal of hostility. Bill's has been deeply repressed—so much so that he has not customarily even entertained hostile thoughts. Mary expresses hostility readily. Her facility in expression gives her catharsis, and appears to relieve his hostile tensions vicariously. It appears, moveover, that Bill is learning from Mary that such expressions are not always followed by dire consequences. It is this (for him) new idea that appears responsible for his "re-created enthusiasm" and for his learning to "roar a little."

Presently we shall discuss changes in need-patterns of husbands and wives. As long as Bill is unable to express his hostility, he needs as a wife someone who will express it for him. To the extent that he becomes able to express it for himself, his need for an expressive wife diminishes. It is significant, then, that Bill has come to feel that Mary is at times too "enthusiastic" and talkative. We interpreted Mary's expressive behavior as growing out of her childhood, in which she was unsuccessful in getting the amount of attention and affection she desired from her mother. From their account of their marital interaction it appears that Bill is providing her with affection and attention. It is consistent with our interpretation to learn that Mary is now able to take the blame for things more easily than she once could, and further, that Mary agrees with Bill that she is too "enthusiastic" and is cooperating in his campaign to "tone her down."

Some Implications of the Theory of Complementary Needs

The theory suggests several questions useful to consider: (1) Granting that there is a demonstrable tendency for men and women to select each other as mates on this basis under certain societal-cultural conditions, does it follow that where there is opportunity for choice of associates in other types of situation, it will occur on this basis? (2) What does the theory assume or imply about changes in need-patterns of spouses? (3) What implications has the theory for marital counseling? (4) Has the theory any implications for marital happiness? In particular, is it implied that the most complementary couples are necessarily the happiest? Let us consider these questions in order.

Imagine yourself about to undertake a dangerous mission as a guerrilla soldier. From a heterogenous platoon that includes your best friend, who is a mediocre soldier, you are permitted to select one companion to accompany you. On what basis will you choose? Will you select the person with whom you are most congenial, the one with whom you like to drink beer and shoot the breeze? Or will you choose the most skilled and trusted soldier in the platoon even though you and he have little in common? On reflection you will probably decide that you will have little opportunity for good conversation but will have much need of skilled help in detecting, avoiding, and, if necessary, destroying the enemy. More generally, this implies that to the degree that a social group is functional, it is the nature of the function rather than complementariness of needs, the relevance of the person's skills to the task rather than his congeniality, that will dictate the selection of recruits to the group. French has conducted a study that confirms this theoretical argument. She found that subjects having a high degree of achievement motivation selected for work partners competent nonfriends; those with high affiliation motivation selected the less competent friends as work partners.[18]

What does the theory assume about changes in needs? In particular does it assume that if a person loses a mate through whatever cause and remarries, he or she will seek to duplicate exactly the first spouse? The answer is not necessarily implied in the theory of complementary needs in mate-selection because the theory does not have a sufficiently developed theory of personality. The writer's view is that as people go through a variety of experiences, they learn and they adapt, with the result that their behaviors change, but still there are discernible continuities. Some theories of personality emphasize the changes; others, the continuities. It seems feasible to take note of both. Let us consider an example. At the time we saw the Carters (described earlier in this chapter) they had a Thurberian complementariness. Let us look at Bill's situation then and in the future. Bill had found security and gratification in a directive and expressive wife. What would happen in, say, twenty years? By that time it seems likely that Bill would have become a professional success; he had been working hard and had received recognition for his ability. It seems doubtful that twenty years later Bill would need, or indeed be able to tolerate, as much directiveness or expressiveness as was emitted by the Mary we met. (We remember that he had already begun to "quiet her down" and to "roar a bit" himself.) And so if Bill were to lose Mary, we have some notion of the probable ways in which the second Mrs. Carter would differ from the first.[19]

What does the theory imply for marital counseling? The chief implication is that when confronted with a person or couple seeking a divorce, the theory suggests to the counselor that he check the relationship for the elements of complementariness that initially brought them together. Of course, there is no assurance that the discovery of the original elements of complementariness will prove any magic key to the restoration of connubial bliss, but it does point to what, at one time at least, was a bond between man and wife. As Martha Winch says, moreover, the theory stimulates the counselor to consider and to work with the present motivations of the spouses rather than to try to reshape them along more conventional lines.[20]

If a couple is complementarily mated, does the theory imply that they will be happy together? Very simply and despite misinterpretations to the contrary, *no!* Given some information about the needs of one person, the theory undertakes to predict the kind of mate the first person will select. It is a theory of mate-selection. It foresees that complementarily mated couples can be happy or unhappy. The grounds for unhappiness are apparent in such remarks as those of Bergler above (page 178): a very masochistic woman is likely to select a sadist for a husband. Presumably such a marriage will be quite conflictful, filled with ambivalence, and may well lead to an early break in the relationship. Accordingly there is no prediction that the more complementary the couple, the happier they will be. Yet some interpreters of the theory seem to believe that its purpose is to predict or to explain happiness.[21]

NOTES

[1] A consideration of some of the intellectual antecedents including the distinction between *agape* and *eros* appears in [Robert F. Winch, *Mate-Selection: A Study of Complementary Needs* (New York: Harper & Row, 1958)], chap. 3.

[2] Emile Durkheim, *The Division of Labor in Society* (translated by George Simpson; New York: Free Press, 1947), p. 56.

[3] Havelock Ellis, *Psychology of Sex* (New York: New American Library, Mentor ed., 1954), p. 198.

[4] [O. Ohmann, "The Psychology of Attraction," chap. 2 in H. M. Jordan (ed.), *You and Marriage* (New York: Wiley, 1942), p. 15].

[5] [J. C.] Flugel, [*The Psycho-Analytic Study of the Family* (London: Hogarth, 1921),] chap. 13; [Therese] Benedek, [*Insight and Personality Adjustment* (New York: Ronald, 1946),] p. 25.

[6] [Theodor Reik, *A Psychologist Looks at Love* (New York: Holt, Rinehart and Winston, 1944),] p. 40.

[7] The logical status of clinical evidence is discussed in the section on "Some Studies Bearing on the Broad Conception of Nurturance" in Chapter 13 of [Winch, *The Modern Family*] and in Chapter 1 of Robert F. Winch, Robert McGinnis, and Herbert R. Barringer (eds.), *Selected Studies in Marriage and the Family* (rev. ed.; New York: Holt, Rinehart and Winston, 1962).

[8] Bela Mittelmann, "Analysis of Reciprocal Neurotic Patterns in Family Relationships," in Victor W. Eisenstein (ed.), *Neurotic Interaction in Marriage* (New York: Basic Books, 1956), pp. 81–100, esp. p. 98.

[9] Edmund Bergler and W. S. Kroger, *Kinsey's Myth of Female Sexuality: The Medical Facts* (New York: Grune & Stratton, 1954), pp. 92–93.

[10] Some thoughts on the dominance of one spouse by the other appear in Chapter 11 in *Mate-Selection* under the heading "The Pygmalion Hypothesis." It is possible that the couples who were not classifiable into one or both of the above dichotomies were near the means of the distributions along one or both dimensions.

[11] Nathan W. Ackerman, *The Psychodynamics of Family Life: Diagnosis and Treatment of Family Relationships* (New York: Basic Books, 1958).

[12] There is evidence of a convergence on nurturance and control (stated in various terms) as the two basic dimensions of interpersonal behavior and of the socially relevant elements of personality. Leary has developed a test of 16 interpersonal variables of personality and has concluded that the 16 variables can be reduced to dominance (our control) and love (our nurturance).—Timothy Leary, *Interpersonal Diagnosis of Personality: A Functional Theory and Methodology for Personality Evaluation* (New York: Ronald, 1957), p. 69. Couch has factor-analyzed the Leary test and agrees that the two factors just mentioned are the principal ones in that test. Couch calls them "interpersonal dominance" and "interpersonal affect," respectively, and he found these same factors to be the principal factors in the analysis of many other types of interpersonal behavioral and test data.—Arthur Stephen Couch, "Psychological Determinants of Interpersonal Behavior." Unpublished doctoral dissertation, Harvard University, 1960, pp. 235 and 554. Schaefer has used a related but different mode of analysis (the Guttman circumplex model) on several empirical studies of maternal behavior and has found two major dimensions that he has called "love vs. hostility" (our nurturance) and "autonomy vs. control" (our control).—Earl S. Schaefer, "A Circumplex Model for Maternal Behavior," *Journal of Abnormal and Social Psychology*, 59: 226–235 (1959). This convergence of results may mean that these are two fundamental dimensions of human interaction or that they are two prevalent and pervasive ideas in the heads of contemporary social psychologists.

[13] Just as the theory of complementary needs was coming to be known, there appeared in the literature a test with an original and attractive feature. This test, the Edwards Personal Preference Schedule, was announced as measuring 15 needs. Its attractive feature was that it was represented as controlling for an important type of response set—"social desirability"—by means of requiring the subject to choose between paired items of presumably matched social desirability. Unfortunately for the replication of the study of complementary needs the attractiveness of a quickly administered and routinely scored test purporting to measure needs lured some investigators away from the replication of the original study. (Of course, the difficulty and cost of the original procedures might have dissuaded them from real replication.) Most of the few correlations found in these studies that were large enough to be assessed as statistically significant were interpreted as inconsistent with the theory of complementary needs. Cf. Charles E. Bowerman and Barbara R. Day, "A Test of the Theory of Complementary Needs as Applied to Couples during Courtship," *American Sociological Review*, 21: 602–605 (1956); James A. Schellenberg and Lawrence S. Bee, "A Re-Examination of the Theory of Complementary Needs in Mate Selection," *Marriage and Family Living*, 22: 227–232 (1960); Irwin Katz, Sam Glucksberg, and Robert Krauss, "Need Satisfaction and Edwards PPS Scores in Married Couples," *Journal of Consulting Psychology*, 24: 205–208 (1960); John Allison Blazer, "Complementary Needs and Marital Happiness," Unpublished M.S. thesis, Richmond Professional Institute, College of William and Mary, 1960. Just how valid are the scales in the PPS and what is the degree of matching of social desirability in the pairs of items with respect to the subjects taking the test are questions that remain open. Mixed evidence on validity appears in Vaughn J. Crandall and Anne Preston, "Verbally Expressed Needs and Overt Maternal Behaviors," *Child Development*, 32: 261–270 (1961). Evidence in support of matched social desirability appears in Allen L. Edwards, *The Social Desirability Variable in Personality Assessment and Research* (New York: Holt, Rinehart and Winston, 1957), chap. 7. A study coming to the contrary conclusion is Norman L. Corah, Marvin J. Feldman, Ira S. Cohen, Walter Gruen, Arnold Meadow, and Egan A. Ringwall, "Social Desirability as a Variable in the Edwards Personal Preference Schedule," *Journal of Consulting Psychology*, 22: 70–72 (1958). There are numerous studies that show that people view those they like as having traits similar to their own and those they dislike as being dissimilar to themselves. Cf. F. E. Fiedler, F. J. Blaisdell, and W. G. Warrington, "Unconscious Attitudes and the Dynamics of Sociometric Choice in a Social Group," *Journal of Abnormal and Social Psychology*, 47: 790–796 (1952); and for an extension to perception of persons of opposite sex, Richard M. Lundy, "Self-Perceptions and Descriptions of Opposite Sex Sociometric Choices," *Sociometry*, 19: 272–277 (1956). Unless completely neutralized, therefore, social desirability enters into research results as an artifact and by producing interspousal correlations in the opposite direction masks any effect of complementary mating.

Another study using a different procedure to measure complementariness finds no evidence of complementary matching in a set of college couples considering marriage. When the couples are segregated into those of short- and long-term acquaintance, however, it is found that the former show evidence of matching on consensus in values and the latter on complementariness. This leads the authors of the study to believe that consensus on values is an early "filtering factor" in the mate-selective process of courtship, while complementariness is a "filtering factor" that operates at a later stage.—Alan Kerckhoff and Keith E. Davis, "Value Consensus and Need Complementarity in Mate Selection," *American Sociological Review*, 27: 295–303 (1962).

[14] The reader will appreciate that it is difficult to present a real case honestly and still preserve the anonymity of the subjects. For this reason names and identifying characteristics have been changed. The case record of which this is a digest runs to well over a hundred pages. Because of space limitations not all points of interpretation can be thoroughly documented.

[15] In this test the subject is presented with a series of pictures and is asked to tell a story about each, what the people in the picture are doing, what led up to this situation, what will be the outcome, etc. The response reported here was given to card 4.

[16] If the reader is disposed to ponder on other possible outcomes for Bill, given the conditions prevailing in his childhood, he should bear two considerations in mind that point to the actual outcome as more likely than any other. In the first place, Bill's mother verges on the dominant type of "overprotective" mother of whom D. M. Levy writes in *Maternal Overprotection* (New York: Columbia University Press, 1943); and, in conformity with that author's findings, Bill shows some of the passive-dependent characteristics of the sons of such women. Neither Bill nor his mother, however, is as "abnormal" as the subjects described by Levy. In the second place, by being a quiet, submissive, yielding person, Bill's father presented Bill with an ego-model precisely suited to Bill's problem of adjusting to his mother. It is probable that for some years he competed unconsciously with his father (and no doubt also with his sister) for his mother's favor, and it seems clear that he formed a similar identification with his father.

[17] Cf. pages 641–646 [of Winch, *The Modern Family*].

[18] Elizabeth G. French, "Motivation as a Variable in Work-Partner Selection," *Journal of Abnormal and Social Psychology*, 53: 96–99 (1956). Also relevant are E. P. Hollander and Wilse B. Webb, "Leadership, Followership, and Friendship: An Analysis of Peer Nominations," in Eleanor E. Maccoby, Theodore M. Newcomb, and Eugene L. Hartley (eds.), *Readings in Social Psychology* (3d ed.; New York: Holt, Rinehart and Winston, 1958), pp. 489–496, esp. pp. 490, 494; Philip M. Marcus, "Expressive and Instrumental Groups: Toward a Theory of Group Structure," *American Journal of Sociology*, 66: 54–59 (1960); Theresa Turk and Herman Turk, "Group Interaction in a Formal Setting: The Case of the Triad," *Sociometry*, 25: 48–55 (1962).

[19] Rosow distinguishes the following determinants of changes in a spouse's need-patterns: maturation; marital interaction; new roles both within and outside the family; and successes, shocks, and failures.—Irving Rosow, "Issues in the Concept of Need-Complementarity," *Sociometry*, 20: 216–233 (1957), esp. pp. 230–231. Cf. also *Mate-Selection*, pp. 296–302.

[20] *Mate-Selection*, chap. 16.

[21] Examples: According to Bernard's interpretation of the theory, it is only possible to determine whether or not a couple is complementarily mated by the outcome—success or failure—of the marriage; Simpson repeats Bernard's misinterpretation; and Izard explains that according to the theory of complementary needs "successful marriages are made up of people whose needs and characteristics complement each other."—Jessie Bernard, *Remarriage: A Study of Marriage* (New York: Holt, Rinehart and Winston, 1956), n., p. 340; George Simpson, *People in Families: Sociology, Psychoanalysis and the American Family* (New York: Crowell, 1960), p. 156; Carroll E. Izard, "Personality Similarity and Friendship," *Journal of Abnormal and Social Psychology*, 61: 47–51 (1960), at p. 47.

COMPLEMENTARY NEEDS IN MATE SELECTION

Problem

The first and most basic of the three propositions of Winch's theory of complementary needs in mate selection asserts that, "in mate selection each individual seeks within his or her field of eligibles for that person who gives the greatest promise of providing him or her with maximum need-gratification." One of the ways in which such need-gratification is secured is by marriage to a person whose personality is complementary rather than similar to (and possibly competitive with) that of the person choosing a mate.

The selection by Winch suggests a number of ways in which traits of two individuals may be considered complementary. In this laboratory problem we will be concerned with only one of these: the pattern which is called "Type I Complementariness." This kind of complement is found when person A is characterized by a given personality trait to a high degree, while in B (the potential mate) the trait is present to a low degree.

To carry out our test of Winch's theory we will use the variable of dominance or control, since this is the aspect of personality for which the evidence is strongest. However, in replicating this aspect of Winch's research, we must introduce a major note of caution. In the original study the sample consists of recently but already married persons. Consequently, any complementarity in dominance between husband and wife may have been the *result* of interaction in marriage, rather than an element which *caused* the husband and wife to choose each other as marital partners. To interpret Winch's findings as "consequence" rather than "cause" would be consistent with a vast body of sociological research which finds that all social groups tend to develop patterns of role differentiation, and that one of the first such differentiations to emerge in a newly formed group is that of differences in leadership or control. "Consequence" rather than "cause" may be even more true for our replication since we are studying marriages of many years duration.

It should be clear, then, that both the original study by Winch and our replication can tell us only if there is or is not complementarity; neither study provides information on whether the complementarity arose as a result of a selective process, or as a result of accommodations made after marriage. However, a study which followed up dating couples over a period of several months (Kerckhoff and Davis, 1962) tends to support the selective-process theory.

The statistical measure which we will use to test for complementarity is known as the coefficient of correlation. (The symbol r is used for this measure.) A correlation coefficient is an index which measures the amount of association between two variables. In our case the two variables are the scores for the husband's control and the wife's control. If there is no association between these two, r would equal .00. If there were total, or perfect, association between them, r would equal 1.00. If the two variables are positively related, so that the higher the husband's score, the higher the wife's score, r will turn out to be a positive number (but always less than 1.00) such as .35 or .62. If it turns out that the two variables are negatively related, that is, the greater the one, the less the other, r will be a negative figure, such as $-.35$ or $-.62$.

Hypothesis

On the basis of Winch's theory, state whether you expect to find a positive or a negative correlation between the husband's and the wife's scores for personal dominance or control needs, and give a brief explanation of why you predict this.

Empirical Indicators for Problem 12

VII. YOUR OWN AND YOUR PARENTS' PERSONALITIES

Please rate . . . your parents (first your father and then your mother) on each of the following descriptions. Using the key below, circle one answer number (in each section) to show the degree to which the description fits . . . your FATHER and . . . your MOTHER.

0 = Never
1 = Rarely
2 = Occasionally
3 = Sometimes
4 = Often
5 = Usually

Father

e   Tries to influence strongly other people's actions —— 0   1   2   3   4   5

f   Takes charge of things when with people ———— 0   1   2   3   4   5

Box 95 = Sum of e and f for FATHER

Mother

e   Tries to influence strongly other people's actions —— 0   1   2   3   4   5

f   Takes charge of things when with people ———— 0   1   2   3   4   5

Box 96 = Sum of e and f for MOTHER

Data Analysis

All the values needed for this calculation are already on the code sheets. You need only add them up and then insert the resulting sums into the correlation formula given on the Tabulation Form and solve for r.

1. *Divide* the code sheets into two roughly equal parts so that you and your partner can each do half of the work.

2. *List* the Control scores for fathers (X) (Box 95) and for mothers (Y) (Box 96), the squares of these scores (X^2, Y^2) (Box 97, 98), and the products of these scores (XY) (Box 99) on the Tabulation Form.

3. *Add* each column to get the total X, total Y, total X^2, total Y^2, and total XY. Then add your half to that of your partner.

4. Insert the values you have just obtained in the correlation formula on the Tabulation Form, and solve for r. Your instructor will have a table of square roots. When you need the square root in order to solve the equation, ask your instructor to look it up for you and then complete your solution of the formula.

Laboratory Report

1. Follow the general directions for writing the Laboratory Report given in Appendix B.

2. *Note* that the conventions associated with the correlation coefficient define the X variable as the independent variable and the Y variable as the dependent variable.

3. Comment in your Discussion on the extent to which data of this type provide evidence of complementarity in mate selection.

REFERENCES

Kerckhoff, A. C., and Davis, K. E. "Value Consensus and Need Complementarity in Mate Selection," *American Sociological Review*, 27 (1962), pp. 295–303.

Tharp, Roland G. "Psychological Patterning in Marriage," *Psychological Bulletin*, 60 (1963), pp. 97–117.

SECTION/COURSE NO. _____ DATE_____ NAME_____

Part I

Control—Father	Control—Mother	Father's Score Squared	Mother's Score Squared	Father's Score X Mother's Score
Box 95	Box 96	Box 97	Box 98	Box 99
X	Y	X²	Y²	XY

Part II

Control—Father	Control—Mother	Father's Score Squared	Mother's Score Squared	Father's Score X Mother's Score
Box 95	Box 96	Box 97	Box 98	Box 99
X	Y	X²	Y²	XY

TOTAL

(Transfer the totals in Parts I and II to the reverse side of this page.)

	X	Y	X²	Y²	XY
Totals from Part I					
Totals from Part II					
Sum of Parts I and II					
Partner's Sum of I and II					
Grand Sum (Σ) (Use these figures in the formula)	ΣX =	ΣY =	ΣX² =	ΣY² =	ΣXY =

$$r = \frac{(N \cdot \Sigma XY) - (\Sigma X \cdot \Sigma Y)}{\sqrt{\left[N \cdot \Sigma X^2 - (\Sigma X)^2\right] \cdot \left[N \cdot \Sigma Y^2 - (\Sigma Y)^2\right]}}$$

$$r = \frac{(\quad \cdot \quad) - (\quad \cdot \quad)}{\sqrt{\left[\quad \cdot \quad - (\quad)^2\right] \cdot \left[\quad \cdot \quad - (\quad)^2\right]}}$$

$$r = \frac{\quad - \quad}{\sqrt{\left[\quad - \quad\right] \cdot \left[\quad - \quad\right]}}$$

$$r = \frac{\quad}{\sqrt{\left[\quad\right] \cdot \left[\quad\right]}}$$

$$r = \frac{\quad}{\sqrt{\quad}}$$

$$r = \frac{\quad}{\quad}$$

$$r = \frac{\quad}{\quad}$$

SECTION/COURSE NO._____ DATE_____ NAME_____

Complementary Needs in Mate Selection

HYPOTHESIS: _____

_____

_____

_____

_____

SAMPLE: _____

_____

_____

_____

INDEPENDENT VARIABLE: _____

_____

_____

_____

_____

DEPENDENT VARIABLE: _____

_____

_____

_____

_____

OTHER FACTORS: _____

_____

_____

_____

SUMMARY OF FINDINGS: _____

_____

_____

_____

_____

_____

_____

_____

_____

DISCUSSION: _____

_____

_____

_____

_____

_____

_____

_____

_____

_____

_____

_____

NOTES FOR INSTRUCTORS USING THIS MANUAL

Criteria for Selecting Laboratory Problems

Each of the problems included in this manual were chosen with the following objectives and criteria in mind:

1. Theoretical Basis. I sought problems which have theoretical relevance for family sociology, and in this process I was guided by a social system or structure-function conceptual framework.

2. Analytical Objectives. To qualify for inclusion, a problem had to go beyond description of family phenomena. The central issues of any science are those of explanation. Accurate description is only a necessary intermediary step. Consequently, after the initial laboratory problems on quantification and the problem establishing the limits and limitations of the sample, each of the laboratory experiences included in this manual is an analytical problem. That is, each problem is designed to enable the student to test relationships between variables.

However, since these laboratory problems are all miniature cross-sectional research designs, rather than experiments in the literal sense, statements of cause and effect are not possible, but only conclusions about relationships and interrelationships.

3. Methodology. I wanted these problems to illustrate and teach certain methodological principles. These are first, the nature of the links among theory, concept, and empirical indicators of concepts; second, the idea of independent and dependent variables; and third, the need for, and use of, control variables to avoid spurious conclusions arising from a confounding of variables.

4. Practicality. With these objectives in mind, I began the search for research problems suitable for replication as laboratory experiences. At this point, practical limitations had to be built into the selection process. First, the research design had to be one which could be replicated with relatively simple questionnaire data. Second, the problem had to be one which could be analyzed within a two-hour laboratory period.

The second of these practical limitations proved the most difficult to meet. The solution adopted for this manual was to replicate only selected aspects of the original studies. In making these often drastic simplifications, I have assumed that, if in the aspect replicated the students findings confirm the original study, the non-replicated aspects of the original study would probably also be confirmed if they were replicated. Obviously, this is not necessarily the case, although I believe it will usually be found to be true.

I would have been unwilling to make this latter assertion prior to experience with this mode of teaching sociology. However, one of the indirect effects of this experience has been to increase my confidence in the validity of the research reports published in sociology. When I first started to use this method of teaching, I spent a considerable amount of time in pointing out the unreliability of much sociological research and in preparing students for laboratory problems which would fail to confirm the original investigation. But such negative experiments have turned out to be rare. And, while there is nothing which can match the thrill of discovering new facts and relationships in one's original research, the experience of discovering that these laboratory replications work is not to be slighted.

The Sampling Problem

Successful use of the laboratory-problem method of this manual requires a sample of approximately 100 cases. In addition, the sample should, if possible, include both men and women respondents and display some variation in social class and religion. This does not mean that a sample containing equal numbers of men and women or of Protestants and Catholics is needed, but there should be enough cases in each group to make the computation of averages meaningful.

As a very rough rule of thumb, I suggest that the minimum number of cases for analysis in any part of a problem be five. For example, where social-class comparisons are called for, if there are not at least five farm families represented in your sample, those which are present should be included with either the white-collar or the blue-collar groups. The instructor should decide which occupational categories to combine them with, on the basis of a rough estimate of the socioeconomic level of the farm students who attend his institution. With a sample from a public university, for example, it would generally be best to include farmers with the blue-collar workers.

These requirements concerning the size and nature of the sample do not rule out use of this manual by the instructor who is teaching a class which cannot provide a sample meeting the criteria. An instructor in this situation can arrange to have the Questionnaire given to other groups of students in his own or nearby institutions. The difficulty with this method of supplementing the sample lies in the time and labor costs of coding the supplemental group of Questionnaires. If, however, this is to be done, the most efficient procedure is to have each member of the class code a couple of extra Questionnaires. An extra laboratory period must then be allowed for coding, since coding the first Questionnaire ordinarily requires a full two-hour laboratory period.

To provide a more convenient method of supplementing the sample, I have prepared a set of code sheets based on Questionnaires completed by students in introductory sociology courses at the University of Minnesota. The set, entitled *DATA DECK of Supplementary Code Sheets,* contains 80 code sheets, selected so that there are equal numbers of men and women, Protestants and Catholics, and children of farm, white-collar, and blue-collar fathers. Instructors wishing to supplement the samples obtained from their own classes may purchase these code sheets from Rand McNally & Company. Order enough *DATA DECKS of Supplementary Code Sheets* to provide one deck for every *two* students in the class, since the students will be working in pairs. The supplementary decks need to be purchased only once, since the same decks can be used again the next time the course is offered.

Another method of supplementing the sample is to add to the code sheets for one class code sheets from previous classes. Eventually, of course, many more code sheets will be accumulated than are necessary. I do not recommend that these be continually accumulated, because with a sample of more than 150 cases, the clerical work of sorting and tabulating takes up too much of the laboratory period.

Even when more than enough code sheets have been accumulated, it is always advisable to administer the Questionnaire to each new class during the first laboratory period and to have the students code it during the second period. These two steps are important parts of the laboratory experience. They give the student the opportunity to participate in the data-gathering and quantification processes which are an integral part of research, and they lend a saliency and reality to the materials which might otherwise not be experienced.

Mechanics of Laboratory Work

Some of the directions listed below are based on the assumption that the problems will be done in two-hour laboratory periods. Although this is preferable, each problem can also be done in the usual one-hour "quiz section" if the students are allowed to complete their calculations and write up the laboratory report as an outside assignment. Alternatively, the entire problem can be done as a home assignment. In the latter case, sets of code sheets can be placed on reserve in the library, or sets can be lent to students for use at home.

Still a third alternative which can be used with very large lecture sections is to do the cross-tabulation as a classroom demonstration. When this alternative is followed, the data can be tallied on the blackboard. These raw data can then be copied down by the students who will be expected to complete the data analysis and laboratory report on an outside assignment. This method has been used successfully with classes of over three hundred students. After two or three such demonstrations, the tabulations can be done in advance and the figures simply written on the blackboard or distributed in mimeographed form. However, I feel it is important to avoid using pretabulated data until the students have watched blackboard demonstrations of the cross-tabulation procedures two or three times and have a firm grasp of what is involved.

1. First Period: Questionnaires. Students are *not* to sign their names. As each completes his Questionnaire, he should turn it in and then leave. The Questionnaire can be completed in 40 to 50 minutes by most students.

2. Second Period: Coding. Before the period in which the coding is done, an identification number must be written in the space provided on the cover of each Questionnaire. Then, (1) Distribute the Questionnaires in random order since it is important that no one codes his own Questionnaire. Coding someone else's Questionnaire gives the student a much more realistic coding experience. (2) The coding is to be done initially on the Coding Worksheet (page 25) and not on the Ditto Master Code Sheet. (3) If the coding is done in class (the recommended procedure), have the class code along with you as you read out the items in the Code. (4) After the coding has been completed, each student is to copy his coding from the Worksheet onto the Ditto Master Code Sheet. Make sure the students remove the tissue before starting to copy, that they write large numbers, and press hard. Have one or two razor blades available for those who need to make corrections. (5) Each student is to sign his name as a coder in the appropriate blank, reinsert the protective tissue, and hand in his Ditto Master Code Sheet, together with the Questionnaire which he has coded. Be sure to collect all Questionnaires, even if you are not going to check the coding or save the Questionnaires, since they should not be allowed to circulate on the campus and possibly influence the way members of a future class will answer the Questionnaire.

3. Dittoing the Code Sheets. It is not necessary or desirable to run off a set of code sheets for every member of the class. It is preferable to have the students work in pairs when sorting and tabulating (but, of course, the laboratory reports should be written individually). Consequently, it is necessary to duplicate only one set of code sheets needs for every *two* students. In addition, run off one set for your own use and another set to put on reserve in the library for those who have missed a laboratory period and must make it up, and for students who are writing term papers. A copy of the Questionnaire should also be put on reserve in the library so it can be consulted by students planning term papers. Call for two or three volunteers to run off the duplicate copies for you.

Save the Ditto Masters, as you may later want to run off more sets.

4. Student Preparation for Laboratory Problems. The problems you select must be announced in advance so that students will have an opportunity to read the study to be replicated in a given problem *before* the laboratory period in which the problem is to be done. See page 5 for comments on the optimum sequence of problems.

5. Hypothesis. Remind students that the hypothesis is to be written before they begin to analyze the data.

6. Blackboard Tabulation for Checking Purposes. The first five or six students to complete their tabulations and calculations should write their summary statistics (means or percentages) on the blackboard so that each student may check the accuracy of his own work and make corrections if needed. To facilitate putting the results on the blackboard, draw an outline table on the blackboard and instruct students to come up and enter their summary statistics as soon as they have completed computing the percentages or means. Differences in the statistics obtained by different stu-

dents may be the result of one or more code sheets getting lost or being added from another set. These and the usual minor clerical errors which occur in the course of most research studies will lead to small differences in the results. These small differences can be ignored if, in general, the results are comparable.

7. The Laboratory Report. Appendix B contains general directions for preparing the Laboratory Reports.

8. Summary of Findings versus Discussion. The most difficult part of the preparation of these reports concerns the distinction between the Summary of Findings and the Discussion. This is because there is a tendency for students to repeat the Summary of Findings as the Discussion, rather than to interpret the findings. Students need reassurance that it is permissible and desirable to interpret and speculate in a scientific report.

9. Grading of Laboratory Reports. Laboratory reports are not examinations. Although grades are usually given for the Laboratory Reports, grading should be secondary. All reasonable questions should be answered, and the students should be helped to make their analysis and write up the results.

Reduction in Clerical Work

One difficulty with these laboratory problems is that a substantial part of each laboratory period is taken up with what is essentially clerical work: sorting, tabulating, adding, figuring percentages, and so on. This is true of most research, but in the case of these laboratory problems there are two steps which can be taken to reduce the amount of clerical work.

1. Students should work in pairs and divide up the work. For example, in a laboratory problem in which social class is the independent variable, one member of the pair might tabulate the code sheets for the middle-class part of the sample, and the other person for the working-class. Similarly the work of figuring percentages and means can be divided. After each person has done his half, each student copies his partner's results onto his own Tabulation Form. Of course, each student, individually, must write his own Laboratory Report, but he draws on the common data and data tabulation.

2. Have the class omit cross-tabulations in later laboratory periods. After four or five laboratory problems have been completed and the students have thoroughly mastered the idea of the cross-tabulation as a method of testing hypotheses, the cross-tabulation and computational part of the laboratory work should

be omitted. To do so, the instructor (or a student committee) will have to compute the statistical data in advance and post the tabulations on the blackboard (but only after the students have written down their hypotheses). This procedure is strongly recommended, not simply because it avoids the tedium of repeating a type of activity already thoroughly mastered, but primarily because it allows time for class discussion and also more time for writing the Laboratory Reports.

Learning to Read Journal Articles

One of the most important skills a student should acquire early in his sociological training is the ability to read and understand articles published in scientific journals. I have found that a highly efficient method of teaching this skill is to have students prepare abstracts of journal articles, *provided* these abstracts follow a form which helps them identify and specify the basic elements in the research report. These are the same elements needed to write the Laboratory Reports for each of the problems in this manual. Consequently, instructors who wish to teach this skill can require their students to use the outline and the abstracting forms given in Appendix B as the basis for preparing two or three abstracts. The abstracting experience can further be coordinated with the laboratory work if the articles which the students are required to abstract are those which are reprinted in this manual.

Tests of Significance

The use of statistics in this manual is with one exception limited to means and percentages. There is no need for undergraduate classes to go beyond this. Since our purpose here is purely illustrative, we assume that all differences are non-chance. Obviously, this is not a sound assumption, but it is a necessary one if the laboratory problems are to be carried out by typical undergraduates within a two-hour period. On the other hand, this assumption is justified somewhat by the fact that each laboratory problem replicates an already established proposition. Statistically oriented instructors can, of course, teach their students to apply inferential statistics to the data analyzed if they so desire, and graduate students writing term papers based on analysis of these data can be required to compute such measures.

Variables in the Questionnaire

Most of the Questionnaire items and measures have been selected on the basis of the variables needed to replicate the articles reprinted in each laboratory problem. In many cases these are quite different from the measures used by the original investigator because it has been necessary to fit them into the format of a simply administered and simply coded Questionnaire. However, other considerations have also entered into the choice of the variables.

First, where measures which meet the format requirements are already available in the published literature, I have tried to use these, sometimes in modified form, rather than create new measures solely for this manual. For example, to measure personality, Schutz's FIRO scales (Schutz, 1958) are used; to measure parent practices, the scales developed by Devereux and his associates (Devereux, Bronfenbrenner, and Suci, 1962) are included; to measure decision patterns, I have used scales modified from those developed by Blood and Wolfe (1960); and to index spousal role orientations, the measure developed by Hurvitz (1960).

Finally, I have tried to include in the Questionnaire measures of fundamental aspects of family structure (such as power and support) and fundamental aspects of the larger social structure (such as social class and religion) in which families are located, and which are intimately interrelated with the family system. I hope that choosing variables of these types will give the Questionnaire a basic significance and a durability which extends beyond the articles which are replicated in the laboratory problems.

Additional Uses of These Materials

If the aim of including in the Questionnaire a set of variables of basic importance to family sociology has been achieved, then it should be possible (after the instructor has had a little experience with the method) for the instructor using this manual and its accompanying Questionnaire to choose other articles from the rapidly growing empirical literature in family sociology and work out the necessary instructions and forms for class replication. Similarly, there are innumerable possibilities for laboratory problems which are not replications of any existing research. However, laboratory problems which are not replications, interesting as they may be to the instructor, miss one of the main pedagogical aims of the laboratory method: to permit the student to demonstrate for himself the validity of the empirical basis of family sociology. Consequently, non-replicative laboratory problems are best avoided except for term papers or for special colloquia, research practica, or seminars in which advanced students explore a specific topic.

On the other hand, the possibilities for such special topic papers and colloquia are very wide. I have conducted a colloquium for undergraduates focused, in successive years, on intrafamily communication, the power structure of the family, and maternal employment. Data for student papers were obtained from the Questionnaire which accompanies this laboratory manual. Each student in such a colloquium is assigned one or two antecedent or consequent variables which he is asked to relate to the central variable of the colloquium. This is done both on the basis of an appropriate conceptual framework and, empirically, on the basis of the cross-tabulations of data from the Questionnaire. Social-position variables, such as social class, religion, and community size, are usually treated as social structural factors influencing the variable on which the colloquium is focused, and family-structure and child-personality variables are treated as dependent variables.

REFERENCES

Blood, R. O., and Wolfe, D. M. *Husbands and Wives.* Glencoe, Ill.: Free Press, 1960.

Devereux, E. C., Bronfenbrenner, U., and Suci, G. J. "Patterns of Parent Behavior in the United States of America and the Federal Republic of Germany: A Cross-National Comparison," *International Social Science Journal,* 14 (1962), pp. 488–506.

Hurvitz, N. "The Measurement of Marital Strain," *American Journal of Sociology,* 5 (1960), pp. 610–615.

Schutz, W. C. *FIRO: A Three Dimensional Theory of Interpersonal Behavior.* New York: Rinehart, 1958.

OUTLINE FOR LABORATORY REPORTS AND ABSTRACTS

Writing the Laboratory Report

Hypothesis. A hypothesis is a statement of the relationship which you expect to prove or to test in a study. The emphasis is on the word *relationship*. That is, the hypothesis should state the way the independent variable is related to the dependent variable (for example, "the greater the number of children in a family, the less the affection received by any one child"). You should base your hypothesis primarily on the study you are replicating. However, if you think that other things you have read or know about or some characteristic of your sample suggest a different hypothesis, then you should feel free to pose a different hypothesis.

1. State the hypothesis in the present tense. This custom is followed because the hypothesis is a statement of what the investigator thinks is the present state of the real world and of the relationships which exist between variables.

2. Give a brief justification or explanation of the hypothesis. That is, give the reasons why you expect such a relationship to hold.

3. Write the hypothesis before coming to class, or at the least before tabulating the data. After the data have been tabulated, do not change the hypothesis to fit the findings. Hypotheses are often proved wrong by the evidence, and this may be the basis for a new understanding of the issue being investigated. Bear in mind, however, that the hypothesis may be correct even if your findings do not support it. This could happen if the sample is inappropriate for the issue being tested or if the measurement of the variables used to test the hypothesis is inadequate.

Sample. 1. Describe how the sample was chosen and how many cases are included. 2. Describe relevant characteristics of the sample such as age, sex, and socioeconomic status. 3. After the first laboratory report, only those characteristics of the sample which might influence your results when you test the hypothesis in that problem should be described.

---

* Although the terms "cause" and "influenced by" are used to describe the independent and dependent variables, it is important to note that most of the problems in this book do not provide clear evidence of cause and effect. For further explanation, see "A Note on Interpreting Cause and Effect," page 199.

Independent Variable (or Variables). The independent variable is that factor which is assumed to be causing change in the dependent variable.* State what this variable is, *and* how it is measured. It is important to specify how a variable is measured because different measurement procedures can produce different results, as in the case of an oral and rectal thermometer.

The Questionnaire items used to measure the variables needed for each replication are reprinted as part of the directions for the replication in a section headed, "Empirical Indicators."

Dependent Variable (or Variables). A dependent variable is that factor which is assumed to be caused by or influenced by changes or variations in the independent variable.* State what the dependent variable is *and* how it is measured.

Other Factors. Confine this listing to those elements which are important for understanding the results of the research. If a control variable is employed, it should be explained here.

Summary of Findings. This should be a literal statement (a statement in words) of the facts or relationships found. State the findings *without* using statistics. However, you may also use specific figures *if* these can be given briefly. For example: "First-born children are more often high in social responsibility, as shown by our finding that 20 per cent of first-born children have high responsibility scores as compared with only 10 per cent of middle or youngest children."

State whether your hypothesis is refuted, accepted, or partially accepted by the data analysis. Remember that your results can differ from those of the original study in certain ways yet still lead to the same conclusion. For example, suppose the original study used a ten-point scale to measure a variable and found that group A had an average of 7.3 as compared to 5.8 for group B. Suppose further that your replication used a five-point scale rather that the original ten-point scale to measure this variable. If the analysis showed group A to have a mean score of 3.5 and group B to have a mean score of 2.4, you would conclude that the replication confirmed the finding of the original study because in both the original study and in your replication group A had a higher score than group B. In short, you should base your summary of the finding and your acceptance or rejection of the hypothesis on what the statistics show about relationships between variables, rather than on the absolute values of the score.

Discussion. This section should provide an *interpretation* of the findings, i.e., (1) what accounts for the findings, or (2) what do the findings mean, or (3) what is the importance of the findings. Example: "The findings are consistent with and support the theory that parents have stricter expectations for first-born children, and tend to let later-born children get away with more. Thus first borns grow up. . . ." The discussion is one of the places where the scientist can (and should) be speculative and imaginative.

A NOTE ON INTERPRETING CAUSE AND EFFECT

The goal of all sciences is to discover cause-and-effect relationships. To establish causality, three criteria have to be met. It must be demonstrated, first, that there is a relationship between two variables; second, that this relationship is due to the variables under examination, and not some other third, "confounding," variable; and third, that the presumed causal or independent variable occurs prior in time to the presumed effect, or, the dependent variable (see Selltiz, *et al.* 1960).

The difficulties in establishing causal sequences in sociology stem primarily from the fact that much research is inadequately designed to provide information on the temporal sequence of variables. In most examples of sociological research, as in most of the problems contained in the present laboratory manual, data are gathered from a cross-section of some population at one particular point in time. Whatever the advantages of cross-sectional research may be in terms of minimizing the costs of data collection, the procedure imposes severe limitations on assessing causality; information obtained at a single point in time provides few clues as to whether one variable occurred *prior* to another. For example, if a status-concern scale and also a racial-prejudice scale are given to a sample, it might be found that those with high scores on status concern also have high prejudice scores. It would be plausible to maintain that status concern brings about feelings of insecurity that are eventually manifested in prejudice. However, this relationship, while interesting, does not constitute proof that status concern *causes* prejudice. It would be equally plausible to argue that persons already prejudiced develop an awareness of status to rationalize their racial views. With cross-sectional data, the researcher may have little besides his own intuitive

judgment to determine which alternative represents the correct causal sequence.

In some instances judgments about the temporal sequence may be easy to make and need not rest heavily on speculation. For example, if we have demonstrated a relationship between religion and fertility plans, it would be relatively safe to say that religion, a characteristic which is usually ascribed at birth, precedes fertility plans rather than vice-versa. Even in this illustration, however, it is not legitimate to maintain that religon *causes* differences in fertility plans. Religious denominations and fertility plans are each known to differ by social class, and it may be that the observed relationship is due to the tendency of one religious group to be higher in social-class standing than the other group, since there is a tendency for persons high in class standing to plan to have fewer children.

Control Variables. The problem just described can be handled with cross-sectional data if we introduce a "control" for social class, the confounding variable. To do this, it is necessary to divide the sample into relatively homogeneous social-class groupings; then within each class group we can compare the relationship between religion and fertility plans. By confining comparisons to each homogeneous class group, the effects of social class are ruled out, or, at least, minimized. Two outcomes are relevant: if the original relationship between religion and fertility was not due to class, the relationship should persist for each comparison; if, however, the relationship was due to class, then holding class constant should make the relationship disappear. Again, however, the use of a control for class does not *prove* causality; it is always possible that class is the wrong variable to control. This additional difficulty illustrates the endless problems involved in establishing cause-and-effect relationships in cross-sectional research designs.

The research procedure capable of demonstrating cause and effect most clearly is the experimental method. In the experiment the researcher first introduces a variable to one group and withholds it from another group, and then observes whether differences between the two groups emerge. If differences do arise, the researcher can attribute them to the experimental variable. Unlike cross-sectional research, experimental variables are introduced at a definite point in time prior to the emergence of the dependent variable, thus clarifying the temporal sequence. Also, it is possible in the controlled experiment to administer the experimental variable to a *randomly selected* group of persons, and in this way to minimize the possibility that other common characteristics and experiences of individuals in the sample may confound the relationship (Selltiz, *et al.*, 1960). Because of these and other advantages, all sciences try to use the experimental method wherever possible. In sociology the use of this method is slowly gaining acceptance (Straus, 1967; Straus, 1968; Zelditch and Hopkins, 1961).

Abstracts of Empirical Research Articles

The outline for preparing Laboratory Reports may be used to abstract journal articles with the following additions:

Reference. At the beginning of the abstract give the complete citation for the material you are abstracting. Use any standard system of citation, such as that of the *American Sociological Review* or the American Psychological Association. The reference should include the author's name, the title of the article, the title of the book or journal in which it appears, the place of publication and the publisher (if a book), volume number (if a journal), the date of publication and the specific page numbers on which the selection appears.

Hypothesis. State the hypothesis which the author is testing, whether or not you agree with it. If a formal hypothesis is not given in the article, state the research problem as succinctly as possible. If there are numerous hypotheses, try to combine them into one, two, or three general hypotheses. (Sometimes you may wish to prepare an abstract which summarizes only one or two of many hypotheses tested in a study.)

Sample. Describe the sampling techniques and sample characteristics of the sample used to test the hypothesis. It is not necessary to describe pretest or preliminary study samples.

Methodology. Classify the research design as either *cross-sectional, longitudinal, experimental,* some combination of these, or possibly other. Describe briefly any other aspects of the research which are necessary for an understanding of the results or any unusual procedures which are of interest in their own right.

Discussion. As in the case of the hypothesis, this should be a summary of the author's discussion. (But you may include your own view or evaluation of his research design and its results, as long as you clearly label your analysis as such.)

REFERENCES

Selltiz, Claire, Jahoda, Marie, Deutsch, Morton, and Cook, Stuart W. *Methods in Social Relations.* New York: Henry Holt, 1960. Chapter 4.

Straus, Murray A. "The Influence of Sex of Child and Social Class on Instrumental and Expressive Family Roles," *Sociology and Social Research,* 52 (1967), pp. 7–21.

Straus, Murray A. "Communication, Creativity, and Problem-Solving Ability of Middle- and Working-Class Families in Three Societies," *American Journal of Sociology,* 73 (1968), pp. 417–420.

Zelditch, Morris, and Hopkins, Terrence K. "Experiments with Organizations," in Amitai Etzioni, ed. *Complex Organizations.* New York: Holt, Rinehart and Winston, 1961.

SECTION/COURSE NO. _____ DATE _____ NAME _____

REFERENCE: _____

_____

_____

HYPOTHESIS OR ISSUE STUDIED: _____

_____

_____

_____

_____

SAMPLE: _____

_____

_____

METHODOLOGY: _____

_____

_____

_____

INDEPENDENT VARIABLE(S): _____

_____

_____

_____

DEPENDENT VARIABLE(S): _____

_____

_____

_____

OTHER FACTORS: _____

_____

_____

SUMMARY OF FINDINGS: _____

_____

_____

_____

_____

_____

_____

_____

_____

_____

DISCUSSION: _____

_____

_____

_____

_____

_____

_____

_____

_____

_____

_____

_____

_____

INSTRUCTIONS FOR EMPIRICAL TERM-PAPER PROPOSALS

Title

The term papers envisioned in this outline are to be based on data from the Questionnaire used for the laboratory problems. Your first task, therefore, is to choose a topic which can be investigated with this data. Copies of the Questionnaire have been put on reserve in the library for your use.

A major purpose of the title of the term-paper proposal is to help you crystallize your thinking and provide a focus for your work. It should sum up or, if that is not possible, formulate *briefly* the main issues with which you are dealing. This can usually be accomplished best by including in the title the independent and the dependent variable. If there are several independent (or dependent) variables, subsume them under a general term such as "community structure" or "personality." The title need not state all the limits and qualifications of your research design, so do not try to crowd too much into the title. Begin with a fairly broad working title. Later, after you have completed much of your research, you may find it appropriate to refine it and narrow its limits further.

Problem and Its Importance

1. The terms "problem" and "importance" cause some confusion because many students think that "problem" means *practical problem,* and that "importance" implies *importance for social welfare.* On the contrary, for purposes of your paper, the most important thing is the *scientific* problem or issue. If the problem also has some practical importance, so much the better. If it does not, that should not be a cause of concern. Remember that the goal of a science is simply *to understand.* If your paper contributes to an understanding of the family, you will already have achieved more than can really be hoped for. If we are to be realistic, we must recognize that the main objective of these papers is to provide you with a learning experience in this area of social-science research.

2. All papers based on materials from this manual should aim at testing a hypothesis concerning a *relationship* between variables. We are not implying that descriptive studies are unimportant, but the nature of

the sample you will be working with and the type of learning which the problems in this manual are designed to provide are best suited to an analytical rather than a descriptive approach.

Summary of Existing Research

One of the most important things you will have an opportunity to learn in working on your research paper is how to search the literature in family sociology for relevant earlier studies and write up a review of what you have found. Such a review could be very extensive; however, for purposes of the term-paper *proposal,* you need only four references as the basis for your review of the literature. Priority should be given to empirical studies; at least two out of the four references should be empirical research designs. For your final term paper you should include as many references as you have found and used. The most comprehensive reference book for research on the family up through 1964 is the *International Bibliography of Research in Marriage and the Family, 1900–1964* by J. Aldous and R. Hill (Minneapolis: University of Minnesota Press, 1967). For publications after 1965, the best single reference source is *Sociological Abstracts.*

A review can cover both substantive and methodological issues. A good review does not simply describe studies in serial order, but relates studies to each other. That is, you should aim at pointing out similarities or differences. The review in the final term paper should also note gaps in knowledge or methodology.

Independent and Dependent Variables

State each variable and also describe how you plan to measure it and to categorize it. For example:

Age at first date. The respondents will be divided into four groups: those who started dating at age 12 or earlier, age 13 to 15, age 16 to 18, and those who have never dated.

There can be more than one *independent* variable if you are interested in how two or three factors affect a given dependent variable, or more than one *dependent* variable if you are interested in how a given independent variable affects two or three dependent variables. But do not use several independent and several dependent variables at the same time, since this will make your analysis too complex for a term paper.

Other Factors

Describe here any control variables you plan to use. Usually your control variable will be social class *or* the sex of respondent. It is usually not possible to use two controls, since this takes a larger sample than is likely to be available to you.

State how the control variable is measured and why you think it important to control for this variable.

Hypothesis

A single general hypothesis is best, but sometimes more than one is needed to take care of differences which you expect to find in different parts of the sample: for example, you may expect to find a positive relation between your variables for men and a negative relationship for women. A general hypothesis and a sub-hypothesis may be appropriate.

Give a brief statement of the reasoning behind your hypothesis: that is, why do you make this prediction?

Sample and Procedure for Obtaining Data

Describe the way the data were obtained and the number of cases in your sample, as well as any special characteristics of your sample.

Mode of Analysis

List the cross-tabulations you plan to make and the computations which must be made (that is, percentages, averages, correlations, etc.). Graduate students should plan to carry out a test of statistical significance in their analysis.

References

As noted above, only four references are needed for the proposal. Be sure to give an accurate and complete citation for each reference. The style of citation employed in this manual is the one used by many sociological journals, and therefore it is a good one to learn and use. But any standard system which lists all the necessary elements is satisfactory.

Some General Points

1. Make a carbon copy of both your term-paper proposal and the final term paper. Turn in the original to your instructor.

2. It will rarely be possible to write a good term-paper proposal until you have done at least *two* of the laboratory problems in this manual, unless, of course, you have had previous research experience.

3. Consult the outline for preparing Laboratory Reports in Appendix B and the first laboratory problems for further instructions and explanation of such things as independent and dependent variables and the hypothesis.

4. In many cases you will want to use the material you have written for the project proposal in the final term paper. However, when you actually start doing the research for the term paper, it may be necessary to change or modify the procedures or other aspects of the study. For example, you may have proposed comparing families with a husband's power score of 14 or more, but find that there are only three such families. In that case you would want to consider making the comparison on the basis of families with scores of 13 or more. Similarly, you may have proposed using an average as the dependent variable. It sometimes happens, however, that averaging covers up important factors. Consequently, if no differences emerge when you are using the average, you may try figuring the percentage of families with a score above or below a certain level.

Remember that a project proposal is a research tool to help you stay on the right track in your research and not wander off; it is not a contract which you must keep at all costs. If the tool you fashioned in your proposal doesn't work well, then you can, and should, sharpen it up.

5. A term paper differs from the Laboratory Reports primarily in that it allows you to make a more detailed analysis since you are not restricted to the two-hour laboratory period. The greater detail in your research design shows up in the way you do your statistical analysis (for example, you may use more than one dependent variable or work out both averages and percentages), but mostly in the review of literature and in the discussion of the findings. A careful review of the literature is essential. In your discussion of your findings you should explore their meaning and implications carefully and relate what you have found to the literature you have previously reviewed. You can, and should, also feel free to speculate about what could account for your findings.

6. Turn in your term paper proposal to your instructor *before* making your analysis, since he may

have comments and suggestions which will be helpful to you.

REFERENCES

Campbell, W. G. *Form and Style in Thesis Writing*. Cambridge, Mass.: Houghton Mifflin, 1954

Schneider, B. R., Jr., and Tjossem, H. K. *Themes and Research Papers*. New York: Macmillan, 1961.

Strunk, Wm., Jr., and White, E. B. *The Elements of Style* Rev. ed. New York: Macmillan, 1962.

Turabin, Kate. *A Manual for Writers of Term Papers, Theses and Dissertations*. Phoenix ed. Chicago: University of Chicago Press, 1955.

Turabin, Kate. *Students' Guide for Writing College Papers*. Phoenix ed. Chicago: University of Chicago Press, 1963

SECTION/COURSE NO._____ DATE_____ NAME_____

TITLE: _____

_____

PROBLEM AND ITS IMPORTANCE: _____

_____

_____

_____

_____

_____

_____

_____

_____

_____

_____

_____

_____

_____

_____

_____

_____

_____

_____

_____

_____

_____

SUMMARY OF EXISTING RESEARCH: _____

_____

_____

_____

_____

_____

_____

_____

_____

_____

_____

_____

_____

_____

_____

_____

_____

_____

_____

_____

_____

_____

_____

INDEPENDENT VARIABLE: _____

_____

_____

_____

_____

DEPENDENT VARIABLE: _____

_____

_____

_____

_____

_____

OTHER FACTORS: _____

_____

_____

_____

_____

_____

HYPOTHESIS(ES): _____

_____

_____

_____

_____

_____

_____

_____

METHOD A—SAMPLE AND PROCEDURE FOR OBTAINING DATA: _____

_____

_____

_____

_____

_____

METHOD B—MODE OF ANALYSIS: _____

_____

_____

_____

_____

_____

_____

_____

_____

_____

REFERENCES (List four): _____

_____

_____

_____

_____

PERCENTAGES FOR INTEGERS FROM 1 TO 144

Computing Percentages for Base Numbers Up to 72. To find what percentage 7 is of 18, turn to the column headed 18. Look down the column to 7 and read the percentage to the right: 38.9 %. For purposes of the problems in this book, round all decimals to whole percentages; in the illustration above, 38.9 % is rounded to 39 %.

Computing Percentages for Base Numbers 73 to 144. Divide in half both the base number and the figure to be converted to a percentage, and proceed as illustrated above. For example, to find what percentage 66 is of 80, find the column headed 40 and read the percentage to the left of 33, e.g., 82.5 %, or, rounded, 83 %. In the case of odd numbered figures, use the next higher number. For example, to find what percentage 83 is of 141, find the column headed 71 and read the percentage to the left of 42, e.g., 59.2 %, or rounded, 59 %.

* Reprinted from Carol L. Stone, *Percentages for Integers 1 to 399* (Pullman, Washington: Washington State University Agricultural Experiment Stations Circular 341, 1958), pp. 3–8.

1	2	3	4	5	6	7	8	9
1 100.0	1 50.0	1 33.3	1 25.0	1 20.0	1 16.7	1 14.3	1 12.5	1 11.1
	2 100.0	2 66.7	2 50.0	2 40.0	2 33.3	2 28.6	2 25.0	2 22.2
		3 100.0	3 75.0	3 60.0	3 50.0	3 42.9	3 37.5	3 33.3
			4 100.0	4 80.0	4 66.7	4 57.1	4 50.0	4 44.4
				5 100.0	5 83.3	5 71.4	5 62.5	5 55.6
					6 100.0	6 85.7	6 75.0	6 66.7
						7 100.0	7 87.5	7 77.8
							8 100.0	8 88.9
								9 100.0

10	11	12	13	14	15	16	17	18
1 10.0	1 9.1	1 8.3	1 7.7	1 7.1	1 6.7	1 6.3	1 5.9	1 5.6
2 20.0	2 18.2	2 16.7	2 15.4	2 14.3	2 13.3	2 12.5	2 11.8	2 11.1
3 30.0	3 27.3	3 25.0	3 23.1	3 21.4	3 20.0	3 18.8	3 17.6	3 16.7
4 40.0	4 36.4	4 33.3	4 30.8	4 28.6	4 26.7	4 25.0	4 23.5	4 22.2
5 50.0	5 45.5	5 41.7	5 38.5	5 35.7	5 33.3	5 31.3	5 29.4	5 27.8
6 60.0	6 54.5	6 50.0	6 46.2	6 42.9	6 40.0	6 37.5	6 35.3	6 33.3
7 70.0	7 63.6	7 58.3	7 53.8	7 50.0	7 46.7	7 43.8	7 41.2	7 38.9
8 80.0	8 72.7	8 66.7	8 61.5	8 57.1	8 53.3	8 50.0	8 47.1	8 44.4
9 90.0	9 81.8	9 75.0	9 69.2	9 64.3	9 60.0	9 56.3	9 52.9	9 50.0
10 100.0	10 90.9	10 83.3	10 76.9	10 71.4	10 66.7	10 62.5	10 58.8	10 55.6
	11 100.0	11 91.7	11 84.6	11 78.6	11 73.3	11 68.8	11 64.7	11 61.1
		12 100.0	12 92.3	12 85.7	12 80.0	12 75.0	12 70.6	12 66.7
			13 100.0	13 92.9	13 86.7	13 81.3	13 76.5	13 72.2
				14 100.0	14 93.3	14 87.5	14 82.4	14 77.8
					15 100.0	15 93.8	15 88.2	15 83.3
						16 100.0	16 94.1	16 88.9
							17 100.0	17 94.4
								18 100.0

Top section (19–27)

19		20		21		22		23		24		25		26		27	
1	5.3	1	5.0	1	4.8	1	4.5	1	4.3	1	4.2	1	4.0	1	3.8	1	3.7
2	10.5	2	10.0	2	9.5	2	9.1	2	8.7	2	8.3	2	8.0	2	7.7	2	7.4
3	15.8	3	15.0	3	14.3	3	13.6	3	13.0	3	12.5	3	12.0	3	11.5	3	11.1
4	21.1	4	20.0	4	19.0	4	18.2	4	17.4	4	16.7	4	16.0	4	15.4	4	14.8
5	26.3	5	25.0	5	23.8	5	22.7	5	21.7	5	20.8	5	20.0	5	19.2	5	18.5
6	31.6	6	30.0	6	28.6	6	27.3	6	26.1	6	25.0	6	24.0	6	23.1	6	22.2
7	36.8	7	35.0	7	33.3	7	31.8	7	30.4	7	29.2	7	28.0	7	26.9	7	25.9
8	42.1	8	40.0	8	38.1	8	36.4	8	34.8	8	33.3	8	32.0	8	30.8	8	29.6
9	47.4	9	45.0	9	42.9	9	40.9	9	39.1	9	37.5	9	36.0	9	34.6	9	33.3
10	52.6	10	50.0	10	47.6	10	45.5	10	43.5	10	41.7	10	40.0	10	38.5	10	37.0
11	57.9	11	55.0	11	52.4	11	50.0	11	47.8	11	45.8	11	44.0	11	42.3	11	40.7
12	63.2	12	60.0	12	57.1	12	54.5	12	52.2	12	50.0	12	48.0	12	46.2	12	44.4
13	68.4	13	65.0	13	61.9	13	59.1	13	56.5	13	54.2	13	52.0	13	50.0	13	48.1
14	73.7	14	70.0	14	66.7	14	63.6	14	60.9	14	58.3	14	56.0	14	53.8	14	51.9
15	78.9	15	75.0	15	71.4	15	68.2	15	65.2	15	62.5	15	60.0	15	57.7	15	55.6
16	84.2	16	80.0	16	76.2	16	72.7	16	69.6	16	66.7	16	64.0	16	61.5	16	59.3
17	89.5	17	85.0	17	81.0	17	77.3	17	73.9	17	70.8	17	68.0	17	65.4	17	63.0
18	94.7	18	90.0	18	85.7	18	81.8	18	78.3	18	75.0	18	72.0	18	69.2	18	66.7
19	100.0	19	95.0	19	90.5	19	86.4	19	82.6	19	79.2	19	76.0	19	73.1	19	70.4
		20	100.0	20	95.2	20	90.9	20	87.0	20	83.3	20	80.0	20	76.9	20	74.1
				21	100.0	21	95.5	21	91.3	21	87.5	21	84.0	21	80.8	21	77.8
						22	100.0	22	95.7	22	91.7	22	88.0	22	84.6	22	81.5
								23	100.0	23	95.8	23	92.0	23	88.5	23	85.2
										24	100.0	24	96.0	24	92.3	24	88.9
												25	100.0	25	96.2	25	92.6
														26	100.0	26	96.3
																27	100.0

Bottom section (28–36)

28		29		30		31		32		33		34		35		36	
1	3.6	1	3.4	1	3.3	1	3.2	1	3.1	1	3.0	1	2.9	1	2.9	1	2.8
2	7.1	2	6.9	2	6.7	2	6.5	2	6.3	2	6.1	2	5.9	2	5.7	2	5.6
3	10.7	3	10.3	3	10.0	3	9.7	3	9.4	3	9.1	3	8.8	3	8.6	3	8.3
4	14.3	4	13.8	4	13.3	4	12.9	4	12.5	4	12.1	4	11.8	4	11.4	4	11.1
5	17.9	5	17.2	5	16.7	5	16.1	5	15.6	5	15.2	5	14.7	5	14.3	5	13.9
6	21.4	6	20.7	6	20.0	6	19.4	6	18.8	6	18.2	6	17.6	6	17.1	6	16.7
7	25.0	7	24.1	7	23.3	7	22.6	7	21.9	7	21.2	7	20.6	7	20.0	7	19.4
8	28.6	8	27.6	8	26.7	8	25.8	8	25.0	8	24.2	8	23.5	8	22.9	8	22.2
9	32.1	9	31.0	9	30.0	9	29.0	9	28.1	9	27.3	9	26.5	9	25.7	9	25.0
10	35.7	10	34.5	10	33.3	10	32.3	10	31.3	10	30.3	10	29.4	10	28.6	10	27.8
11	39.3	11	37.9	11	36.7	11	35.5	11	34.4	11	33.3	11	32.4	11	31.4	11	30.6
12	42.9	12	41.4	12	40.0	12	38.7	12	37.5	12	36.4	12	35.3	12	34.3	12	33.3
13	46.4	13	44.8	13	43.3	13	41.9	13	40.6	13	39.4	13	38.2	13	37.1	13	36.1
14	50.0	14	48.3	14	46.7	14	45.2	14	43.8	14	42.4	14	41.2	14	40.0	14	38.9
15	53.6	15	51.7	15	50.0	15	48.4	15	46.9	15	45.5	15	44.1	15	42.9	15	41.7
16	57.1	16	55.2	16	53.3	16	51.6	16	50.0	16	48.5	16	47.1	16	45.7	16	44.4
17	60.7	17	58.6	17	56.7	17	54.8	17	53.1	17	51.5	17	50.0	17	48.6	17	47.2
18	64.3	18	62.1	18	60.0	18	58.1	18	56.3	18	54.5	18	52.9	18	51.4	18	50.0
19	67.9	19	65.5	19	63.3	19	61.3	19	59.4	19	57.6	19	55.9	19	54.3	19	52.8
20	71.4	20	69.0	20	66.7	20	64.5	20	62.5	20	60.6	20	58.8	20	57.1	20	55.6
21	75.0	21	72.4	21	70.0	21	67.7	21	65.6	21	63.6	21	61.8	21	60.0	21	58.3
22	78.6	22	75.9	22	73.3	22	71.0	22	68.8	22	66.7	22	64.7	22	62.9	22	61.1
23	82.1	23	79.3	23	76.7	23	74.2	23	71.9	23	69.7	23	67.6	23	65.7	23	63.9
24	85.7	24	82.8	24	80.0	24	77.4	24	75.0	24	72.7	24	70.6	24	68.6	24	66.7
25	89.3	25	86.2	25	83.3	25	80.6	25	78.1	25	75.8	25	73.5	25	71.4	25	69.4
26	92.9	26	89.7	26	86.7	26	83.9	26	81.3	26	78.8	26	76.5	26	74.3	26	72.2
27	96.4	27	93.1	27	90.0	27	87.1	27	84.4	27	81.8	27	79.4	27	77.1	27	75.0
28	100.0	28	96.6	28	93.3	28	90.3	28	87.5	28	84.8	28	82.4	28	80.0	28	77.8
		29	100.0	29	96.7	29	93.5	29	90.6	29	87.9	29	85.3	29	82.9	29	80.6
				30	100.0	30	96.8	30	93.8	30	90.9	30	88.2	30	85.7	30	83.3
						31	100.0	31	96.9	31	93.9	31	91.2	31	88.6	31	86.1
								32	100.0	32	97.0	32	94.1	32	91.4	32	88.9
										33	100.0	33	97.1	33	94.3	33	91.7
												34	100.0	34	97.1	34	94.4
														35	100.0	35	97.2
																36	100.0

n	37	38	39	40	41	42	43	44	45
1	2.7	2.6	2.6	2.5	2.4	2.4	2.3	2.3	2.2
2	5.4	5.3	5.1	5.0	4.9	4.8	4.7	4.5	4.4
3	8.1	7.9	7.7	7.5	7.3	7.1	7.0	6.8	6.7
4	10.8	10.5	10.3	10.0	9.8	9.5	9.3	9.1	8.9
5	13.5	13.2	12.8	12.5	12.2	11.9	11.6	11.4	11.1
6	16.2	15.8	15.4	15.0	14.6	14.3	14.0	13.6	13.3
7	18.9	18.4	17.9	17.5	17.1	16.7	16.3	15.9	15.6
8	21.6	21.1	20.5	20.0	19.5	19.0	18.6	18.2	17.8
9	24.3	23.7	23.1	22.5	22.0	21.4	20.9	20.5	20.0
10	27.0	26.3	25.6	25.0	24.4	23.8	23.3	22.7	22.2
11	29.7	28.9	28.2	27.5	26.8	26.2	25.6	25.0	24.4
12	32.4	31.6	30.8	30.0	29.3	28.6	27.9	27.3	26.7
13	35.1	34.2	33.3	32.5	31.7	31.0	30.2	29.5	28.9
14	37.8	36.8	35.9	35.0	34.1	33.3	32.6	31.8	31.1
15	40.5	39.5	38.5	37.5	36.6	35.7	34.9	34.1	33.3
16	43.2	42.1	41.0	40.0	39.0	38.1	37.2	36.4	35.6
17	45.9	44.7	43.6	42.5	41.5	40.5	39.5	38.6	37.8
18	48.6	47.4	46.2	45.0	43.9	42.9	41.9	40.9	40.0
19	51.4	50.0	48.7	47.5	46.3	45.2	44.2	43.2	42.2
20	54.1	52.6	51.3	50.0	48.8	47.6	46.5	45.5	44.4
21	56.8	55.3	53.8	52.5	51.2	50.0	48.8	47.7	46.7
22	59.5	57.9	56.4	55.0	53.7	52.4	51.2	50.0	48.9
23	62.2	60.5	59.0	57.5	56.1	54.8	53.5	52.3	51.1
24	64.9	63.2	61.5	60.0	58.5	57.1	55.8	54.5	53.3
25	67.6	65.8	64.1	62.5	61.0	59.5	58.1	56.8	55.6
26	70.3	68.4	66.7	65.0	63.4	61.9	60.5	59.1	57.8
27	73.0	71.1	69.2	67.5	65.9	64.3	62.8	61.4	60.0
28	75.7	73.7	71.8	70.0	68.3	66.7	65.1	63.6	62.2
29	78.4	76.3	74.4	72.5	70.7	69.0	67.4	65.9	64.4
30	81.1	78.9	76.9	75.0	73.2	71.4	69.8	68.2	66.7
31	83.8	81.6	79.5	77.5	75.6	73.8	72.1	70.5	68.9
32	86.5	84.2	82.1	80.0	78.0	76.2	74.4	72.7	71.1
33	89.2	86.8	84.6	82.5	80.5	78.6	76.7	75.0	73.3
34	91.9	89.5	87.2	85.0	82.9	81.0	79.1	77.3	75.6
35	94.6	92.1	89.7	87.5	85.4	83.3	81.4	79.5	77.8
36	97.3	94.7	92.3	90.0	87.8	85.7	83.7	81.8	80.0
37	100.0	97.4	94.9	92.5	90.2	88.1	86.0	84.1	82.2
38		100.0	97.4	95.0	92.7	90.5	88.4	86.4	84.4
39			100.0	97.5	95.1	92.9	90.7	88.6	86.7
40				100.0	97.6	95.2	93.0	90.9	88.9
41					100.0	97.6	95.3	93.2	91.1
42						100.0	97.7	95.5	93.3
43							100.0	97.7	95.6
44								100.0	97.8
45									100.0

46		47		48		49		50		51		52		53		54	
1	2.2	1	2.1	1	2.1	1	2.0	1	2.0	1	2.0	1	1.9	1	1.9	1	1.9
2	4.3	2	4.3	2	4.2	2	4.1	2	4.0	2	3.9	2	3.8	2	3.8	2	3.7
3	6.5	3	6.4	3	6.3	3	6.1	3	6.0	3	5.9	3	5.8	3	5.7	3	5.6
4	8.7	4	8.5	4	8.3	4	8.2	4	8.0	4	7.8	4	7.7	4	7.5	4	7.4
5	10.9	5	10.6	5	10.4	5	10.2	5	10.0	5	9.8	5	9.6	5	9.4	5	9.3
6	13.0	6	12.8	6	12.5	6	12.2	6	12.0	6	11.8	6	11.5	6	11.3	6	11.1
7	15.2	7	14.9	7	14.6	7	14.3	7	14.0	7	13.7	7	13.5	7	13.2	7	13.0
8	17.4	8	17.0	8	16.7	8	16.3	8	16.0	8	15.7	8	15.4	8	15.1	8	14.8
9	19.6	9	19.1	9	18.8	9	18.4	9	18.0	9	17.6	9	17.3	9	17.0	9	16.7
10	21.7	10	21.3	10	20.8	10	20.4	10	20.0	10	19.6	10	19.2	10	18.9	10	18.5
11	23.9	11	23.4	11	22.9	11	22.4	11	22.0	11	21.6	11	21.2	11	20.8	11	20.4
12	26.1	12	25.5	12	25.0	12	24.5	12	24.0	12	23.5	12	23.1	12	22.6	12	22.2
13	28.3	13	27.7	13	27.1	13	26.5	13	26.0	13	25.5	13	25.0	13	24.5	13	24.1
14	30.4	14	29.8	14	29.2	14	28.6	14	28.0	14	27.5	14	26.9	14	26.4	14	25.9
15	32.6	15	31.9	15	31.3	15	30.6	15	30.0	15	29.4	15	28.8	15	28.3	15	27.8
16	34.8	16	34.0	16	33.3	16	32.7	16	32.0	16	31.4	16	30.8	16	30.2	16	29.6
17	37.0	17	36.2	17	35.4	17	34.7	17	34.0	17	33.3	17	32.7	17	32.1	17	31.5
18	39.1	18	38.3	18	37.5	18	36.7	18	36.0	18	35.3	18	34.6	18	34.0	18	33.3
19	41.3	19	40.4	19	39.6	19	38.8	19	38.0	19	37.3	19	36.5	19	35.8	19	35.2
20	43.5	20	42.6	20	41.7	20	40.8	20	40.0	20	39.2	20	38.5	20	37.7	20	37.0
21	45.7	21	44.7	21	43.8	21	42.9	21	42.0	21	41.2	21	40.4	21	39.6	21	38.9
22	47.8	22	46.8	22	45.8	22	44.9	22	44.0	22	43.1	22	42.3	22	41.5	22	40.7
23	50.0	23	48.9	23	47.9	23	46.9	23	46.0	23	45.1	23	44.2	23	43.4	23	42.6
24	52.2	24	51.1	24	50.0	24	49.0	24	48.0	24	47.1	24	46.2	24	45.3	24	44.4
25	54.3	25	53.2	25	52.1	25	51.0	25	50.0	25	49.0	25	48.1	25	47.2	25	46.3
26	56.5	26	55.3	26	54.2	26	53.1	26	52.0	26	51.0	26	50.0	26	49.1	26	48.1
27	58.7	27	57.4	27	56.3	27	55.1	27	54.0	27	52.9	27	51.9	27	50.9	27	50.0
28	60.9	28	59.6	28	58.3	28	57.1	28	56.0	28	54.9	28	53.8	28	52.8	28	51.9
29	63.0	29	61.7	29	60.4	29	59.2	29	58.0	29	56.9	29	55.8	29	54.7	29	53.7
30	65.2	30	63.8	30	62.5	30	61.2	30	60.0	30	58.8	30	57.7	30	56.6	30	55.6
31	67.4	31	66.0	31	64.6	31	63.3	31	62.0	31	60.8	31	59.6	31	58.5	31	57.4
32	69.6	32	68.1	32	66.7	32	65.3	32	64.0	32	62.7	32	61.5	32	60.4	32	59.3
33	71.7	33	70.2	33	68.8	33	67.3	33	66.0	33	64.7	33	63.5	33	62.3	33	61.1
34	73.9	34	72.3	34	70.8	34	69.4	34	68.0	34	66.7	34	65.4	34	64.2	34	63.0
35	76.1	35	74.5	35	72.9	35	71.4	35	70.0	35	68.6	35	67.3	35	66.0	35	64.8
36	78.3	36	76.6	36	75.0	36	73.5	36	72.0	36	70.6	36	69.2	36	67.9	36	66.7
37	80.4	37	78.7	37	77.1	37	75.5	37	74.0	37	72.5	37	71.2	37	69.8	37	68.5
38	82.6	38	80.9	38	79.2	38	77.6	38	76.0	38	74.5	38	73.1	38	71.7	38	70.4
39	84.8	39	83.0	39	81.3	39	79.6	39	78.0	39	76.5	39	75.0	39	73.6	39	72.2
40	87.0	40	85.1	40	83.3	40	81.6	40	80.0	40	78.4	40	76.9	40	75.5	40	74.1
41	89.1	41	87.2	41	85.4	41	83.7	41	82.0	41	80.4	41	78.8	41	77.4	41	75.9
42	91.3	42	89.4	42	87.5	42	85.7	42	84.0	42	82.4	42	80.8	42	79.2	42	77.8
43	93.5	43	91.5	43	89.6	43	87.8	43	86.0	43	84.3	43	82.7	43	81.1	43	79.6
44	95.7	44	93.6	44	91.7	44	89.8	44	88.0	44	86.3	44	84.6	44	83.0	44	81.5
45	97.8	45	95.7	45	93.8	45	91.8	45	90.0	45	88.2	45	86.5	45	84.9	45	83.3
46	100.0	46	97.9	46	95.8	46	93.9	46	92.0	46	90.2	46	88.5	46	86.8	46	85.2
		47	100.0	47	97.9	47	95.9	47	94.0	47	92.2	47	90.4	47	88.7	47	87.0
				48	100.0	48	98.0	48	96.0	48	94.1	48	92.3	48	90.6	48	88.9
						49	100.0	49	98.0	49	96.1	49	94.2	49	92.5	49	90.7
								50	100.0	50	98.0	50	96.2	50	94.3	50	92.6
										51	100.0	51	98.1	51	96.2	51	94.4
												52	100.0	52	98.1	52	96.3
														53	100.0	53	98.1
																54	100.0

55		56		57		58		59		60		61		62		63	
1	1.8	1	1.8	1	1.8	1	1.7	1	1.7	1	1.7	1	1.6	1	1.6	1	1.6
2	3.6	2	3.6	2	3.5	2	3.4	2	3.4	2	3.3	2	3.3	2	3.2	2	3.2
3	5.5	3	5.4	3	5.3	3	5.2	3	5.1	3	5.0	3	4.9	3	4.8	3	4.8
4	7.3	4	7.1	4	7.0	4	6.9	4	6.8	4	6.7	4	6.6	4	6.5	4	6.3
5	9.1	5	8.9	5	8.8	5	8.6	5	8.5	5	8.3	5	8.2	5	8.1	5	7.9
6	10.9	6	10.7	6	10.5	6	10.3	6	10.2	6	10.0	6	9.8	6	9.7	6	9.5
7	12.7	7	12.5	7	12.3	7	12.1	7	11.9	7	11.7	7	11.5	7	11.3	7	11.1
8	14.5	8	14.3	8	14.0	8	13.8	8	13.6	8	13.3	8	13.1	8	12.9	8	12.7
9	16.4	9	16.1	9	15.8	9	15.5	9	15.3	9	15.0	9	14.8	9	14.5	9	14.3
10	18.2	10	17.9	10	17.5	10	17.2	10	16.9	10	16.7	10	16.4	10	16.1	10	15.9
11	20.0	11	19.6	11	19.3	11	19.0	11	18.6	11	18.3	11	18.0	11	17.7	11	17.5
12	21.8	12	21.4	12	21.1	12	20.7	12	20.3	12	20.0	12	19.7	12	19.4	12	19.0
13	23.6	13	23.2	13	22.8	13	22.4	13	22.0	13	21.7	13	21.3	13	21.0	13	20.6
14	25.5	14	25.0	14	24.6	14	24.1	14	23.7	14	23.3	14	23.0	14	22.6	14	22.2
15	27.3	15	26.8	15	26.3	15	25.9	15	25.4	15	25.0	15	24.6	15	24.2	15	23.8
16	29.1	16	28.6	16	28.1	16	27.6	16	27.1	16	26.7	16	26.2	16	25.8	16	25.4
17	30.9	17	30.4	17	29.8	17	29.3	17	28.8	17	28.3	17	27.9	17	27.4	17	27.0
18	32.7	18	32.1	18	31.6	18	31.0	18	30.5	18	30.0	18	29.5	18	29.0	18	28.6
19	34.5	19	33.9	19	33.3	19	32.8	19	32.2	19	31.7	19	31.1	19	30.6	19	30.2
20	36.4	20	35.7	20	35.1	20	34.5	20	33.9	20	33.3	20	32.8	20	32.3	20	31.7
21	38.2	21	37.5	21	36.8	21	36.2	21	35.6	21	35.0	21	34.4	21	33.9	21	33.3
22	40.0	22	39.3	22	38.6	22	37.9	22	37.3	22	36.7	22	36.1	22	35.5	22	34.9
23	41.8	23	41.1	23	40.4	23	39.7	23	39.0	23	38.3	23	37.7	23	37.1	23	36.5
24	43.6	24	42.9	24	42.1	24	41.4	24	40.7	24	40.0	24	39.3	24	38.7	24	38.1
25	45.5	25	44.6	25	43.9	25	43.1	25	42.4	25	41.7	25	41.0	25	40.3	25	39.7
26	47.3	26	46.4	26	45.6	26	44.8	26	44.1	26	43.3	26	42.6	26	41.9	26	41.3
27	49.1	27	48.2	27	47.4	27	46.6	27	45.8	27	45.0	27	44.3	27	43.5	27	42.9
28	50.9	28	50.0	28	49.1	28	48.3	28	47.5	28	46.7	28	45.9	28	45.2	28	44.4
29	52.7	29	51.8	29	50.9	29	50.0	29	49.2	29	48.3	29	47.5	29	46.8	29	46.0
30	54.5	30	53.6	30	52.6	30	51.7	30	50.8	30	50.0	30	49.2	30	48.4	30	47.6
31	56.4	31	55.4	31	54.4	31	53.4	31	52.5	31	51.7	31	50.8	31	50.0	31	49.2
32	58.2	32	57.1	32	56.1	32	55.2	32	54.2	32	53.3	32	52.5	32	51.6	32	50.8
33	60.0	33	58.9	33	57.9	33	56.9	33	55.9	33	55.0	33	54.1	33	53.2	33	52.4
34	61.8	34	60.7	34	59.6	34	58.6	34	57.6	34	56.7	34	55.7	34	54.8	34	54.0
35	63.6	35	62.5	35	61.4	35	60.3	35	59.3	35	58.3	35	57.4	35	56.5	35	55.6
36	65.5	36	64.3	36	63.2	36	62.1	36	61.0	36	60.0	36	59.0	36	58.1	36	57.1
37	67.3	37	66.1	37	64.9	37	63.8	37	62.7	37	61.7	37	60.7	37	59.7	37	58.7
38	69.1	38	67.9	38	66.7	38	65.5	38	64.4	38	63.3	38	62.3	38	61.3	38	60.3
39	70.9	39	69.6	39	68.4	39	67.2	39	66.1	39	65.0	39	63.9	39	62.9	39	61.9
40	72.7	40	71.4	40	70.2	40	69.0	40	67.8	40	66.7	40	65.6	40	64.5	40	63.5
41	74.5	41	73.2	41	71.9	41	70.7	41	69.5	41	68.3	41	67.2	41	66.1	41	65.1
42	76.4	42	75.0	42	73.7	42	72.4	42	71.2	42	70.0	42	68.9	42	67.7	42	66.7
43	78.2	43	76.8	43	75.4	43	74.1	43	72.9	43	71.7	43	70.5	43	69.4	43	68.3
44	80.0	44	78.6	44	77.2	44	75.9	44	74.6	44	73.3	44	72.1	44	71.0	44	69.8
45	81.8	45	80.4	45	78.9	45	77.6	45	76.3	45	75.0	45	73.8	45	72.6	45	71.4
46	83.6	46	82.1	46	80.7	46	79.3	46	78.0	46	76.7	46	75.4	46	74.2	46	73.0
47	85.5	47	83.9	47	82.5	47	81.0	47	79.7	47	78.3	47	77.0	47	75.8	47	74.6
48	87.3	48	85.7	48	84.2	48	82.8	48	81.4	48	80.0	48	78.7	48	77.4	48	76.2
49	89.1	49	87.5	49	86.0	49	84.5	49	83.1	49	81.7	49	80.3	49	79.0	49	77.8
50	90.9	50	89.3	50	87.7	50	86.2	50	84.7	50	83.3	50	82.0	50	80.6	50	79.4
51	92.7	51	91.1	51	89.5	51	87.9	51	86.4	51	85.0	51	83.6	51	82.3	51	81.0
52	94.5	52	92.9	52	91.2	52	89.7	52	88.1	52	86.7	52	85.2	52	83.9	52	82.5
53	96.4	53	94.6	53	93.0	53	91.4	53	89.8	53	88.3	53	86.9	53	85.5	53	84.1
54	98.2	54	96.4	54	94.7	54	93.1	54	91.5	54	90.0	54	88.5	54	87.1	54	85.7
55	100.0	55	98.2	55	96.5	55	94.8	55	93.2	55	91.7	55	90.2	55	88.7	55	87.3
		56	100.0	56	98.2	56	96.6	56	94.9	56	93.3	56	91.8	56	90.3	56	88.9
				57	100.0	57	98.3	57	96.6	57	95.0	57	93.4	57	91.9	57	90.5
						58	100.0	58	98.3	58	96.7	58	95.1	58	93.5	58	92.1
								59	100.0	59	98.3	59	96.7	59	95.2	59	93.7
										60	100.0	60	98.4	60	96.8	60	95.2
												61	100.0	61	98.4	61	96.8
														62	100.0	62	98.4
																63	100.0

n	64	65	66	67	68	69	70	71	72
1	1.6	1.5	1.5	1.5	1.5	1.4	1.4	1.4	1.4
2	3.1	3.1	3.0	3.0	2.9	2.9	2.9	2.8	2.8
3	4.7	4.6	4.5	4.5	4.4	4.3	4.3	4.2	4.2
4	6.3	6.2	6.1	6.0	5.9	5.8	5.7	5.6	5.6
5	7.8	7.7	7.6	7.5	7.4	7.2	7.1	7.0	6.9
6	9.4	9.2	9.1	9.0	8.8	8.7	8.6	8.5	8.3
7	10.9	10.8	10.6	10.4	10.3	10.1	10.0	9.9	9.7
8	12.5	12.3	12.1	11.9	11.8	11.6	11.4	11.3	11.1
9	14.1	13.8	13.6	13.4	13.2	13.0	12.9	12.7	12.5
10	15.6	15.4	15.2	14.9	14.7	14.5	14.3	14.1	13.9
11	17.2	16.9	16.7	16.4	16.2	15.9	15.7	15.5	15.3
12	18.8	18.5	18.2	17.9	17.6	17.4	17.1	16.9	16.7
13	20.3	20.0	19.7	19.4	19.1	18.8	18.6	18.3	18.1
14	21.9	21.5	21.2	20.9	20.6	20.3	20.0	19.7	19.4
15	23.4	23.1	22.7	22.4	22.1	21.7	21.4	21.1	20.8
16	25.0	24.6	24.2	23.9	23.5	23.2	22.9	22.5	22.2
17	26.6	26.2	25.8	25.4	25.0	24.6	24.3	23.9	23.6
18	28.1	27.7	27.3	26.9	26.5	26.1	25.7	25.4	25.0
19	29.7	29.2	28.8	28.4	27.9	27.5	27.1	26.8	26.4
20	31.3	30.8	30.3	29.9	29.4	29.0	28.6	28.2	27.8
21	32.8	32.3	31.8	31.3	30.9	30.4	30.0	29.6	29.2
22	34.4	33.8	33.3	32.8	32.4	31.9	31.4	31.0	30.6
23	35.9	35.4	34.8	34.3	33.8	33.3	32.9	32.4	31.9
24	37.5	36.9	36.4	35.8	35.3	34.8	34.3	33.8	33.3
25	39.1	38.5	37.9	37.3	36.8	36.2	35.7	35.2	34.7
26	40.6	40.0	39.4	38.8	38.2	37.7	37.1	36.6	36.1
27	42.2	41.5	40.9	40.3	39.7	39.1	38.6	38.0	37.5
28	43.8	43.1	42.4	41.8	41.2	40.6	40.0	39.4	38.9
29	45.3	44.6	43.9	43.3	42.6	42.0	41.4	40.8	40.3
30	46.9	46.2	45.5	44.8	44.1	43.5	42.9	42.3	41.7
31	48.4	47.7	47.0	46.3	45.6	44.9	44.3	43.7	43.1
32	50.0	49.2	48.5	47.8	47.1	46.4	45.7	45.1	44.4
33	51.6	50.8	50.0	49.3	48.5	47.8	47.1	46.5	45.8
34	53.1	52.3	51.5	50.7	50.0	49.3	48.6	47.9	47.2
35	54.7	53.8	53.0	52.2	51.5	50.7	50.0	49.3	48.6
36	56.3	55.4	54.5	53.7	52.9	52.2	51.4	50.7	50.0
37	57.8	56.9	56.1	55.2	54.4	53.6	52.9	52.1	51.4
38	59.4	58.5	57.6	56.7	55.9	55.1	54.3	53.5	52.8
39	60.9	60.0	59.1	58.2	57.4	56.5	55.7	54.9	54.2
40	62.5	61.5	60.6	59.7	58.8	58.0	57.1	56.3	55.6
41	64.1	63.1	62.1	61.2	60.3	59.4	58.6	57.7	56.9
42	65.6	64.6	63.6	62.7	61.8	60.9	60.0	59.2	58.3
43	67.2	66.2	65.2	64.2	63.2	62.3	61.4	60.6	59.7
44	68.8	67.7	66.7	65.7	64.7	63.8	62.9	62.0	61.1
45	70.3	69.2	68.2	67.2	66.2	65.2	64.3	63.4	62.5
46	71.9	70.8	69.7	68.7	67.6	66.7	65.7	64.8	63.9
47	73.4	72.3	71.2	70.1	69.1	68.1	67.1	66.2	65.3
48	75.0	73.8	72.7	71.6	70.6	69.6	68.6	67.6	66.7
49	76.6	75.4	74.2	73.1	72.1	71.0	70.0	69.0	68.1
50	78.1	76.9	75.8	74.6	73.5	72.5	71.4	70.4	69.4
51	79.7	78.5	77.3	76.1	75.0	73.9	72.9	71.8	70.8
52	81.3	80.0	78.8	77.6	76.5	75.4	74.3	73.2	72.2
53	82.8	81.5	80.3	79.1	77.9	76.8	75.7	74.6	73.6
54	84.4	83.1	81.8	80.6	79.4	78.3	77.1	76.1	75.0
55	85.9	84.6	83.3	82.1	80.9	79.7	78.6	77.5	76.4
56	87.5	86.2	84.8	83.6	82.4	81.2	80.0	78.9	77.8
57	89.1	87.7	86.4	85.1	83.8	82.6	81.4	80.3	79.2
58	90.6	89.2	87.9	86.6	85.3	84.1	82.9	81.7	80.6
59	92.2	90.8	89.4	88.1	86.8	85.5	84.3	83.1	81.9
60	93.8	92.3	90.9	89.6	88.2	87.0	85.7	84.5	83.3
61	95.3	93.8	92.4	91.0	89.7	88.4	87.1	85.9	84.7
62	96.9	95.4	93.9	92.5	91.2	89.9	88.6	87.3	86.1
63	98.4	96.9	95.5	94.0	92.6	91.3	90.0	88.7	87.5
64	100.0	98.5	97.0	95.5	94.1	92.8	91.4	90.1	88.9
65		100.0	98.5	97.0	95.6	94.2	92.9	91.5	90.3
66			100.0	98.5	97.1	95.7	94.3	93.0	91.7
67				100.0	98.5	97.1	95.7	94.4	93.1
68					100.0	98.6	97.1	95.8	94.4
69						100.0	98.6	97.2	95.8
70							100.0	98.6	97.2
71								100.0	98.6
72									100.0

Index

PB-8382-1-SB
75-57T